1,000,000 Books

are available to read at

Forgotten Books

www.ForgottenBooks.com

Read online
Download PDF
Purchase in print

ISBN 978-0-265-12751-3
PIBN 10275826

This book is a reproduction of an important historical work. Forgotten Books uses state-of-the-art technology to digitally reconstruct the work, preserving the original format whilst repairing imperfections present in the aged copy. In rare cases, an imperfection in the original, such as a blemish or missing page, may be replicated in our edition. We do, however, repair the vast majority of imperfections successfully; any imperfections that remain are intentionally left to preserve the state of such historical works.

Forgotten Books is a registered trademark of FB &c Ltd.
Copyright © 2018 FB &c Ltd.
FB &c Ltd, Dalton House, 60 Windsor Avenue, London, SW19 2RR.
Company number 08720141. Registered in England and Wales.

For support please visit www.forgottenbooks.com

1 MONTH OF FREE READING

at

www.ForgottenBooks.com

By purchasing this book you are eligible for one month membership to ForgottenBooks.com, giving you unlimited access to our entire collection of over 1,000,000 titles via our web site and mobile apps.

To claim your free month visit:
www.forgottenbooks.com/free275826

* Offer is valid for 45 days from date of purchase. Terms and conditions apply.

English
Français
Deutsche
Italiano
Español
Português

www.forgottenbooks.com

Mythology Photography **Fiction**
Fishing Christianity **Art** Cooking
Essays Buddhism Freemasonry
Medicine **Biology** Music **Ancient Egypt** Evolution Carpentry Physics
Dance Geology **Mathematics** Fitness
Shakespeare **Folklore** Yoga Marketing
Confidence Immortality Biographies
Poetry **Psychology** Witchcraft
Electronics Chemistry History **Law**
Accounting **Philosophy** Anthropology
Alchemy Drama Quantum Mechanics
Atheism Sexual Health **Ancient History**
Entrepreneurship Languages Sport
Paleontology Needlework Islam
Metaphysics Investment Archaeology
Parenting Statistics Criminology
Motivational

FIFTY-FOURTH
ANNUAL REPORT

OF THE

Chamber of Commerce

OF

Greater SAN FRANCISCO.
Chamber of Commerce,

SUBMITTED TO A MEETING HELD

JANUARY 19TH, 1904

TOGETHER WITH

LIST OF OFFICERS AND STANDING COMMITTEES FOR THE YEAR 1904-1905, RESOLUTIONS AND MEMORIALS, BY-LAWS, HARBOR REGULATIONS, COMMERCIAL STATISTICS, ETC.

SAN FRANCISCO:
COMMERCIAL PUBLISHING COMPANY
1904

F
844S
G78
1903/04

July 29, 1932

04663-S

OFFICERS AND STANDING COMMITTEES
1904

GEORGE ALMER NEWHALL..............President
E. R. DIMOND......................Vice-President
C. H. BENTLEY..............Second Vice-President

TRUSTEES:

Frank L. Brown	Wm. H. Marston
W. J. Dutton	Thos. Rickard
J. A. Folger	James Rolph, Jr.
Wm. L. Gerstle	Henry Rosenfeld
Rufus P. Jennings	Jas. B. Smith
H. D. Loveland	Wm. R. Wheeler

STANDING COMMITTEES

FINANCE:
E. R. Dimond   Thos. Rickard   J. A. Folger

LIBRARY:
F. L. Brown   Wm. L. Gerstle   Wm. H. Marston

MEMBERSHIP:
James B. Smith   Thos. Rickard   H. D. Loveland

ARBITRATION:
H. Rosenfeld   Wm. R. Wheeler   R. P. Jennings
James Rolph, Jr.   C. H. Bentley

APPEALS:
Wm. L. Gerstle   James A. Folger   W. J. Dutton
W. H. Marston   F. L. Brown

FOREIGN COMMERCE AND REVENUE LAWS:
W. R. Wheeler   C. H. Bentley   R. P. Jennings

INTERNAL TRADE AND IMPROVEMENTS:
W. J. Dutton   Jas. B. Smith   F. L. Brown

HARBOR AND SHIPPING:
Wm. H. Marston   H. Rosenfeld   James Rolph, Jr.

RECEPTION AND ENTERTAINMENT:
Rufus P. Jennings   Thos. Rickard   H. D. Loveland

SECRETARY, TREASURER AND LIBRARIAN:
E. Scott

PRESIDENT'S ANNUAL REPORT

To the Members of the Chamber of Commerce of San Francisco, California.

Gentlemen—We have again in the history of our Chamber reached the end of another year, and it is my pleasant duty to once more lay before you our Annual Report and call your attention to the future outlook.

Much work has been done during the past year and a great many subjects have been acted upon. The administration of the affairs of the Chamber has been largely in the hands of our First Vice-President, Mr. Edward R. Dimond, your President having been absent for five months during the year. The thanks of the Chamber are extended to Mr. Dimond for the energetic and active manner in which he has carried on the work.

As is my custom, I will call your attention to a number of the transactions which have engaged the attention of your Board of Directors and which are as follows:

A NEW CUSTOM HOUSE.

Last year we were pleased to report that an appropriation had been secured for the building of a new custom house, and it is with much pleasure that I now inform you that a contract has been awarded for the erection of same, and we hope before long to see a handsome new building in place of the one that has served us so long and well all these years.

SUBMARINE CABLE TO ALASKA.

Your Chamber took an active interest in this matter and the result of our efforts is that a new cable is an assured fact in this portion of our Union.

GOVERNMENT TRANSPORTATION.

Strong efforts have been made to induce the War Department to retain in San Francisco the Government transports. This, as you all know, has been successful, and our recent advices from Washington show that San Francisco will always receive a very large proportion of this business.

PURCHASING OF GOVERNMENT SUPPLIES.

Another matter of great interest to San Francisco is the purchasing of Government supplies for the different governmental departments. Much correspondence has been had with the Government in this regard, and we are pleased to say that our replies have been favorable, and that California, and especially San Francisco, will receive a just proportion of this business.

ELECTRIC LIGHT SHIPS.

An effort has been made by your Chamber, and we are pleased to say, successfully, in favor of electric lights on the lightship at entrance of this harbor. This, of course, as is well known, will insure a steady light for the incoming and outgoing vessels.

PURCHASE OF CALAVERAS BIG TREES.

Action has been taken by your Trustees favoring the purchase by the National Government of the Calaveras Grove of Big Trees and converting same into a national park. The recent reports to the daily press inform us that President Roosevelt has recommended this action to Congress.

LIFE-SAVING STATION AT HALFMOON BAY.

After a careful investigation by the Harbor and Shipping Committee of your Board of Trustees, Senator Perkins has introduced a bill in Congress in favor of a life-saving station at Halfmoon Bay, and we are assured that it will meet with the approval of both Houses.

ISTHMIAN CANAL.

The canal subject is one that this Chamber has always taken a very active interest in and we are pleased to say that the President has seen fit to recommend that a canal be secured; therefore, your Board of Trustees have endorsed the action of the President in this regard.

AMERICAN CONSULAR SERVICE.

As is well known, the foreign consular service is of great benefit and service to the world, and as new business is being opened up in South Africa, your Board of Trustees have taken action favoring an increase of American consuls in this new business district. And not only has action been taken in regard to this part of the world, but also in favor of general consular reform, leaning to a Civil Service in the consular department rather than that consuls be appointed for political reasons.

CUBAN RECIPROCITY.

Your Board, after due consideration, has declared itself against the Cuban Reciprocity for the reason that it was thought that such action would interfere with a number of our own products.

NATIONAL EXPOSITION AT SHANGHAI.

For some time the question of an American National Exposition at Shanghai has been agitated, and your Board has seen fit to favor such an exposition, and will do all it can to promote such an enterprise, as it is our belief that Shanghai will be one of the principal ports for the increasing trade with Northern China, which is of so much importance to this city.

HARBOR IMPROVEMENTS.

Harbor improvements have also had our close attention, and efforts have been made in favor of improving Islais Creek, and also for better facilities for handling foreign commerce in our port.

INCREASE OF THE NAVY.

In the matter of the proposed increase of ships and personnel of the navy, your Chamber has strongly endorsed all measures of this kind, as they believe that the seaboard should be fully protected.

ARBITRATION.

Another matter that has consumed a good deal of the time of your Trustees has been the arbitration clause in bills of lading to cover disputes arising in the settlement of claims involving nominal amounts. This your Board of Trustees has heartily endorsed. Also in favor of revising the rules and regulations adopted by the Chamber in regard to commercial transactions.

AMERICAN MERCHANT MARINE.

Your Chamber has placed itself on record as being strongly in favor of the revival of the American Merchant Marine engaged in foreign carrying trade.

CHINESE TREATY.

Much interest has been shown by the people of our State in securing benefits to the Pacific Coast in the Chinese Treaty. This your Board of Trustees has endorsed.

PARCELS POST.

Another effort has been made in regard to foreign parcels post, as it is the wish of your Trustees to have this system extended to all foreign countries, inasmuch as it is considered of great advantage in the commercial world in forwarding samples of goods to and from foreign countries.

PHILIPPINE COMMISSION.

Governor Taft having seen fit to appoint a Commission of forty native Filipinos to visit this country as representatives of the Philippine Islands at the World's Fair to be held in St. Louis, your

Chamber, in conjunction with other commercial organizations of this city, have undertaken to entertain them during their stay here.

In this connection I might say that co-operation with other commercial bodies in the section tributary to the Bay of San Francisco for the improvement of water ways leading to the Bay; also in having further improvements made in this harbor in the way of removing hidden rocks, etc., has been encouraged and strong action in this direction taken by this body.

OUR REPRESENTATIVE IN WASHINGTON, D. C.

We cannot fail to again mention the excellent work of our representative in the National Capital. Your Trustees, after reviewing his work for the past year, have concluded to retain his services for another year. Individually, I am of the opinion that this should be made a permanent office of the Chamber, in view of the fact that so much more can be accomplished when we have a man of our own to assist us with matters pertaining to Government affairs.

COMMITTEES.

The thanks of the Chamber are due to our various committees.

The Finance Committee has enabled us to carry our work on and has left a good balance in the treasury. Cerdit for this is due to Mr. E. R. Dimond, our First Vice-President and chairman of this committee.

Our Library Committee, under the chairmanship of Mr. Edward L. Eyre, has increased the number of volumes in our possession. One of the specialties of this committee has been to receive and go through the various bills pending in Congress, and we wish to extend our thanks to this committee for its labors in this direction.

Our Foreign Commerce and Revenue Laws Committee, under the chairmanship of Mr. A. D. Field, has done committee work that has materially added to the importance of our foreign commerce.

Our Internal Trade and Improvement Committee, by the active and energetic work of its chairman, Mr. Wm. J. Dutton, has materially improved matters in this regard.

Mr. Wm. H. Marston, chairman of the Harbor and Shipping Committee, has been unceasing in his efforts to improve matters pertaining to the water front, and great credit is due to this committee for their unceasing efforts.

Mr. Rufus P. Jennings, chairman of the Reception and Entertainment Committee, has on many occasions demonstrated the advantage of this committee in the manner in which our visitors have been received and given a Godspeed on their departure.

Mr. Chas. M. Yates, the chairman of our Membership Committee, deserves the thanks of this Chamber for the increase of forty during the year.

It is very gratifying to the Board of Trustees to see the manner in which members of the commercial world are appreciating their efforts:

Our Committees on Arbitration and Appeals are doing everything in their power to improve these departments of our Chamber.

EXPORTS.

The exports from San Francisco by sea during 1903 amounted to more than $50,000,000 and the imports to more than $36,000,000, showing a large balance in our favor.

REAL ESTATE.

This has been an unusually active year in the history of the city, there being 552 more sales and $314,645 larger valuations than the previous year, which were supposed to be the banner year.

The mortages of 1903 aggregate $30,889,988, while the releases amount to $21,346,699, thus making the net sum borrowed $9,543,289. In other words, there was $47,710,157 invested in San Francisco realty during the year and only $9,543,289 of the total amount was borrowed, showing clearly that $38,166,868 was absolutely new money invested in real estate in the city and county of San Francisco.

BANK CLEARANCES.

Our bank clearances have steadily increased. While in our annual report last year we surpassed all other years in these clearances, yet for the year 1903 we have again taken a step forward, as the clearances amounted to $1,520,198,682.07. An increase of $146,836,656.76 over 1902, or more than $12,000,000 per month.

The manufactures in San Francisco during 1903 we estimate at a little over $150,000,000 in valuation. While our customs collections show some difference, they would have amounted to over $9,000,000 if the duty on coal and tea had not been removed, but they did actually show $7,621,160.

The population of the city is steadily increasing and is now estimated to be between 440,000 and 450,000 people.

The present estimates of production for 1903 are as follows: Gold, $17,500,000; silver, $600,000; copper, $6,000,000.

The approximate value of all metals and minerals produced in California during 1903 is $36,000,000.

Oranges figured quite largely in the produce of the State, yielding 25,000 carloads, of which 2,000 carloads were grown in the northern portion of the State. The lemon crop amounted to 3,200 carloads—some 150 carloads being produced north of Tehachapi. The walnut crop amounted to 11,500,000 lbs. The almond crop to 6,000,000 lbs., while our wine amounted to 32,000,000 gallons. The amount of brandy produced in the State was 5,700,000 gallons, fiscal year. The bean crop amounted to 117,500,000 lbs., while the salmon pack amounted to 3,420,000 cases. Wheat was unusually small, owing to the dry season. This amounted to 9,517,500 centals. Barley was 8,750,000 centals. Fuel oil amounted to 22,000,000 barrels, at an average price of 75 cents per barrel. The raisin crop amounted to 112,000,000 lbs.; canned fruit pack, 2,600,000 cases; hops, 47,000 bales, of 186 lbs. each; beet sugar, 154,000,000 lbs.; dried fruits as follows: prunes,

115,000,000 lbs.; peaches, 30,000,000 lbs.; apricots, 19,000,000 lbs.; apples, 9,000,000 lbs.; plums, 2,200,000 lbs.; nectarines, 600,000 lbs.; figs, 7,500,000 lbs.; grapes, 400,000 lbs.; pears, 4,500,000 lbs.; silver prunes, 400,000 lbs.

Wool amounted to 22,500,000 lbs; butter, 32,000,000 lbs.; cheese, 6,750,000 lbs. The value of all dairy products was about $19,000,000. Quicksilver amounted to 26,750 flasks, worth $43 each; honey, 3,650,000 lbs., and canned tomatoes, 840,000 cases.

Before closing I cannot neglect to again refer to the financial condition of San Francisco, and call particular attention to the advance made by our city.

We have lost by death some ten members: Louis Simon, January 27; J. H. Hecht, February 24; Samuel Sachs, March 13; G. F. Swift, March 29; Irving M. Scott, April 28; Wm. P. Thomas, April 29; R. G. Sneath, May 3; Wm. B. Hooper, July 16; Isador Schwartz, September 14; J. J. Smith, October 11.

And now in closing I wish to extend to the Board my hearty thanks for their co-operation and support, and to express my personal thanks to the members for their active co-operation during the year, and for the compliment in again electing me President of the Chamber.

Great credit is due to the press of San Francisco for their co-operation and support given to us in all matters pertaining to the public good.

GEORGE A. NEWHALL,
President.

SECRETARY'S ANNUAL REPORT

To the Honorable President, Board of Trustees and Members:

I again have the honor of presenting to you the usual annual reports and synopsis of transactions, which show in a measure the work of the Chamber during the past year and which relate almost entirely to subjects presented and acted upon by the Chamber and Board of Trustees. To form, however, a more complete idea of the work of the Chamber, it would be necessary to look over the general correspondence which covers very many subjects not included in the synopsis of transactions, hundreds of letters having been received requesting information upon the general resources and industries of the State, and hundreds more requesting specific information bearing upon almost every conceivable industry. This miscellaneous correspondence has steadily increased from year to year. I have encouraged it as much as possible, by replying to every letter and furnishing the best information obtainable in line with the requests made.

The report of the Treasurer shows a prosperous condition of the finances of the Chamber.

In addition to the regular meetings, one special meeting of the Chamber and four special meetings of the Board have been held during the year.

The rooms of the Chamber have been loaned for various purposes fifteen times; in some cases the meetings lasted several days.

The additions to the library have been very gratifying; 269 volumes and pamphlets have been donated and 13 purchased. This does not, however, represent the actual number of volumes, as many of the works included in the list under one subject comprise a number of volumes. A special feature in our library is the number of publications which we obtain from the National Government, which has been largely increased since the establishment of the Bureau of the Chamber in Washington. We not only receive the principal publications of the different departments, but the Congressional Record and copies of all bills introduced in Congress in any way affecting the Pacific Coast.

I respectfully suggest to the members of the Chamber a careful examination of the statistics contained in the annual report, as it will not only enable them to realize the increase of our commerce during the year, but will assist them in comparing the commercial importance of this city with that of others throughout the country.

The annual reports of the Chamber are in great demand among commercial organizations throughout the world, as it is realized that they are carefully compiled and contain the best available information upon the subjects mentioned.

Thanking the officers and members of the Chamber, as well as the gentlemen of the press, for their courtesy and assistance during the year, I remain,

Yours respectfully,

E. SCOTT,

Secretary.

January 19, 1904.

TREASURER'S ANNUAL REPORT
Year Ending January 2, 1904.

1903, January 2—
Balance cash on hand............................		$ 5,996 08
Received since dues............................	$7,270 00	
Received repayment telegram	12 08	
Received from sale of old books................	5 00	
Received from Guatemala Relief Fund...........	4 39	
Received from interest on deposits in Savings Banks	150 48	
Received subscriptions to Washington (D. C.) Bureau	3,647 50	
		11,089 45
		$17,085 53

DISBURSEMENTS:

Rent, thirteen months.........................	$ 830 00	
Salary Secretary, Treasurer and Librarian.......	2,400 00	
Salary William M. Bunker, Washington..........	3,800 00	
Salary C. W. Burks	720 00	
Wages Janitor.................................	65 00	
Sundry petty bills	252 37	
Postage	231 50	
Telephones	104 61	
Telegrams	202 22	
Gas for light and fuel..........................	15 25	
Stationery	111 83	
Printing, miscellaneous	101 50	
Printing 1,750 copies Annual Report, 1903.......	550 50	
Compiling statistics Annual Report, 1903........	100 00	
Accountant	15 00	
Library expense—new books	123 90	
Taxes and insurance	19 67	
Expense collecting dues and premium on bond....	155 27	
Entertainments	19 91	
Moving office	239 04	
Expense Mercantile Joint Committee............	23 34	
Expense visit of William M. Bunker, etc.........	97 50	
		$10,178 41

1904, January 2—
Balance cash on hand.........................		$6,907 12
In Security Savings Bank, term deposit..........	$1,140 79	
In San Francisco Savings Union, term deposit....	1,087 49	
In San Francisco Savings Union, ordinary deposit.	4,678 84	
		$6,907 12

SPECIAL FUND, GUATEMALA EARTHQUAKE SUFFERERS.

1903, January 2—
Balance cash on hand		$1,004 45
January and March, disbursed for supplies shipped	$1,000 06	
June 30, transferred to Chamber of Commerce....	4 39	
		$1,004 45

E. SCOTT, *Treasurer.*

Approved:
(Signed) E. R. DIMOND,
Chairman of Finance Committee.

ADDITIONS TO LIBRARY, 1903

DONATED.

1. State Mining Bureau—
    Copper Resources of California, April, 1902 (1 volume).
    Register of Mines and Minerals, El Dorado County (pamphlet).
    Map of El Dorado County, California.
    Mineral Map of Lake County, California.
    Register of Mines and Minerals, Lake County, California (pamphlet).
    Register of Mines and Minerals of Placer County, California (pamphlet).
    Map of Placer County, California.
    Register of Mines and Minerals, San Diego County, California (pamphlet).
    May of San Diego County, California.
    Register of Mines and Minerals, San Bernardino County, California (pamphlet).
    Map of San Bernardino County, California.
    Register of Mines and Minerals, Inyo County, California (pamphlet).
    Map of Inyo County, California.
    Bulletin No. 25 (pamphlet).
    Gold Production, California (pamphlet).
    Bulletin No. 26 (pamphlet).
    The Saline Deposits of California, May, 1902 (1 volume).
2. Johannesburg Chamber of Commerce, Monthly Report, December, 1902 (pamphlet).
3. First Annual Report of The Merchants' Exchange, July, 1902 (pamphlet).
4. Statistics of Railways in the United States, 1901 (1 volume).
5. Special Consular Report, Creameries in Foreign Countries, 1902 (pamphlet).
6. Tests of Gold and Silver in Shales from Western Kansas, 1902 (pamphlet).
7. Perth Chamber of Commerce, Twelfth Annual Report, June, 1902 (pamphlet).
8. Bulletin No. 2, United States Department of Agriculture; The Root Rot of Taro, by T. F. Sedgwick, 1902 (pamphlet).
9. Annual Report of Lighthouse Board, June 30, 1902 (1 volume).

Additions to Library. 17

10. American Chamber of Commerce, Paris; Bulletin No. 20, January, 1903 (1 volume).
11. Water Supply and Irrigation Papers of the United States Geological Survey, No. 70, 1902 (pamphlet).
12. Stored Goods as Collateral for Loans, Vol. XXV, 1902 (pamphlet).
13. Report of the White Range Gold Mines, Altunga Goldfield, South Australia, 1902 (pamphlet).
14. Bulletins of Statistics of the Republic of Mexico, July and August, 1902 (pamphlets).
15. Bulletins of the United States Geological Survey, Nos. 195, 196, 199, 201, 1902 (pamphlets).
16. The Action of Ammonium Chloride upon Silicates, Department of the Interior, Bulletin No. 207, 1902 (pamphlet).
17. Bulletin of the Chamber of Commerce of Cochin China, August, 1902 (pamphlet).
18. The American Merchant Marine, Marvin (1 volume).
20. Monthly Summary of Commerce and Finance of the United States, October, November and December, 1902; January, February, March, April, May, June, July, August, September and October, 1903 (pamphlets).
21. Monthly Summary of the Commerce of the Philippine Islands, February, April, May, June, July, August, September, November and December, 1902; February, March, April, May, June and July, 1903 (pamphlets).
22. Result of a Census of New South Wales, March, 1901 (pamphlet).
23. Imports and Exports of Gold and Silver, and Imports and Exports of Merchandise into and from the United States, June 30, 1902 (pamphlet).
24. Annual Review of the Foreign Commerce of the United States, June 30, 1902 (pamphlet).
25. Imported Merchandise Entered for Consumption in the United States, and Duties Collected Thereon, 1827-1902 (pamphlet).
26. Annual Report of the War Department, June 30, 1902 (pamphlet).
27. Drawback Paid on Imports, 1902 (pamphlet).
28. Imports of Merchandise into the United States, 1902 (pamphlet).
29. Exports of Domestic Merchandise from the United States, 1902 (pamphlet).
30. Estadistica Comercial de la Republica de Chile, ano 1901 (pamphlet).
31. Consular Reports, April, May, July, August, September, October and November, 1902 (8 pamphlets).
32. Message from the President of the United States, in Regard to Lands Held for Ecclesiastical or Religious Uses in the Philippine Islands, etc., 1901 (pamphlet).

Additions to Library.

33. Annual Reports of the War Department, June 30, 1901; Parts 3, 4 and 5 (3 volumes).
34. Mineral Resources of the United States, 1900 (pamphlet).
35. Public Laws and Resolutions Passed by the United States Philippine Commission, 1901 (pamphlet).
36. Annual Report of the Department of the Interior, 1901 (1 volume).
37. Annual Report of the Supervising Inspector-General, Steamboat Inspection Service, 1900 (pamphlet).
38. Report of the Secretary of the Interior, 1901 (pamphlet).
39. Mineral Resources of the United States, 1900 (1 volume).
40. Water Supply and Irrigation Papers, Nos. 17, 18, 19, 20, 41, 42, 44, 58, 59, 60 and 64, 1901 and 1902 (11 pamphlets).
41. Distribution of the Agricultural Exports of the United States, 1897-1901 (pamphlet).
42. Annual Reports of the Auditor for the Treasury Department, 1898, 1899, 1900, 1901 and 1902 (5 pamphlets).
43. Laws Governing the Steamboat Inspection Service, February 20, 1902 (pamphlet).
44. Progress of the Beet-Sugar Industry in the United States, 1901 (pamphlet).
45. General Rules and Regulations Prescribed by the Board of Supervising Inspectors of Steamboats, January, 1902 (pamphlet).
46. Preliminary Report of the Commissioner of Internal Revenue, July 24, 1901 (pamphlet).
47. Annual Reports, 1901, Commissioner of Internal Trade (1 volume).
48. Official Records of the Union and Confederate Navies in the War of the Rebellion, Series 1, Vols. 14 and 15 (2 volumes).
49. Report for 1902, Trinidad Chamber of Commerce (pamphlet).
50. Abstract of the Twelfth Census, 1900 (1 volume).
51. Year Book, Albany Chamber of Commerce, 1903 (pamphlet).
52. Annual Report of the Department of the Interior, 1901 (1 volume).
53. Bulletin de la Chambre d'Agriculture de Cochinchine, December, 1902; November, 1902 (pamphlets).
54. Exports Declared for the United States, quarter ended September 30, 1902 (pamphlet).
55. Census of New Zealand, 1901 (pamphlet).
56. Annual Report of the Wellington Harbor Board, September 30, 1902 (pamphlet).
57. Annales, Minister de Agriculture, France, December, 1902 (pamphlet).
58. Municipal Reports of San Francisco, 1900-1901 (1 volume).
59. Annual Report of the Lighthouse Board, June 30, 1900 (1 volume).

Additions to Library. 19

60. Annual Report of the Lighthouse Board, June 30, 1902 (1 volume).
61. The Seven Colonies of Australasia, 1901-1902 (1 volume).
62. Monthly Summary of Commerce and Finance of the United States, January and February, 1903.
63. American Chamber of Commerce, Paris, Bulletin No. 19, October, 1902.
64. Report of the Committee of the Manila Chamber of Commerce, December, 1902.
65. Twentieth Annual Report of the Proceedings of the Napier Chamber of Commerce, November, 1892.
66. Bulletins Nos. 20, 21 and 22, Boston Merchants' Association, February, 1903 (pamphlet).
67. Jahresbericht der Handelskammer zu Hamburg uber das Jahr 1902.
68. Bericht der Handelskammer in Bremen uber das Jahr 1902.
69. Twenty-fifth Annual Report of the Board of Trade of San Francisco, 1902 (pamphlet).
70. Twenty-sixth Annual Report of the Board of Trade of San Francisco, 1903 (pamphlet).
71. Nineteenth Annual Report of the Los Angeles Board of Trade, 1902.
72. Boston Merchants' Association Bulletin (souvenir number).
73. Commercial Relations of the United States, Vol. II, 1902.
74. The Production of Coal in 1900, by Edward W. Parker (pamphlet).
75. Report of the Forester for 1902 (pamphlet).
76. Circular No. 24, United States Bureau of Forestry (pamphlet).
77. Irrigation Institutions, by Elwood Mead (1 volume).
78. Bulletin No. 206, Department of the Interior (pamphlet).
79. Bulletins Nos. 204 and 205, Department of the Interior (2 pamphlets).
80. Nineteenth Report of the United States Civil Service Commission, July 1, 1901, to June 30, 1902.
81. California Miners' Association Annual, 1902.
82. The Argonauts of California, by C. W. Haskins.
83. Review of the World's Commerce During the Year 1901 (pamphlet).
84. Report on Certain Economic Questions in the English and Dutch Colonies in the Orient, by Jeremiah W. Jenks, 1902.
85. Annual Report of the Lighthouse Board, year ending June 30, 1902.
86. Report of the United States Philippine Commission to the Secretary of War for the Period from December 1, 1900, to October 15, 1901.

87. Regulation of Immigration—Report of the Committee on Immigration.
88. United States Geological Reports, 1901—
   Production of Aluminum and Bauxite.
   Production of Arsenic.
   Production of Asbestos.
   Production of Asphaltum and Bituminous Rock.
   Production of Bismuth.
   Production of Abrasive Materials.
   Production of Antimony.
   Production of Gas-Pot Clays.
   Production of Barytes.
   Production of Borax and Bromine.
   Production of Cement.
   Production of Chromic Iron Ore.
   Production of Copper.
   Production of Flint and Feldspar.
   Production of Flourspar and Cryolite.
   Production of Fuller's Earth.
   Production of Graphite.
   Production of Gypsum.
   Production of Iron Ores.
   Production of Lead.
   Production of Lithium.
   Production of Manganese Ores.
   Production of Magnesite.
   Production of Mica.
   Production of Mineral Paints.
   Production of Mineral Waters.
   Production of Monazite.
   Production of Nickel and Cobalt.
   Production of Peat.
   Production of Platinum.
   Production of Precious Stones.
   Production of Quicksilver.
   Production of Salt.
   Production of Talc and Soapstone.
   Production of Sulphur and Pyrite.
   Production of Titanium.
   Production of Tungsten, Molybdenum, Uranium and Nanandium.
   Production of Zinc.
   The Occurrence of Strontium Ores.
   The Stone Industry.
   The Utilization of Iron and Steel Slags.

Additions to Library. 21

Statistics of the American Iron Trade.
The Manufacture of Coke.
Statistics of the Clay Working Industries.
89. United States Bankruptcy Law, Amended to February 5, 1903 (pamphlet).
90. Conservative Lumbering at Sewanee, Tenn., 1903 (pamphlet).
91. The Redwood, Department of Agriculture, 1903 (pamphlet).
92. Message from the President of the United States, June 17, 1902.
93. Report of the Taft Philippine Commission, January 25, 1902 (pamphlet).
94. University of California Register, 1901-1902 (1 volume).
95. Report of the Librarian of Congress, year ending June 30, 1902.
96. Bulletin No. 2, California Miners' Association (pamphlet).
97. Preliminary Report of the Income Account of Railways, year ending June 30, 1902.
98. Biennial Report of the President of the University of California, 1900-1902.
99. Annual Report of the Secretary of War, 1902 (pamphlet).
100. Monthly Bulletin of the International Bureau of American Republics.
101. Annual Report of the Quartermaster-General, June 30, 1902 (pamphlet).
102. United States Naval Reserve and State Naval Militia, 1890 (pamphlet).
103. Knaggs' Almanac, 1902.
104. Hamburg's Handel im Jahre 1902.
105. Eighteenth Report of the United States Civil Service Commission, July, 1900-June, 1901.
106. Annual Wool Review, 1902.
107. Water Supply and Prevention of Waste in Leading European Cities.
108. Associacao Commercial do Porto, 1902 (pamphlet).
109. Monthly Report, Johannesburg Chamber of Commerce, December, 1902.
110. Second International Conference of American States, Held at the City of Mexico, from October, 1901, to February, 1902.
111. List of Lights and Fog Signals on the Pacific Coast of the United States, and of the Lights and Gulf Signals of the Dominion of Canada on the Coast of British Columbia, corrected to February 1, 1903 (pamphlet).
112. International Commercial Congress, Philadelphia Commercial Museum, 1899 (1 volume).
113. United States Geological Survey, Monographs, Vols. XLII, XLIII.
114. Sinopsis Estadistica 1, Jeographica de la Republica de Chile, year 1901 (pamphlet).

115. United States Department of Agriculture, Circular No. 25, Division of Foreign Markets, 1903 (pamphlet).
117. Department of Agriculture, Bulletin No. 35, Eucalyptus Cultivated in the United States, 1902 (pamphlet).
118. Department of Agriculture, Bulletin No. 27, The Hardy Catalpa, 1902.
119. Review of the World's Commerce, Department of State, 1902.
120. Letter from the Secretary of the Treasury.
121. Customs Tariff for the Philippine Archipelago, September, 1901.
122. Statistical Abstract of the United States, 1902.
123. Our Foreign Trade in Agricultural Products, 1891-1900 (pamphlet).
124. Bulletin No. 196, United States Geological Survey (pamphlet).
125. The Redwood.
126. List of Beacons, Buoys and Day Marks on the Pacific Coast of the United States, January, 1903.
127. Annual Report, Commissioner of Navigation, 1902 (volume).
128. Republica de Chile, Tarifa de Avalous, 1903 (1 volume).
129. Defects of the Financial Statements of the City of New York, with Suggestions for Improved Forms (pamphlet).
130. Wilmington Board of Trade Journal, March and April, 1903 (pamphlet).
131. Annual Report of the Auckland Chamber of Commerce, February, 1903.
132. Chambre d'Agriculture de Cochinchine, 1901 (pamphlet).
133. Exports Declared by the United States, quarter ending December 31, 1902.
134. Results of a Census of New South Wales, March 31, 1901 (pamphlet).
135. Resumen de la Importacion y de la Exportation, Enero de 1903.
136. Bulletin No. 24, Department of Agriculture, 1903 (pamphlet).
137. Consular Reports, May, 1903; Commerce, Manufactures, etc. (pamphlet).
138. Report of the Forester for 1902 (pamphlet).
139. Annual Report of the Lighthouse Board, year ended June 30, 1902.
140. Bloomer's International Cryptograph (1 volume).
141. Monthly Summary of Commerce of the Philippine Islands, October and June, 1902.
142. Annual Report of the Department of the Interior, Vol. II, 1901.
143. Report of the United States Philippine Commission, Vol. X, 1902.
144. Commerce and Navigation of the United States, Vols. I and II, 1902.
145. The Woodsman's Handbook, Part 1, Bulletin 36, Department of Agriculture (pamphlet).

146. Twelfth Annual Report of the Geelong Chamber of Commerce, 1902 (pamphlet).
147. Twenty-third Annual Report of the Peoria Board of Trade, 1902 (pamphlet).
148. Fiftieth Anniversary Dinner, Bengal Chamber of Commerce, 1903 (pamphlet).
149. Bulletin No. 21, American Chamber of Commerce of Paris, April, 1903 (pamphlet).
150. Annual Report Johannesburg Chamber of Commerce, 1903 (pamphlet).
151. Annual Report Yokohama Foreign Chamber of Commerce, 1903 (pamphlet).
152. A New Method of Turpentining, Orcharding, Department of Agriculture (pamphlet).
153. Results of a Census of New South Wales, March, 1901 (pamphlet).
154. New South Wales Statistical Register, 1901 and previous years (1 volume).
155. Special Consular Report, Briquettes as Fuel in Foreign Countries (pamphlet).
156. Register for 1902-1903, Leland Stanford, Jr., University, April, 1903 (pamphlet).
157. Bulletin No. 10, Treasury Department, April, 1903 (pamphlet).
158. Boletin de Estadistica Fiscal, Diciembre de 1902, Republica Mexicana (pamphlet).
159. Results of a Census of the Colony of New Zealand, March, 1901 (1 volume).
160. Civil Report of Brigadier-General Leonard Wood, Governor of Cuba, Vols. I, II, III, IV, V and VI, January 1 to May 1, 1902.
161. Consular Reports, July, 1903; Commerce, Manufactures, etc.
162. Yearbook of the Department of Agriculture, 1902.
163. Bulletin de lo Societe de Geographie Commerciale de Paris, 1903.
164. Fifty-fourth Annual Report of the Cincinnati Chamber of Commerce, 1902 (1 volume).
165. Congressional Records, Fifty-seventh Congress, Second Session, Vols. I, II and III.
166. Congressional Records, Index to Vol. XXXVI, Parts 1, 2 and 3.
167. Trust Laws; Act to Regulate Commerce and Acts Supplementary Thereto, 1887-1903 (pamphlet).
168. Report of the Buffalo Merchants' Exchange, 1902.
169. Annual Report of the Southampton Chamber of Commerce, 1902-1903.
170. Boston Merchants' Association Bulletin, No. 25, June, 1903.
180. Seventh Annual Report of the Interstate Commerce Commission, 1902.

Additions to Library.

181. Seventieth Annual Report of the Philadelphia Board of Trade, January 26, 1903.
182. Annual Statistical Report of the New York Produce Exchange for the Year 1902.
183. The Philadelphia Maritime Exchange Annual, 1903.
184. Annual Report Milwaukee Chamber of Commerce, 1902-1903 (1 volume).
185. Annual Report of the Cleveland Chamber of Commerce, 1903 (1 volume).
186. Annual Report of the Melbourne Chamber of Commerce, 1902-1903 (pamphlet).
187. Annual Report Hongkong Chamber of Commerce, 1902 (1 volume).
188. Forty-second Annual Report of the Cape Town Chamber of Commerce, 1902 (pamphlet).
189. Year Book and Directory Pittsburg Chamber of Commerce, 1903 (1 volume).
190. Annual Report Brisbane Chamber of Commerce, 1902-1903 (pamphlet).
191. One Hundred and Eighteenth Report by the Directors of the Chamber of Commerce and Manufactures of the City of Edinburgh, 1903 (pamphlet).
192. Annual Report New York Produce Exchange, 1902-1903 (1 volume).
193. Official Record of the Union and Confederate Navies in the War of the Rebellion, Series 1, Vol. XVI.
194. Officers of the Army of the United States, September 20, 1903 (pamphlet).
195. Official Army Register for 1903 (1 volume).
196. Hamburg's Handel und Schiffahrt, 1902.
196. Report of the Bengal Chamber of Commerce, 1902 (1 volume).
198. Exports Declared for the United States for Quarter Ending March 31, 1903 (pamphlet).
199. Thirty-sixth Report of Boston Port and Seaman's Aid Society, 1903 (pamphlet).
200. Bulletin de la Chambre d'Agriculture de Cochinchine, April and May, 1903 (pamphlet).
201. Exports of Manufactures from the United States and Their Distribution, 1790 to 1902 (1 volume).
202. Bulletin No. 3, United States Census Office, 1903 (pamphlet).
203. The Japan Correspondence, 1903 (1 volume).
204. Report Sixth Annual Convention of the National Live Stock Association, 1903 (1 volume).
205. Annual Report of the Chief of Engineers, United States Army, 1903 (1 volume).

206. Summary of Yokohama City, Annual Statistics No. 1, 1903 (pamphlet).
207. The Results of Reciprocity with Brazil, by Lincoln Hutchinson (pamphlet).
208. Boletin de Estadistica Fiscal, Republica Mexicana, April and May, 1903 (2 pamphlets).
209. Estadistica Comercial de la Republica de Chile, 1902 (1 volume).
210. Bulletins Nos. 215 and 216, United States Geological Survey, 1901 to 1903 (2 pamphlets).
211. Volume XLV, United States Geological Survey, Monographs.
212. Navigation Laws of the United States (1 volume).
213. California Hydrography, United States Geological Survey, 1903 (pamphlet).
214. Markets for Agricultural Implements and Vehicles, Bureau of Statistics Department of Commerce and Labor (pamphlet).
215. Bulletins Nos. 43 and 44, United States Department of Agriculture (2 pamphlets).
216. Monthly Report of the Yokohama Chamber of Commerce.
217. Report of the Ninth Annual Meeting of the Lake Mohonk Conference on International Arbitration, 1903 (pamphlet).
218. Universita Commerciale Luigi Bocconi, Milano, 1902-1903 (pamphlet).
219. Bulletin 22, United States Department of Agriculture, The Present Status of Rice Culture in the United States, 1903 (pamphlet).
220. Bulletin 35, United States Department of Agriculture, Recent Foreign Explorations, 1903 (pamphlet).
221. Bulletin 113, United States Department of Agriculture, Irrigation of Rice in the United States, 1902 (pamphlet).
222. Report No. 6, United States Department of Agriculture, Rice; Its Cultivation, Production and Distribution in the United States and Foreign Countries, 1893 (pamphlet).
223. Year Book Springfield Board of Trade, 1903 (pamphlet).
224. The Water Supply of the City of New York (1 volume).
225. Memoria del Superintendente de Aduanas Sobre la Renta y el Comercio Exterior en 1902, Republica de Chile (pamphlet).
226. Statistical Atlas, Twelfth Census of the United States (1 volume).
227. United States Geological Survey, Monographs XLIV (1 volume).
228. Statistics of Railways in the United States, 1902 (1 volume).
229. Bulletin de la Chambre d'Agriculture de Cochinchine, February, 1903 (pamphlet).
230. Statistische Mittheilungen betreffend Bremens Handel und Schiffahrt, 1902 (pamphlet).
231. Geographic Tables and Formulas, United States Geological Survey, 1903 (pamphlet).

Additions to Library.

232. Forty-ninth Annual Report Commercial Exchange, Philadelphia, 1903 (pamphlet).
233. Bulletin 36, United States Department of Agriculture, 1903 (pamphlet).
234. Le Commerce du Monde, 1903 (pamphlet).
235. Consular Reform and Commercial Expansion, 1903 (pamphlet).
236. Annual Report of the Commissioner of Navigation, 1903 (1 volume).
237. Annual Report Upon the Improvement of Rivers and Harbors in California Tributary to and North of San Francisco Bay, and of Pearl Harbor, Hawaii, 1903 (pamphlet).
238. Annual Statistical Report of The Merchants' Exchange, 1902-1903 (pamphlet).
239. The Rise and Progress of the Standard Oil Company (1 volume).
240. Fifty-third Annual Report Adelaide Chamber of Commerce, 1903 (pamphlet).
241. First Biennial Report of the Board of Architecture, 1903 (pamphlet).
242. First Annual Report Johannesburg Chamber of Commerce, 1903 (pamphlet).
243. The Regulation of Commerce Through a Dispensing Power, Nimmo, 1903 (pamphlet).
244. Why the Frye-Payne Shipping Bill Should be Passed at the Next Session of Congress, by Joseph Nimmo, Jr. (pamphlet).
245. The Relations of the Frye-Payne Shipping Bill to the Commercial Interests of the Pacific Coast, by Nimmo, 1900 (pamphlet).
246. Report on Cuba, by H. D. Dumont, May, 1903 (pamphlet).
247. Annual Report of the Hawaiian Sugar Company, of Makaweli, Kauai, 1902 (pamphlet).
248. The Foreign Buyers' Catalogue.
249. Boletin de Estadistica Fiscal, ano fiscal de 1901-1902, Republica Mexicana (pamphlet).
250. The Blue Book of California Manufacturers and Producers (pamphlet).
251. Thirteenth Annual Report of the Perth Chamber of Commerce, 1903 (pamphlet).
252. Report of the Committee of the Bengal Chamber of Commerce, 1902, Vol. 1.
253. Boletin de Estadistica Fiscal, February and March, 1903, Republica Mexicana (pamphlet).
254. Bulletins Nos. 211, 212 and 217, United States Geological Survey (3 pamphlets).
255. Bulletins Nos. 32, 33, 41 and 42, United States Department of Agriculture (5 pamphlets).
256. Annual Report of the Department of the Interior, 1902, Vol I.

257. Bulletins Nos. 209, 210 and 213, United States Geological Survey (3 pamphlets).
258. Bulletin No. 3, United States Census Office (pamphlet).
259. List of Merchant Vessels of the United States, 1903 (1 volume).
260. Geological Atlases of the United States, Nos. 93 and 95 (2 pamphlets).
261. Atlas to Accompany Monograph XLV, United States Geological Survey (pamphlet).
262. Folios 282, 283, 284, 285, 286, 287, 289, 291 and 292, United States Geological Survey, 1903.
263. Exports Declared by the United States During the Four Quarters Ending June 30, 1902 (1 volume).
264. List and Station of the Commissioned and Warrant Officers of the Navy of the United States, and the Marine Corps on the Active List, July 1, 1903 (pamphlet).
265. Bulletin de la Chambre d'Agriculture de Cochinchine, 1903 (pamphlet).
266. Statistics of the Port of Hannibal, Brazil, for 1902 (pamphlet).
267. Report of the Country Recently Examined in the Davenport and Murchison Ranges, Along the Frew River and Eastward of Tennant's Creek, etc., South Australia (pamphlet).
268. Statistics of the Colony of New Zealand, 1901 (1 volume).
269. California Blue Book, 1903.

LIST OF BOOKS PURCHASED FOR THE LIBRARY DURING YEAR 1903-1904.

Century Dictionary and Cyclopedia.
Whitaker Almanac, 1903.
The World Almanac and Encyclopedia, 1903.
Mead Irrigation Institution.
Argonauts of California, by C. W. Haskins.
Kelly's Directory of Merchants, Manufacturers and Shippers of the World, 1903.
Around the Capital.
Chronicle and Directory of China and Japan, 1903
Statesman's Year Book, 1903.
Directories, San Francisco, 1878-1879, 1881-1882 and 1883-1884.
Annual Statistician, 1903-1904.

E. SCOTT, *Librarian.*

REPORTS OF WILLIAM M. BUNKER

REPRESENTATIVE IN WASHINGTON, D. C.

OUTLINE REVIEW OF THE ACTS ADOPTED AT THE SECOND SESSION OF THE FIFTY-SEVENTH CONGRESS.

Report presented at Quarterly Meeting, April 21, 1903.

The first act adopted at the second session of the Fifty-seventh Congress amends Section 20 of an act simplifying the laws in relation to the collection of the revenues, approved March 10th, 1890. The act provides that any merchandise deposited in any public or private bonded warehouse may be withdrawn for consumption within three years from the date of original importation on payment of the duties and charges to which it may be subject by law at the time of such withdrawal, this providing that the same rate of duty shall be collected thereon as may be imposed by law upon like articles of merchandise imported at the time of the withdrawal.

The first act affecting the Pacific Coast relates to grants of land to the Territory and State of Washington for school purposes, and prescribing the conditions under which sections, fractional in quantity, are given a United States title.

The Pacific Coast gains through the passage of an act establishing a lighthouse and fog signal station at Mukilteo Point, near the city of Everett, Washington.

An act approved January 12th authorizes the issuance of a patent to the County of Clallam, Washington, for a parcel of land 222 feet in width in the town site of Port Angeles.

An act of general interest amends the internal revenue laws, so that all distilled spirits in internal revenue bonded warehouses shall be entitled to the same allowance for loss, from leakage or evaporation, which now exists in favor of distilled spirits produced, gauged and so deposited prior to January 1st, 1891, and subject to the same conditions and limitations.

The act relating to Hawaiian silver coinage and silver certificates, approved January 14th, deals with silver coins and silver certificates. The last section provides that the cost of transporting Hawaiian coins from the Islands to the Mint at San Francisco, and the return of a like amount in the subsidiary coins of the United States to the Islands, shall be borne by the United States, providing the expense be kept within ten thousand dollars.

An act of general interest, approved January 15th, provides for the rebates of duties imposed by law on all coal of every form and description imported into the United States from foreign countries for a period of one year from and after the passage of the act.

By act No. 30, certain real property in the town of Juneau, and District of Alaska, upon which the public school building of the town of Juneau is now situated, being all of block 23, except lots numbered 5 and 6, is granted to the town of Juneau for school purposes.

One of the most important acts of Congress is Public—No.33, entitled "An act to promote the efficiency of the militia and for other purposes." The act provides for the reorganization of the militia of the United States and in twenty-five sections deals with the subject in greal detail.

One of the most important acts of the session, and one in which San Francisco through commercial connections has a direct interest, is that providing for the payment in part of judgments rendered under an act of the Legislative Assembly of the Territory of Hawaii for property destroyed in suppressing the bubonic plague in the Territory in 1899 and 1900, and authorizing the Territory to issue bonds for the payment of the remaining claims. One million dollars is appropriated out of any money in the United States Treasury not otherwise appropriated, to pay in part the judgments rendered under an act of the Legislative Assembly of the Territory of Hawaii by the Fire Claims Commission of that Territory for property destroyed in the years 1899 and 1900. The act was approved January 29, 1903, to take effect from and after its passage.

An act approved January 31st provides for the compulsory attendance of witnesses before registers and receivers of the land office. Witnesses shall have the right to receive their fee for one day's attendance in advance. The fees and mileage of the witnesses shall be the same as that provided by law in the District Courts of the United States in the districts in which such land offices are situated; and the witnesses shall be entitled to receive their fees for attendance in advance from day to day of the hearing.

Act No. 49 enables the Secretary of Agriculture to more effectually suppress and prevent the spread of contagious and infectious diseases of live stock. The Secretary is authorized and directed from time ti time to establish such ruels and regulations concerning the exportation and transportation of live stock from any place within the United States where he may have reason to believe contagious diseases exist, into and through any State of Territory and to foreign countries, and all such rules and regulations as he makes shall have the force of law.

The act to amend an act entitled "An act to establish a uniform system of bankruptcy throughout the United States," approved July 1st, 1898, was approved February 5th. It contains nineteen sections and covers five pages.

Act No. 65 provides for free homesteads on the public lands of actual and bona fide settlers in the north one-half of the Colville Indian Reservation, Washington, and reserves the public lands for that purpose.

California has more than a passing interest in the act approved February 9th, providing for the erection of a building for the use and accommodation of the Department of Agriculture. The cost of the building is fixed at $1,500,000. As the Agricultural Department has of late years shown a specially friendly interest in the development of the agricultural resources of California, and has made this development a feature of departmental policy, Californians will be largely benefited by this new and much needed building.

The appropriations for the diplomatic and consular service for the fiscal year ending June 30, 1904, show a number of salary increases, which are mainly due to altered classification. The Consul-General to Tientsin, assigned formerly to the third class and with a salary of three thousand dollars, is now in the second class, with a salary of three thousand five hundred dollars a year. For the preparation, printing, publication and distribution by the Department of State of the diplomatic, consular and other commercial reports, forty thousand dollars are allowed. The Secretary of State is authorized to expend not exceeding six thousand five hundred dollars for services of employees in the Bureau of Foreign Commerce; the sum of two thousand dollars for the cost of cablegrams in instructing consular officers to report upon matters of immediate importance to commerce and industry, and of cablegrams of cousuls on such subjects; also to defray the extra expense imposed upon consular officers in collecting data, and not exceeding two hundred and fifty thousand dollars in the purchase of such books, maps and periodicals as may be necessary to the editing of diplomatic, consular and other commercial reports. There is a provision that all terms of measure, weight and money shall be reduced to and expressed in terms of measure, weight and coin of the United States, as well in the foreign terms, and that each issue of diplomatic, consular and other commercial reports shall not exceed ten thousand copies. These reports will now be issued by the Bureau of Manufactures, Department of Commerce, although the collection of the data will be subject to approval by the Secretary of State. The Bureau of Manufactures and the Department of State will work together to promote foreign commerce. Under the new dispensation, the creation of a Department of Commerce, the commercial reports of consuls shall have greater practical value than ever before.

Act No. 86 defines what shall constitute and provide for assessments on oil mining claims. Where oil lands are located under the provisions of Title 32, Chapter 36, Revised Statutes of the United States, as placer mining claims, the annual assessment labor upon such claims may be done upon any one of a group of claims lying contiguous and owned by the same person or corporation, not exceeding five claims in all: Provided, that said labor will tend to the development or to determine the oil-bearing character of such contiguous claims.

Admittedly the most important measure passed at the second session of the Fifty-seventh Congress was the act to establish the Department of Commerce and Labor. The creation of this Department has engaged the attention of federal officials, congressmen and publicists, and the Department, as formed by Congress, is the result of several years of discussion and study. The functions of the Department may not be enumerated, because it is seen in the very inception of the enterprise that experience alone will enable the Secretary of the Department to shape its policy. The main purpose of the Department is the expansion of domestic and foreign commerce.

Through methods that are rendered necessary by the increase in the volume of domestic and foreign commerce since 1897, the expansion of commerce made a Department of Commerce indispensable. While the volume of business was comparatively small it was possible for the Treasury and other departments to safeguard commercial interests at home and abroad. With the increase of commerce since 1897, and bearing in mind that commercial activity of foreign countries, the Government of the United States finds it necessary to make new and modern arrangements for safeguarding the commercial interests of the people.

An act of interest to commercial people, and more especially those using transportation, is No. 103, approved February 19th. The act further regulates commerce with foreign nations and among the States. It deals with the failure upon the part of any carrier to file and publish the tariffs, or rates and charges, or strictly to observe such tariffs until changed according to law, and makes such failure a misdemeanor. The offending corporation shall be subject to a fine not less than one thousand dollars, nor more than twenty thousand dollars for each offense. It shall be unlawful for any person or corporation to offer, grant, or give, or to solicit, accept or receive any rebate, commission, or discrimination in respect of the transportation of any property in interstate or foreign commerce by any common carrier subject to said act to regulate commerce and the acts amendatory thereto, whereby any such property shall by any device whatever be transported at a less rate than that named in the tariffs published and filed by such carrier. The four sections of the act go into minute details.

An act approved February 24th established a lighthouse and fog-signal at the southwest point of Burrows Island, Rosario Strait, Washington, and appropriates fifteen thousand dollars for the construction of the same.

An act making appropriations for the legislative, executive and judicial expenses of the government for the fiscal year ending June 30th, 1904, and for other purposes, has no special interest for California beyond the fact that it makes allowances for salaries paid federal officials in the State.

An act approved February 25th grants the Central Arizona Railway Company the right of way for railroad purposes through the San Francisco Mountains forest reserve in Arizona.

On account of the intimate trade relations between San Francisco and Alaska, our merchants are interested in Act No. 135 amending the Civil Code of Alaska, providing for the organization of private corporations, and for other purposes. This act is long and elaborate, and covers nine printed sheets. It deals with various forms of litigation, makes rules for municipal elections, provides for street improvements, fire protection, water supply, lights, wharfage, maintenance of public schools, protection of public health, police protection, and the expenses of assessment and collection of taxes, etc. Many sections of the act deal with the formation and operation of private corporations in Alaska. The purposes include the construction, ownership, and operation of railroads, tramways, street railways, wagon roads, canals, flumes, telegraph and telephone lines, and the acquisition and operation of mines. The act provides for the operation of manufacturing and agricultural industries, and goes into particularities of corporate law.

Act No. 137 established a standard of value and provides for a coinage system in the Philippine Islands. Its thirteen sections describe the unit of value in the islands, which shall be the gold peso, consisting of 12.9 grains of gold, .9 fine, the said gold peso to become the unit of value when the government of the Philippine Islands shall have coined and ready for or in circulation not less than five millions of the silver pesos hereinafter provided for in this act; and the gold coins of the United States, at the rate of one dollar for two pesos hereinafter authorized to be coined, shall be legal tender for all debts, public or private, in the Philippine Islands. The act describes the method of coinage, and names in detail various conditions and limitations.

In the Deficiency Appropriation Act (No. 156), there is an allowance of $250,000 for work on barracks and quarters in the Philippine Islands, and for acquiring sites. For logs and cordwood purchased by the United States from the Alaska Commercial Company in Alaska, $17,486.84 is allowed. The Secretary of the Treasury is authorized and required to amend and adjust the accounts of the Alaska Commercial Company, the North American Transportation and Trading Company, and the Alaska Exploration Company for supplies furnished and services rendered the sick, destitute and starving natives of Alaska in the year 1900. The act also appropriates money for the support of the Department of Commerce and Labor.

The act to regulate the immigration of aliens into the United States (No. 162) was passed after elaborate discussion and careful consideration, and has attracted a great deal of attention throughout the United States. It contains 38 sections and covers 11 printed pages.

OF SPECIAL INTEREST TO CALIFORNIA.

An act placing a fog-bell and lens-lantern light on the southeastern end of Southhampton Shoal, San Francisco Bay, at a cost not to exceed thirty thousand dollars, was approved February 10, 1903.

An act granting to the State of California six hundred and forty acres of land in lieu of section sixteen, township seven south, range eight east, San Bernardino meridian, now occupied by the Torros band or villages of Mission Indians, was approved February

11th. Section sixteen becomes a part of the reservation heretofore set apart for the use and occupancy of these Indians.

The act (No. 144) making appropriations for the current and contingent expenses of the Indian Department allows $1,600 for the Mission-Tule Agency of California. The allowance for the general incidental expenses of the Indian service in California, including traveling expenses of various agents and support and civilization of Indians at the Round Valley, Hoopa Valley, and Tule River Agencies, and the pay of employees at said agencies, amounts to $15,000. In this bill is an allowance of $10,000 for the maintenance at Omaha, in the discretion of the Secretary of the Interior, of a warehouse for the receipt, storage and shipping of goods for the Indian service. There is an allowance of the same amount for the maintenance of a similar institution at St. Louis. The allowance of $10,000 for a warehouse at San Francisco was eliminated from the bill, owing to the vigorous opposition of senators from Nebraska and Missouri. It is thought that the next Congress will abolish the warehouse at Omaha and St. Louis and establish one at San Francisco, which is admittedly the best location for the purpose. The Secretary of the Interior is authorized to use any part of the $100,000 appropriated for the removal and support of the Mission Indians in California, and is expected to buy land, develop water, and invest such money as may be necessary in agricultural implements, harness, wagons, horses, subsistence supplies, and other necessaries. For the support and education of 450 pupils at the Indian School, Riverside, $75,150 is appropriated.

Act No. 157, making appropriations for sundry civil expenses of the Government for the fiscal year ending June 30, 1904, and for other purposes, contains the following items of interest to California:

For continuation of Fresno Post-office and Court-house Building, $25,000.

For continuation of Los Angeles Post-office and Court-house, $212,500.

For rental of temporary quarters for the accommodation of Government officers, and for electric current for power purposes at Los Angels, $12,500.

For continuation of building San Francisco Custom-house, $125,000. For quarters and bath-house and improvements at the quarantine station, San Diego, $6,000.

For fog-bell and lens-lantern light on the southeastern end of Southampton Shoal, San Francisco Bay, $30,000.

For a fog-signal and dwelling for its keeper at Piedras Blancas light station, $15,000.

For constructing, equipping and outfitting complete for service, a first-class steam light-vessel, with steam fog-signal, for Blunt's Reef, $90,000.

The Fish Commission appropriations include one of $4,620 for the Baird and Fort Gaston stations.

For the protection and improvement of the Sequoia National Park, and the construction and repair of bridges, fences, etc., $10,000.

For Crater Lake, National Park, Oregon, $2,000.

For support of reindeer stations in Alaska, and the introduction of reindeer from Siberia for domestic purposes, $25,000.

For continuing improvement of San Francisco Harbor by removel of Blossom Rock, $50,000.

Continuing improvement of Oakland Harbor, $131,000.

Completing harbor improvements, San Diego, $192,850.

Continuing improvement in San Pablo Bay by constructing a channel between the Straits of Carquinez and Golden Gate or Point Pinole, and Point Wilson or Lone Tree Point, $300,000.

Improving Stockton and Mormon Channels, $50,000.

Continuation of stone wall on the boundary line of the Reservation Presidio, $5,000.

For the constructing of buildings at and enlargements of such military posts as in the judgment of the Secretary of War may be necessary, etc., $1,500,000, to be immediately available.

For defraying the expenses of the California Debris Commission in carrying on the work authorized by the Act of Congress approved March 1st, 1893, $15,000.

For traveling and incidental expenses in the Territory of Alaska, $10,000.

In Act No. 159, making appropriations for the service of the Post-office Department for the fiscal year ending June 30th, 1904, there is provided:

"Additional compensation to the Oceanic Steamship Company for transporting the mails by its steamer sailing from San Francisco to Tahiti; all mails made up in the United States destined for the Island of Tahiti, $45,000. A further provision authorizes the Postmaster-General to spend such sums as may be necessary, not exceeding $55,000, to cover one-half of the cost of transportation, compensation and expense of clerks to be employed in assorting and punching mails in transit on steamships between the United States and other postal administrations in the International Postal Union, and not exceeding $40,000 for transferring the foreign mail from incoming steamships in New York Bay to the several steamships and railway piers, and between the steamship piers in New York City and Jersey City, and the post-office and railway stations, and for transferring the foreign mail from incoming steamships in San Francisco Bay to the piers."

Act No. 160, making appropriations for the Naval Service for the fiscal year ending June 30, 1904, contains the usual items covering the expenses of the Naval Training School at Yerba Buena Island, the expense of Mare Island Navy Yard, etc.

Act No. 161, increasing the limit of cost of certain public buildings, authorizing the purchase of sites for public buildings, authorizing the erection and completion of public buildings, and for other purposes, is of special interest to San Francisco, in that it contains this item of increase:

"United States Custom-house at San Francisco, California, from $1,000,000 to $1,500,000: Provided, that the Secretary of the Treasury may, in his discretion, provide space in said Customhouse for the Sub-Treasury."

(Signed) WILLIAM M. BUNKER,
Washington Representative Chamber of Commerce of San Francisco.

April 21, 1903.

THE COMMERCIAL PROSPECTS OF CALIFORNIA.

Report presented at Quarterly Meeting, July 21, 1903.

Mr. President and Gentlemen of the Chamber of Commerce of San Francisco:

I thank you for this audience. To address you is an honor. To speak for you at Washington, three thousand miles from home, is a double distinction. In return for your confidence, your compliments and your appreciation I can only say you have beggared me in thanks.

The Washington Bureau of the Chamber was born of necessity. The growth of San Francisco commerce called for commercial work at Washington. New and complex issues were arising. Old issues were not disposed of. It was essential that each commercial issue be followed to its logical conclusion. The Chamber of Commerce of San Francisco, the parent commercial organization of the Pacific Coast, after a thorough survey of the situation, very properly decided to take an initiative. Eighteen months ago you named me as your Washington representative and authorized me to represent you in the departments and before the committees at Washington. Under the official guidance of your President and Board of Trustees I have looked after the commercial interests of the city, State and Coast. While Congress was in session I co-operated with the Congressional delegation, a delegation, I may say, so far above the average as to form a bright and shining contrast. To that delegation you, gentlemen, and the people of California are indebted for active, earnest and successful work in the halls of Congress.

The Chamber of Commerce has accomplished more than was expected, and has made a record of which the members may be proud. For five years the city vainly asked for a new Custom House. The last Congress made the desired appropriation. In the argument before the House Committee on Public Buildings and Grounds for an appropriation for a new Custom House you spoke through your Washington representative. The document showing the value and necessity of a new home for the customs officials, a new and properly appointed office building, was prepared by your direction, by your representative, and filed with the Committee. In his successful effort to raise the appropriation from $1,000,000 to $1,500,000 that same document was borrowed by Senator Perkins for use with the Conference Committee. In the argument in favor of the bill providing for the irrigation of the arid and semi-arid lands you spoke to the House Committee on Irrigation through your representative. The address in the latter instance dealt in detail with the trade and commerce of the Pacific Coast, and was printed and circulated as an official document of the United States Senate and House of Representatives.

THE NEW CUSTOM HOUSE WILL BE BUILT ON PROPER LINES.

The new Custom House should meet the demands of the most ambitious and exacting San Franciscan. It is already known that the competing architects consist of D. W. Willard & Babb, Cook & Willard, associates, Redlands, Cal.; A. F. Rosenheim, Los Angeles, Cal.; Whidden & Lewis, Portland, Ore.; Thomas R. Kimball, Omaha, Neb.; Eames & Young, St. Louis, Mo.; Reid & Reid, San Francisco; Newton J. Tharp, San Francisco; John G. Howard, Berkeley, Cal.; Clinton Day, San Francisco; Bliss & Faville, San Francisco; William Mooser, San Francisco; Shea & Shea, San Francisco. Seven of the twelve are San Francisco men, and all save two are Pacific Coast men. The judges who will make the selection are Frank Miles Day, Philadelphia, Pa.; William M. Akin, New York; E. B. Green, Buffalo, N. Y.; John M. Carrere, New York; Supervising Architect Taylor of the Treasury Department, Washington, D. C.

In the course of an interview with Hon. James K. Taylor, Supervising Architect of the Treasury, a few days since, I learned facts and figures relating to the character and dimensions of the structure. The new Custom House will contain 2,400,000 cubic feet. There will be 25,000 square feet on each floor. The five floors will therefore square in the aggregate 125,000 feet. The sum of $1,440,000 will be allowed for the estimated cost of the building. Of the $1,500,000 appropriated, $60,000 will be retained for contingencies. The architectural competition will cover a period from five to five and one-half months. This length of time will permit the transfer of plans to and from Washington, and also allow for the necessary correspondence. Mr. Taylor has visited this city, is familiar with the climatic conditions, and appreciates the value of sunshine. The new Custom House will be built on lines permitting the greatest possible use of natural light. The structural effects will be all we San Franciscans can ask. In the light of our previous experience with public buildings these structural details are interesting and suggestive. Mr. Taylor recognizes that the shade so necessary in the heat of an Eastern summer, where much of the Custom House work is performed under almost intolerable conditions, is more than dispensable here. The new Custom House will, therefore, have all the available light and sunshine. This and kindred matters have been given due weight in preparing the specifications.

THE DEPARTMENT OF COMMERCE AND LABOR IS LAYING A BROAD FOUNDATION.

The Chamber of Commerce of San Francisco was one of the earliest and most strenuous advocates of a Department of Commerce and Labor. At your request your Washington representative advocated the Department bill at a meeting of the House Committee on Inter-State and Foreign Commerce. The action of the Chamber commended itself to Hon. George B. Cortelyou, who had already been unofficially selected for the position of Secretary of the Department. Since his appointment Mr. Cortelyou has borne the Chamber in mind. The choice of this gentleman is for many reasons one of the best that could have possibly been made. By instinct and education an organizer, equipped by experience for the most exacting executive position, raised from place to place through proven merit, firm, forceful and tireless, and above all, ambitious for the practical success of his Department, it seems to me from my Washington viewpoint that we may expect this official to meet his high ideals. For the first time in the history of the country domestic and foreign commerce will be systematically and scientifically served. This service was impossible under the old arrangement of bureaus dealing scatteringly with commercial affairs. The functions of the Department may not be detailed because it is in process of organization. In the course of an interview with Secretary Cortelyou that gentleman gave me facts that I am at liberty to state. It is known that the newly created Bureau of Corporations, of which Hon. James R. Garfield is Commissioner, is fully organized and hard at work. The Bureau of Manufactures will be organized as soon as its duties shall have been determined. The bureaus transferred from the State, Treasury and Interior Departments are being reorganized under the direction of the Secretary.

In order to systemize the new departments Mr. Cortelyou created this Commission on Organization:

Carroll D. Wright, Commissioner of Labor, Chairman.
S. N. D. North, Census Office, Vice-Chairman.
James R. Garfield, Commissioner of Corporations.
O. H. Tittmann, Superintendent, Coast and Geodetic Survey.
Geo. M. Bowers, Commissioner of Fish and Fisheries.
F. P. Sargent, Commissioner-General of Immigration.
O. P. Austin, Chief of the Bureau of Statistics.
Frank H. Hitchcock, Chief Clerk, Department of Commerce and Labor, Secretary.

The Commissioners found existing bureaus were in several cases during the same work; that some bureaus were doing valueless work, and that consolidation would insure better results. They found, as expected, that the changed conditions in our foreign trade had not been officially met. The conditions, and not officials, were blameworthy. In the absence of a Department of Commerce there was no department properly qualified for modern commercial work. If any intelligent and thinking man doubts the need of a Department of Commerce, that doubt will be dispelled by the reports of the commission organized to gather facts and figures for Secretary Cortelyou.

There is curiosity regarding the special advantages commerce will derive from the Department of Commerce and Labor. These may not be defined until the Commission shall have assembled facts and figures relating to trade and commerce, and until the lines of each bureau shall have been definitely fixed. Until this work has been done, the Commission reports are filed, and the suggestions of the men of affairs have been considered, no man can measure the probable effects of the Department work.

THE FIRST STEP TOWARD CONSULAR REFORM.

The general utility of the Department of Commerce has already been shown. A special case relates to the Consular Service. The service was last reorganized in 1856. The change was a slight modification of the laws of 1796. The service is archaic and inefficient. The best that can be said of it is that it is better than it was. Every effort to make a system of this service has been successfully defeated by politicians who have for patronage reasons opposed a higher standard of consular qualifications. The law creating the Department of Commerce and Labor wisely transferred to this Department the Bureau of Foreign Commerce, which had previously been a branch of the Department of State. Under the new dispensation the consular reports on trade and commerce will be edited and published under the direction of the Department of Commerce and Labor. This Department will write to consular officers for specific commercial information, with the expectation and intention of receiving specific and satisfactory replies. The consular officers, already fairly active in the promotion of trade, will now face a condition instead of a theory. If their commercial reports fall below the standard of the Department of Commerce and Labor, the State Department will be asked to use its influence in the right direction and deal with the situation. This is the first step toward consular reform since 1856.

A MESSAGE FROM SECRETARY CORTELYOU.

It is a pleasure and a privilege to present to you, gentlemen, the compliments of Secretary Cortelyou, and to be able to say for him that he appreciates the progress of the Pacific Coast, the importance of Pacific Ocean commerce, and the splendid development of San Francisco, and the State. In felicitating you on the prosperity and prospects of the community, he said that he recalls with interest and pleasure his visit with the McKinley party. As soon as his Department is in running order, he will revisit the State for the purpose of renewing his acquaintance with Californians and studying our commercial conditions and necessities. You have a direct interest in this visit, as you have in this Department. The Department of Commerce and Labor already ranks fourth among the National Departments with respect to numerical strength. It is the youngest and lustiest. Organized on business lines for business purposes, and directed by a man of force and foresight, its sphere of influence must steadily expand. To this Department, more than to any other, the business men of the country will look for relief and assistance. The business interests of California, and especially those of San Francisco, are so diversified and so swiftly increasing, that we are bound to have the largest use for this business Department of the Government. I betray no confidence in saying that the Department appreciates our commerce, our advantages in the Asiatic trade, and the necessity of officially fostering this trade. And I am in position to say that the trade interest of the Pacific will receive the first attention of the Department.

THE EFFECTS OF ECONOMIC CHANGES.

Within two years our economic conditions have completely changed. The first step of civilization is agricultural. The second is industrial. Within two years California has taken the second step. Californians cannot be blamed for conjuring with fuel oil and electric power, and for the moment forgetting that theirs is the land of floral, fruit and climatic superiority. Their modified rapture is distinctly creditable. The absence of brag and bluster means much. If we may trust the signs of the times the people see their new opportunities. And what opportunities! After annexation and expansion, the long-distance transmission of electric energy and the find of fuel oil came as two brighter blessings. These agents cut the cost of motive power in halves. The reduced expense for motive power is the prime cause of the increased and increasing industrial activity. The agricultural, commercial and industrial activities, in a sense inter-dependent, are harmoniously working for general progress. These changed conditions were the subject of an address delivered by your representative before a meeting of the Commercial Museum of Philadelphia.

OUR GROWING TRADE WITH ASIA.

Contributing causes for the new activity in Asiatic trade are our acquisition of the Philippines, the annexation of the Hawaiian Islands, and the idea in the great financial centers of the country that the stimulation of American trade in Asia is inseparable from the maintenance of American supremacy in the trading world. There is no sentiment in this idea. It is born of events. The men who conceived it are close calculators. In this connection cycles of Cathay are nothing to them. They think in business periods. Your President and the Trustees saw the dawn of this new era when they asked me to report on the effect of the Trans-Siberian Railway. After seeing what I saw and hearing what I heard in Japan, China and Siberia, in 1899, I was not surprised when we sold Asia $43,000,000 wirth of goods in 1902, as against $15,000,000 worth in 1892. I saw that if the Asiatic demand for American products maintained the existing ratio of progress our goods would be wanted in ever-increasing quantities. I saw that Asia could and would absorb a large part of the surplus food stuffs of the Pacific Coast. Then, as now, there was talk of Eastern Siberia dominating the Asiatic flour market. This talk is baseless. Emotional travelers saw, as they still see, in the flowered plains of the Amur and Trans-Baikail regions the finest of wheat lands. The wheat of Eastern Siberia is poor stuff. The climatic conditions are against the farmer and can never be modified. To China alone the exports of American flour from San Francisco were 386,508 barrels in 1892. In 1902 San Francisco shipped 590,044 barrels to China. The exports of American flour to China, Hongkong and Russian China in the ten months ending with April, 1902, amounted to 1,486,047 barrels, valued at $4,423,692, and in ten months of 1903, 1,437,472 barrels, valued at $4,676,491. This slight reduction in the total quantity shipped is due to the fact that the shipments of 1902 were above the normal, by reason of the light importations of flour in 1901, during the war period in China. These are Bureau of Statistics figures. To the ordinary man the term "Asiatic trade" lacks special significance. He knows it relates to trade with Asia, and that we are constantly exporting to and importing from Asia. He does not realize that all the leading countries of the earth are competing for the trade of several hundred million Asiatics, and that this trade is really the great commercial prize of the day. He does not realize that this trade may be the making of his trade, calling or business.

THE WHOLE COUNTRY HAS AN INTEREST IN THE ASIATIC TRADE.

The Pacific Mail liner Korea, sailing from San Francisco for Asia on the 19th of June, carried as part of her cargo 4,000 tons (not barrels) of flour. This is the largest single shipment of flour ever made from San Francisco by a liner. This shipment concerns the mechanics, the manufacturers and the merchants east of the Rocky Mountains, as well as those of the Pacific Coast. The steamer that carried this freight was built at Newport News by Atlantic Coast mechanics. The machinery used in harvesting the wheat from which this flour was made was in part, at least, manufactured in Atlantic or Middle Western States. It may represent a dozen States. The machinery with which the flour was milled was partially made east of the Rocky Mountains. In addition to the 4,000 tons of flour the Korea carried 3,500 tons of miscellaneous freight, of which at least 3,000 tons were articles of what the Pacific Coast calls Eastern manufacture. That cargo, similar to those carried by steamers of the other trans-Pacific lines, proves the oneness of the country. The manifest of the steamer mirrors our products, from the Atlantic to the Pacific, from Maine to Mexico, speaking for the thousand and one interwoven interests of mechanic, manufacturer, merchant and general public. So vast and sweeping is this American trade with Asia that no community escapes its reflected influence. But we have not done with the demand for Pacific Coast breadstuffs by countries across the Pacific. The values of Pacific Coast breadstuff exports to Asia and Oceania in the first ten months for three fiscal years to April 1st were: 1901, $5,110,494; 1902, $5,835,168; 1903, $10,983,211.

Mark the increase in the first ten months of the fiscal year 1903 over the first ten months of the fiscal year 1902, $4,948,043, or 40 per cent.

The breadstuff exports which make this striking showing are corn, oats, flour and wheat.

Food for Asia and Australasia, and food for American thought! While San Francisco, as the metropolis of the Pacific, is bound to be the biggest beneficiary of American trade with Asia and Oceania, every section of the country must share in this trade advantage. As the Pacific Coast faces Asia, so face we the fact that with its vast natural wealth, and the aid of the trans-continental railways and ocean steamers, the Coast holds the strategic position with respect to Asiatic trade. The distance from London to Shanghai is 10,500 miles. The distance from San Francisco to Shanghai is 5,586 miles. The distance from London to Yokohama is 11,665 miles. The distance from San Francisco to Yokohama is 4,536 miles. This Coast is the natural base for the Asiatic trade campaign. This city, third in commercial rank, seventh in the volume of business, the assured ultimate terminal point of nearly every trans-continental railway in the United States, is the recognized focal point of the Asiatic trade campaign. Why was our strategic position so long ignored? The answer covers several reasons. The industrial activities of the region east of the Mississippi River long absorbed the attention of financiers. Then there were European markets to exploit. We may assume that export trade to Europe has reached the limit for this decade. The line of least resistance in export trade leads to the Asiatic East.

The present base line of rate reckoning is between the United States and Europe. This line was created by economic development. The activities of the trans-Mississippi region and the growth of Pacific Ocean commerce are changing the currents of trade. The flow towards the Pacific Coast and thence across the ocean to Asia has gained irresistible force.

RELATION OF THE ASIATIC TRADE TO AMERICAN INVESTMENTS.

The primary geographic advantage of the Pacific Coast must be used for its full value by the American leaders of finance and trade. Unless this is done the United States will lose influence in the Asiatic markets. None of this influence can be spared if we would insure the integrity of American securities. The expansion of American trade in Asia is more than a thing to be desired; it is a necessity. In this way, and in this way only, can our financiers maintain the equilibrium of American investments. To-day London fixes the price of silver, New York the price of cotton, and Chicago the price of wheat, corn and provisions. San Francisco, third in commercial importance among American cities, and the local financial city of the Pacific Coast, will finally fix the world's price for several of the great commodities. The signs so read.

THE POTENTIAL INFLUENCE OF THE CHAMBER.

The Pacific Coast is now an integral part of the country. East and West have a community of interest. They draw closer day by day. The prejudices due to wide separation are no more. The spirit that developed the Atlantic States on commercial and indusrial lines has finally reached the Coast. It has mingled with the buoyant spirit of the Pacific. As a result we have in the present public enterprise an effective blend. Each section, East and West, appreciates the fact that each needs the other in its business. California cannot grow, San Francisco cannot grow, the other Coast cities cannot grow without creating a larger market for Eastern products. Therefore the East favors California, San Francisco and the other Coast cities. Among the agencies that have exploited commercial and industrial California in the East, none can claim greater credit than the Chamber of Commerce of San Francisco. Your President and Board of Trustees saw and utilized their opportunity nearly two years ago. They anticipated the awakening of the State. They were first in the field of promotion that has proved most fruitful. They began their campaign of commercial education at the National Capital. They planned their work on broad lines. The results have vindicated their judgment. Trade and commerce and the allied industrial interests have been systematically and successfully, and better still, legitimately promoted under the Chamber's direction. The debt of this community to the Chamber may not be measured. The man who owns real estate, the manufacturer, the artisan, the day laborer, in fact, every one eager for the material progress of the city must thank the Chamber in part for the present high tide of local prosperity.

REPORT

Presented at Annual Meeting, January 19, 1904.

To the Hon. President, Board of Trustees and Members of the Chamber of Commerce of San Francisco.

Gentlemen—The Washington Bureau of the Chamber begins its third year under flattering auspices. The finished work speaks for itself. The future offers larger opportunities. The Bureau is the natural sequel to previous prompt action by the Chamber administration. It is only one link in a long chain of events. The past and the present may be pertinently joined. The broad and strong foundations of the San Francisco commerce of to-day were at least partially laid by the Chamber of Commerce of San Francisco. The home records and the files at Washington show that the Chamber has fairly earned its power and prestige. The commercial history of California is the history of the Chamber. Chamber initiatives have succeeded. The Chamber was the first to properly appraise the American-Asiatic trade. It forced the facts to the front. These same facts affect the trade issues of to-day. The President of the Chamber and his associated Trustees saw the impending changes in Asiatic trade. While public men were discussing the effects on the Pacific Coast of the Trans-Siberian Railroad, and were needlessly alarmed, the Chamber arranged an official inspection of the Thans-Siberian route. It initiated a study of the new transportation facilities. It planned a commercial reconnoissance of Northeastern Asia. As the representative of the Chamber I had the honor and the privilege of studying commercial conditions in China, Japan and Siberia, and latter following the lines of trade between Asia and Europe. The enquiry into the Asiatic trade involved interviews with consular representatives and a special study of trade in Northern China and Eastern Siberia. Public interest centered in Northern China and Eastern Siberia. These regions were the first beneficiaries of the Thans- Siberian Railway. The records of the Chamber show that its reports of Asiatic trade conditions were fair, full and faithful. The Asiatic demand for American bread stuffs, the demand for American merchandise and the results that would follow Russian tariff changes were discussed in detail. The necessity of officially safeguarding American trade in the Russian-Asiatic region was aggressively demonstrated. The several reports made to the Chamber were later circulated officially by the Washington authorities. In view of the political and commercial crisis in Manchuria and the changes that threaten American trade in Northeastern Asia, it is distinctly appropriate that the work of the Chamber in promoting, protecting and exploiting trade interests, should be borne in mind.

The Chamber went to the very foundation of American trade with that portion of Siberia directly tributary to the Pacific Coast. The facts and figures were presented in 1899. Up to that time no one had taken a trade census of Eastern Siberia. In one of the reports issued by the Chamber the commercial and vital statistics of Vladivostock, Khabarovsk, Blagovestchensk, Stretyinsk, and other cities and towns of Eastern Siberia were printed in the English language for the first time. The business of each place was studied and classified. The social facts relating to trade and figures covering the industrial activity were, through the Chamber, presented to the American public. Incidentally, the value of consular reform was emphasized and the advanced views of the Chamber were fortified.

THE BUSINESS NECESSITY FOR CONSULAR REFORM.

The Chamber was one of the first commercial organizations to stand for consular service reform. The vast foreign trade of San Francisco widened the horizon of this commercial community and showed the necessity for a more practical consular service. The service has been bettered in the last few years. The service is better to-day than it was a year ago. But the service will not meet the demands of commerce until a consular reform bill shall have been passed. The chief needs of the consular service are:

A regularly graded classification, including all salaried consuls, or consul-generals, based on the amounts of salary, and so arranged as to permit the interchange of consular posts within the same grade, by order of the President alone, or advancement by promotion from grade to grade.

The fixing of salaries for the higher grades sufficiently adequate to encourage capable men to enter the service as a career, and provision for the turning of all fees received at salaried posts into the Government Treasury; and

The establishment of a system of competitive examination, open to all, for entrance to the lower grades, of transfers and promotions based upon superior capacity shown in actual service and of retention during good behavior.

As the representative of the Chamber I attended the annual meeting at Baltimore on the 11th ult., of the National Consular Reform Committee, of which Hon. H. A. Garfield is President, and assisted in the discussion of the reform measure which Congress will be asked to adopt. The consular bill introduced by Hon. Henry Cabot Lodge, Senator from Massachusetts, and the bill introduced by Hon. Robert Adams, Jr., representing the Second Pennsylvania District, were carefully analyzed and compared. The Adams bill, as amended in committee, was finally made the committee measure. The friends of consular reform may be felicitated on the successful agitation of the consular reform issue. While it is true that no consular reform bill has been passed since 1856 and the service lacks system, the fact remains that active and aggressive agitation for consular reform has bettered the service. All that may be done by simple agitation has been done, and well done, and yet the need of consular improvement is greater to-day than ever. The changes in the currents of trade insure an increasing demand for better men in the service. The foreign competition in export trade grows fiercer. All the leading countries of the world are working for a larger share of the export trade. This is no mere assertion. No one who reads the commercial reports, the official statements and the popular literature of the business nations of the world can fail to notice the increased competition in export trade. The American people have standardized their business interests, have raised the efficiency of their manufacturing plants, have multiplied their transportation facilities, and have taken many strides of commercial progress. And yet, the consular service dealing directly with export trade is ruled by laws nearly fifty years old. In order to keep pace with our own commercial progress, in order to offset the aggressive action of foreign traders, the American Government must raise its consular service to a higher standard of efficiency, a standard that may only be reached through recognition of merit, and independent selection. The demand for reform is based on business needs. These needs are not of one class and are not limited to a few localities. They are especially imperative in British South Africa, where American exports have increased from Three Million Dollars to over Thirty-three Million Dollars in the last ten years; in Eastern Asia, with which, through an increasing tonnage, we are coming into closer contact, and in many other parts of the world. The state of affairs that permits uninformed and untrained men to represent the business interests of the country in foreign lands is absurdly artificial. In practical business life there is an ever increasing demand for the highest business ability. In the consular service there are men who have never had any business training, others who have demonstrated their lack of business ability, and others still, who for various reasons, are barely tolerable as consular officers. As the consular service is a business department of the Government and the consuls are supposed to do business in a business way, it follows, that only men familiar with business and who have the business instinct should be placed in consular positions.

DEPARTMENT OF COMMERCE AND LABOR.

The Chamber of Commerce of San Francisco early advocated the creation of a new department dealing directly in a public way with the strictly commercial affairs of the country. The Chamber memorialized Congress in favor of the needed department. Plans for the creation of this new branch of the public service were advocated by the representative of the Chamber at Washington at hearings of the House Interstate and Foreign Commerce

Committee. The department has shown its value. Scattered bureaus that formerly worked at cross purposes have been welded into a symmetrical system. Order has been devolved from confusion. The department is operated on business lines. Private business in the active cities and towns of the United States gets no greater care than that given public business by the new department. This is the general verdict. My own satisfactory experience is an incidental factor. The orderly and purposeful progress of the department may be accepted as an earnest of future achievements. The appropriation necessary to the proper operation of the department should be promptly voted. Money is needed for special probing of foreign markets, foreign methods, and foreign trade demands. The export trade of Germany is not based on lucky hits. That trade is not accidental. That trade is born of official inquiries in foreign countries. Trained investigators found bottom facts and bottom figures. These facts and figures were scattered throughout commercial Germany. The German traders moved in the light of accurate information. The American Government has finally organized a department to develop American trade. Given the necessary funds, and given them promptly, the Department of Commerce and Labor will be able to stimulate foreign trade at a time when such stimulation will advantageously affect every part of the country. If the funds of the Department of Commerce and Labor a few months since had allowed the Secretary to send to Asia a specially arranged expedition the export trade of the United States would have been benefited to an amount larger than the annual expenses of the foreign inquiry division. The Department has many and varied functions. At present the various bureaus are assembling guiding information. With this information domestic and foreign trade may be fostered, promoted and protected. The Pacific Coast has a special use for the Department of Commerce and Labor, a greater use, perhaps, than any other section of the country. This because the trade fields of the Pacific are without parallel.

THE PACIFIC COAST BASE FOR AMERICAN-ASIATIC TRADE.

The Pacific Coast line of 12,424 miles is the natural American base for Asiatic trade. No other western nation has an equally good base for this trade. Circumstances have conspired in favor of the Pacific Coast. San Francisco has been especially favored. It is the duty of San Francisco and Pacific Coast people generally to see that these favoring trade conditions are brought to national attention. The distance from London to Shanghai is 10,500 miles, as against 5,841 miles from San Francisco to Shanghai. It is 2,100 miles from San Francisco to Honolulu. It is 6,855 miles from San Francisco to the Philippines via the Hawaiian Islands. San Francisco has a Shanghai transportation advantage over London of 4,659 miles. San Francisco has relative transportation advantages over London with respect to other Asiatic ports. These advantages have been made more apparent through the annexation and expansion policies of the Government. And yet neither the Government nor the public has fully grasped the significance of the situation. American public men who have crossed the Russia Empire on the Trans-Siberian Railway in the last two years have praised the enterprise of Russia, and have seen in the march of that empire to Pacific waters a magnificent and commendable national policy. These observing Americans assert that Russia needs a Pacific trade base. They do not hesitate to say that in the absence of an Asiatic trade base the Russian Empire will fail to meet its manifest destiny. They do not hesitate to say in interviews, addresses, books and magazines that this trade base must be fixed in the living present. These views are being freely printed and broadly circulated. If a Pacific trade base is needed by Russia for the healthy extension of Russian-Asiatic trade, how much more necessary to the Asiatic trade interests of the United States is a broad and liberal policy on the part of the American Government that will permit the proper and natural use of Pacific Coast geographical advantages in American-Asiatic trade development.

Is it not clear that the American base should be hurriedly developed? The distance from New York to San Francisco is 3,200 miles. The distance from Dalny, the Russian city of Manchuria, to St. Petersburg is over 6,000 miles. It is also over 6.000 miles from St. Petersburg to Vladivostock; these distances show the strategic trade advantages of San Francisco. The distinguished American, more particularly the American public men who have simply praised the great eastern march of Russia, have missed the lesson of that march. They have failed to see or at least to mention that while the Russian nation marches in an eastern direction, the American nation marches westerly, and that in a trade sense, the two nations are making for the same point. The promotion policy pursued by Russia is more than interesting to the American people. It is a warning.

THE RADIATING INFLUENCE OF PACIFIC OCEAN TRADE.

The Government has an economic interest in Pacific Ocean trade. The expansion of this trade has made the Pacific Coast a natural official base. There are numerous illustrations in point. They effect various branches of the Government. The great military depot for quartermaster stores of the United States army is at Jeffersonville, Indiana, 867 miles from New York and over 2,300 miles from San Francisco. The depot was opened in the early part of the Civil War. Its location at that time, and for the next quarter of a century, suited the service. But to-day, after a lapse of more than forty years, after the country has altered its trade methods after the country has expanded thousands of miles, in short, after the commercial, military and population conditions of the country have in nearly every respect changed, the purchase of supplies deliverable at Jeffersonville for use in the Philippines, over 9,000 miles from the Jeffersonville depot, is against good business judgment. Most supplies used by the army at Pacific Coast points and in the Island possessions can be more easily and more cheaply bought at San Francisco and other Pacific Coast points than in eastern cities. This fact is admitted by army officers. But there is no military warehouse at San Francisco and there is the rub. Army supplies are often purchased for future use and must be stored in military buildings. Certain supplies for use in the Pacific Island possessions that could be advantageously bought in San Francisco, if deliverable at San Francisco, are bought elsewhere, because the Government requires delivery at Jeflersonville. In the absence of military warehouse accommodations at San Francisco these supplies, to be carried in stock and used as needed, must be delivered at Jeffersonville. The present interest of the service and the prospective emergency demands of the service certainly justify the War Department in erecting at San Francisco a large and modern warehouse.

A SAN FRANCISCO WAREHOUSE FOR INDIAN SUPPLIES.

Various agencies have worked many months for the establishment at San Francisco of a permanent warehouse for Indian supplies. At the second session of the Fifty-Seventh Congress an item providing for such a warehouse was favored by the Senate and thrust aside by the House Committee. Under the date of January, 1903, Hon. W. A. Jones, Commissioner of Indian Affairs, wrote to the Secretary of the Interior, recommending an appropriation of ten thousand dollars for the maintenance at San Francisco of a permanent warehouse for Indian supplies. There are reasons for assuming that an appropriation of this kind will carry in the present Congress. The economic necessity of this warehouse has impressed itself on the Government and may no longer be avaded. The reasoning that applies to other branches of the Government as to the use of this Pacific Coast base applies with equal force to Indian affairs. Commissioner Jones officially says that there is much more reason for a permanent warehouse in San Francisco than in some of the cities where such warehouses are maintained.

IMMIGRANT STATION AT SAN FRANCISCO.

The Committee on Commerce, through Senator Perkins, has favorably reported on the bill providing for the erection of buildings for an immigrant station at San Francisco. The bill appropriates $200,000 for the erection of the station. It is endorsed by

Secretary Cortelyou of the Department of Commerce and Labor, who says that in order to avoid the difficulties arising from attempts to communicate with the detained aliens, the buildings should be located on Government land in the harbor of San Francisco. Isolation from the mainland is also deemed necessary for sanitary reasons, from the fact that communicable diseases are peculiarly prevalent among aliens from Oriental countries.

THE CALAVERAS BIG TREE PARKS.

Hon. George C. Perkins, senior Senator from California, and Hon. James N. Gillett, have respectively introduced into the Senate and House a bill to acquire title to the two groves of big trees in Calaveras County, with a view to making national parks thereof. The bills are identical. They provide that the Secretary of the Interior shall buy the groves at a sum not exceeding $200,000. The Chamber has instructed its representative at Washington, D. C., to promote the passage of the measure, which is being actively pushed. The Outdoor Art League of California, the Woman's Auxiliary of the American Park and Outdoor Art Association, a national organization, and many affiliated improvement clubs, as well as many public men, are co-operating with the people of California in their efforts to preserve the big trees. The office of the Washington representative of the Chamber is a correspondence center for the organizations working for this great national measure. The favorable influences, stimulated by the Outdoor Art League of California, the directing agency of the great salvation enterprise, represent all the centers of thought of the country. These influences are working harmoniously on the theory that the preservation of these peerless products of nature is a national affair.

GOVERNMENT TESTS OF REDWOOD.

The Government is studying the chemistry of structural materials. An investigation directed by the Geological Survey has made excellent progress. The reports serve the lumbering interests and are of popular and practical value. Pacific Coast woods are being tested by the University of California. Hon. Addison

G. Foster, of Washington, is the author of a Senate bill appropriating $50,000 for testing the tensile strength of fir and other woods. This amount is to be used in continuing the tests now in progress. As it is desirable that redwood, an exclusive product of California, shall be specifically named in the Foster bill as one of the woods used for tesing purposes, the aid of the Chamber has been invoked by the redwood interests. The proper steps have been taken for amending the bill, and the indications promise official recognition of redwood. As redwood is superior to pine for permanent structural use the value of official tests of redwood, on scientific lines, is beyond dispute. The growing popularity of redwood in eastern markets enhances the importance and emphasizes the necessity of scientific endorsement.

THE VALUE OF UNITED ACTION.

As Pacific Coast interests grow greater and become more diversified, united action by Pacific Coast representatives is indispensable. The Coast has a common cause. Its representatives should make a common cause in the halls of national legislation. In years past, needless internectine strife has cost the Pacific Coast states millions. Appropriations by the National Government that should have been made have been lost through wrangles of Pacific Coast committees and the reflected influences of these wrangles at Washington. The representatives of other States have fanned and utilized Pacific Coast prejudices. These clever gentlemen have outwardly mourned and inwardly rejoiced at the miscarriage of Pacific Coast appropriation. Happily, conditions have changed. The representatives in the Senate and House of the several Pacific Coast States and Territories are working harmoniously for Pacific Coast interests. They have learned, through varied experience, that desired wholesale legislation can only be secured through united effort. There is a disposition to pool issues and pull together. The men from the Pacific realize that division of sentiment means defeat; they realize that the Administration, the great Deparements, the Senate, the House, and the Bureaus that influence legislation have been too often halted by prejudiced protests. The men from the Pacific realize that their respective constituencies have a community of interest. They are no longer pulled to and fro by local prejudices. They work together for Pacific Coast progress. It is to-day as it should be, all for one, and one for all. The other States have in times past reaped rich harvests from crops of discord on the shares of the Pacific. The new era, the era of peace among Pacific Coast representatives at Washington, should bring the Pacific Coast States into their own. The change comes none too soon. The Pacific and trans-Pacific developments have multiplied the legislative needs of the Pacific Coast. In the light of the progress and prospects of Pacific Coast States, the coloring of legislation through local prejudices were treason to the people who have made the far West. The Coast is developing with such rapidity and on so many lines that favoring legislation at Washington is of national concern. For the Pacific Coast offers a great and growing home market for American products and is the great Asiatic trade base. The members of the California delegation, to the last man, are working for the commercial pre-eminence of the Pacific Coast. They are industriously and intelligently forwarding the commercial interests of the State. They richly deserve popular confidence and popular support.

I have the honor to be,

Very respectfully yours,

WILLIAM M. BUNKER,

Representative at Washington, D. C., of the Chamber of Commerce of San Francisco.

Washington, D. C., January 12, 1904.

SEVENTH BANQUET, CHAMBER OF COMMERCE.

The seventh banquet of the Chamber was held in the Maple Room of the Palace Hotel Saturday, January 23d, at 6:30 p. m., about one hundred members of the Chamber participating, and the following invited guests, namely:

F. J. Symmes, President, and L. M. King, Secretary, The Merchants' Association; N. P. Chipman, President, California State Board of Trade; A. A. Watkins, President, Board of Trade of San Francisco; Mr. Hugh Craig, ex-President of the Chamber of Commerce; Chas. H. Spear, President, Board of State Harbor Commissioners; Hon. John G. Brady, Governor of Alaska; Professors Bernard Moses and Carl C. Plehn, University of California, and Wm. H. Seeley.

President George A. Newhall was toastmaster, with the honorary guests seated to his right and left.

President's Report

The President, Mr. Newhall, presented and read his annual report reviewing the work of the Chamber during the past year and giving statistics of the principal products of the State, and a general forecast of the increasing prosperity of the State and city.

Secretary's Report

The Secretary presented and read his annual report calling attention to the reports of the officers and of statistics which would be printed in the Annual Report.

Banquet.

Treasurer's Report

The Treasurer presented financial report for the quarter and year ending January 2, 1904, approved by the Chairman of the Finance Committee, showing cash balance on hand in savings banks, $6,907.12, which was duly approved and ordered placed on file.

Librarian's Report

The Librarian reported the additions to the library during the year, which was ordered received and placed on file.

Report Washington Bureau

The Secretary presented and read a portion of the report of Mr. William M. Bunker, the Washington representative of the Chamber, reviewing the acts of the present Congress pertaining to our commercial matters, and also touching upon the possibilities of the commerce of San Francisco and the Pacific Coast. Report of Mr. Bunker was ordered received and placed on file, and published in the Annual Report.

Report Nominating and Election Committee

The Secretary presented the report of the Nominating and Election Committee, certifying to the officers and Trustees elected at the annual election held January 12th.

The following addresses were made:

Address of Mr. F. J. Symmes

Mr. Symmes, President of the Merchants' Association, spoke, stating that the field of the work of the Merchants' Association was in the city, while that of the Chamber of Commerce practically covered our relations with the world; also called attention to the importance of fostering our trade with the Central and South American States bordering on the Pacific Ocean, stating that in our great desire to develop the Oriental trade that possibly this had been somewhat overlooked.

Address of Mr. Hugh Craig

Mr. Hugh Craig, ex-President of the Chamber, spoke, calling special attention to the work of the Chamber of Commerce in times past, particularly when it was under the leadership of the fathers of some of those who are now its present officers, besides speaking of the work of the Chamber during many years past.

Address of Mr. N. P. Chipman

Mr. N. P. Chipman, President of the California State Board of Trade, spoke of the resources of California, and what is being done to advertise them.

Address of Mr. A. A. Watkins

Mr. A. A. Watkins, President of the Board of Trade of San Francisco, made an appropriate address.

Address of Professor Bernard Moses

Professor Bernard Moses, of the University of California, an ex-member of the Philippine Commission, spoke, calling attention to the future development of the Philippine Islands, and of our trade in the Far East.

Address of Mr. Chas. H. Spear

Mr. Chas. H. Spear, President of the State Board of Harbor Commissioners, made an address touching upon the work and policy of the Board, and the work it had on hand. He stated that it was the desire of the Board of Commissioners to discontinue all improvements that could not be classified as permanent, and outlined the future improvements which were contemplated and which would be suitable for the growing commerce and trade which would be centered at this port. He also stated that it was a mistake to suppose that the harbor of San Francisco was such an expensive port, and compared it with others, dwelling upon the fact that the ports of Boston and Seattle, whose waterfront is owned by private corporations, were more expensive to shippers than the harbor of San Francisco, which was under the control of the State.

Address of Professor Carl C. Plehn Professor Carl C. Plehn, Dean of the College of Commerce of the University of California, spoke of the work of that institution in the way of promoting scientific commerce, the College of Commerce doing for commerce what the College of Agriculture was doing for the farmer.

Address of Mr. A. Sbarboro Mr. A. Sbarboro, President of the Manufacturers' and Producers' Association of California, discussed the wine industry of California, its past history and development, and called attention to the great future which was before it.

Address of Mr. H. D. Loveland Mr. H. D. Loveland, President of the Pacific Coast Jobbers' and Manufacturers' Association, spoke, calling attention to the work of that organization and its benefits in securing traffic regulations of interest to this coast.

Address of Governor John G. Brady, of Alaska Governor John G. Brady, of Alaska, spoke of the conditions prevailing in that district, and also stated that great efforts should be made to spread abroad information concerning the vast resources of Alaska, which to-day were practically unknown.

The banquet then terminated, the addresses of all the gentlemen having been exceedingly appropriate, and received with appreciation by those present.

FORM OF CALL FOR MEETING OF THE CHAMBER OF COMMERCE.

Hon......................................

President Chamber of Commerce of San Francisco:

Sir—The undersigned, in accordance with Article I of the By-Laws, respectfully request that you will call a Special Meeting of the Chamber on.................19..., at........o'clock for the purpose of....................................... and we hereby agree to attend said meeting personally.

(To be signed by at least five members.)

CORRESPONDENTS

Annual reports are exchanged with the following commercial organizations, and are furnished to all Foreign Consuls, local commercial and industrial associations and libraries. Members of the Chamber of Commerce of San Francisco traveling abroad will be furnished with a circular letter of introduction on application to the Secretary.

The American Chamber of Commerce, Paris, France.
The Chamber of Commerce of Calais, Calais, France.
The Chamber of Commerce of Havre, Havre, France.
The Camera do Comercio, Oporto, Portugal.
The Chamber of Commerce, London, England.
The Chamber of Commerce, Liverpool, England.
The Chamber of Commerce, Glasgow, Scotland.
The Chamber of Commerce, Bristol, England.
The Chamber of Commerce, Southampton, England.
The Chamber of Commerce, Genoa, Italy.
The Chamber of Commerce, Sydney, N. S. W.
The Chamber of Commerce, Melbourne, Australia.
The Chamber of Commerce, Geelong, Australia.
The Chamber of Commerce, Auckland, New Zealand.
The Hongkong Chamber of Commerce, Hongkong, China.
The Yokohama Foreign Chamber of Commerce, Yokohama, Japan.
The Chamber of Commerce, Canterbury, New Zealand.
The Chamber of Commerce, Adelaide, South Australia.
The Chamber of Commerce of Bengal, Calcutta, India.
The Chamber of Commerce, Hamburg, Germany.
The Vancouver Board of Trade, Vancouver, B. C.
The British Columbia Board of Trade, Victoria, B. C.
The Chamber of Commerce, Newcastle, Australia.
The British Chamber of Commerce, Paris, France.
The Chamber of Commerce of the State of New York, New York, N. Y.
The Chamber of Commerce, Boston, Mass.
The Board of Trade and Transportation, New York, N. Y.
The Philadelphia Maritime Exchange, Philadelphia, Pa.
The Baltimore Board of Trade, Baltimore, Md.
The Chamber of Commerce, New Orleans, La.

The Chamber of Commerce, Cincinnati, Ohio.
The New York Produce Exchange, New York, N. Y.
The Chamber of Commerce, Savannah, Ga.
The Chamber of Commerce, Galveston, Texas.
The Chicago Board of Trade, Chicago, Ill.
The Peoria Board of Trade, Peoria, Ill.
The Pittsburg Chamber of Commerce, Pittsburg, Pa.
The Chicago Chamber of Commerce, Chicago, Ill.
The Bath Board of Trade, Bath, Maine.
The Chamber of Commerce, Sault St. Marie, Mich.
The Merchants' Exchange, St. Louis, Mo.
The Omaha Board of Trade, Omaha, Neb.
The Board of Trade, Newark, N. J.
The Chamber of Commerce, Cleveland, Ohio.
The Philadelphia Board of Trade, Philadelphia, Pa.
The Chamber of Commerce, Richmond, Va.
The Chamber of Commerce, Aberdeen, Wash.
The Chamber of Commerce, Spokane, Wash.
The Chamber of Commerce, Tacoma, Wash.
The Chamber of Commerce, Seattle, Wash.
The Humboldt County Chamber of Commerce, Eureka, Cal.
The Portland (Or.) Chamber of Commerce, Portland, Ore.
The Astoria Chamber of Commerce, Astoria, Ore.
The Chamber of Commerce, Los Angeles, Cal.
The Chamber of Commerce, San Diego, Cal.
The Chamber of Commerce, Salt Lake City, Utah.
The Oakland Board of Trade, Oakland, Cal.
The Fresno Chamber of Commerce, Fresno, Cal.
The Sacramento Board of Trade, Sacramento, Cal.
The Stockton Board of Trade, Stockton, Cal.
The Board of Trade of San Francisco, San Francisco, Cal.
The Merchants' Association, San Francisco, Cal.
California State Board of Trade, San Francisco, Cal.
Milwaukee Chamber of Commerce, Milwaukee, Wis.
Merchants' Exchange, Memphis, Tenn.
Chamber of Commerce of Amsterdam.
Chamber of Commerce of Bulawayo, Matabebeland, South Africa.
Parliamentary Library, Ottawa.
New York State Library, Albany, N. Y.
Chamber of Commerce, Edinburgh, Scotland.
Chamber of Commerce, Johannesburg, S. A. R.
Perth Chamber of Commerce, Western Australia.
Chamber of Commerce, New Haven, Conn.
Chamber of Commerce, Bremen, Germany.
Commercial and Industrial Association, Montgomery, Ala.

Interstate Commerce Commission, Washington.
University of California Library, Berkeley, Cal.
Merchants' and Manufacturers' Association, Baltimore, Md.
Chamber of Commerce and Factory of Ghent.
Board of Trade, Springfield, Mass.
Free Public Library, San Francisco, Cal.
Leland Stanford, Jr., University Library, Palo Alto, Cal.
Staten Island Chamber of Commerce, Staten Island, N. Y.
The State Historical Society of Wisconsin, Madison, Wis.
Nagasaki Chamber of Commerce, Nagasaki, Japan.
Business Men's Association, Pueblo, Colo.
Chamber of Commerce, Kobe, Japan.
Philadelphia Commercial Museum, Philadelphia, Pa.
Imperial University, Kyoto, Japan.
University of Pennsylvania, Philadelphia, Pa.
American Chamber of Commerce, Manila, P. I.
Yokohama Chamber of Commerce (Japanese), Yokohama, Japan.
Chamber of Commerce, Kyoto, Japan.
The Commercial Club, St. Paul, Minn.
Wellington Harbor Board, Wellington, N. Z.
Commercial Club, Cedar Rapids, Iowa.
Tokyo Chamber of Commerce Yaesucho, Tokyo, Japan.
National Board of Trade, Philadelphia, Pa.
Manila Chamber of Commerce, Manila, P. I.
Boston Merchants' Association, Boston, Mass.
Chamber of Commerce, Buffalo, N. Y.
The American Chamber of Commerce in Berlin, Germany.
The Netherland Chamber of Commerce in America, 68 Broad St., N. Y.
The Commercial Club of Fargo, N. D.
Deutsches Export-Informations-Bureau, Cologne, Germany.

SYNOPSIS OF TRANSACTIONS

JANUARY, 1903.

Consular Reform

In compliance with the report of the Committee on Foreign Commerce and Revenue Laws, to whom the matter had been referred, a resolution was adopted by the Board of Trustees in favor of H. R. Bill 16,023, Fifty-seventh Congress, Second Session, providing for the improvement of the consular service.

International Arbitration

The Committee on Foreign Commerce and Revenue Laws, to whom the subject of International Arbitration had been referred, reported in favor of the request of the Lake Mohonk Conference on International Arbitration, requesting the recommendation of the Chamber regarding this matter. Resolution adopted approving recommendation of the committee.

American National Exposition in China

The Committee on Foreign Commerce and Revenue Laws reported in favor of Senate Bill 6,125, Fifty-seventh Congress First Session, providing for the establishment of an American Exposition in Shanghai, China, to be supported by the United States Government, suggesting, however, that the suitability of the City of Canton for this purpose be carefully considered. Resolution adopted by the Board of Trustees approving the action of the committee.

Military Instruction Camp

In compliance with a request from the San Miguel Improvement Club for the co-operation of the Chamber in endeavoring to induce the Congress to make an appropriation for the purchase of the Nacimiento Ranch in San Luis Obispo and Monterey Counties for a military instruction camp. Resolution adopted by the Board of Trustees that as the Honorable the Secretary of War had approved of this selection, the California delegation at Washington be requested to endeavor to have the Congress make the appropriation named by the Secretary of War for the purchase of this property.

In Memoriam The Secretary announced the death of Messrs. Chas. Meinecke, Oliver Eldridge and W. C. Gibbs, members of the Chamber of Commerce. Resolution adopted that the matter be referred to the President of the Chamber to take appropriate action.

Bills of Lading Letter presented from the Chamber of Commerce of Melbourne, Australia, asking the custom of the port of San Francisco as to the signing of bills of lading. Secretary instructed to advise the Chamber of Commerce of Melbourne that according to the custom of the port of San Francisco, bills of lading for shipments by steamer or sail vessels are not signed until the goods are in the possession of the carriers.

Submarine Cable in Alaska Letter presented from Mr. J. W. Ivey, representing the interests of Alaska in Washington, requesting the co-operation of the Chamber in endeavoring to induce the Congress to make an appropriation to lay a submarine cable from the northwest part of Washington to the southwest part of Alaska. Resolution adopted that the California delegation be requested to induce the Congress to make an appropriation for this purpose, substantially as provided for in House Document 231, Fifty-seventh Congress, Second Session.

State Civil Service

Request presented from the Municipal League of Los Angeles, requesting the co-operation of the Chamber to induce the State Legislature to enact a bill providing for the Civil Service in this State. Resolution adopted by the Board of Trustees that the matter be laid on the table.

Lewis & Clark Centennial, 1905

Letters presented from the Lewis and Clark Centennial Exposition to be held in the City of Portland, Oregon, in 1905, requesting the endorsement and approval of the Chamber of Commerce of said exposition. Resolution adopted that the matter be referred to the Committee on Foreign Commerce and Revenue Laws.

Cuban Reciprocity; California Wines

Correspondence presented from the California Wine Association and Mr. William M. Bunker in Washington relative to having the duty on California wines placed as low as possible in the proposed Cuban Reciprocity Treaty, should it be likely that said treaty be adopted. Resolution adopted approving above correspondence.

National Finance and Currency

Request presented from the Chamber of Commerce of the State of New York to have the Chamber co-operate with them with a general view of rendering money conditions more elastic. Resolution adopted by the Board of Trustees that the matter be laid on the table.

Pacific Ocean Cable

Copies of cablegrams presented conveying messages of congratulation to the officials of the Commercial Pacific Cable Company and the officers of the Honolulu Chamber of Commerce, upon the completion of the submarine cable from this city to Honolulu. Resolution adopted by the Board of Trustees confirming the cablegrams.

Icrease of Officers in the Navy

A letter presented from the Portland, Oregon, Chamber of Commerce requesting the Chamber to co-operate with them in endeavoring to induce the National Congress to increase the capacity of the Naval Schools or otherwise provide for the requisite number of thoroughly educated officers of the Navy. Resolution adopted by the Board of Trustees that the Secretary communicate with Mr. Bunker in Washington, requesting him to advise the Board as to the feeling in the Navy Department and among officials in regard to this matter.

Governmental Transportation

Resolution adopted by the Board of Trustees that a communication be sent to Mr. E. H. Harriman, President of the Southern Pacific Company, again calling his attention to the necessity of continued efforts on behalf of retaining the Government transportation system at San Francisco.

Interstate Commerce Commission

Communication presented from the Interstate Commerce Law Convention, requesting the cooperation of the Chamber in aid of the so-called "Elkins Bill" in Congress, to provide additional power to the Interstate Commerce Commission. Resolution adopted by the Board of Trustees that the matter be referred to the special committee having this matter in hand, viz: Messrs. A. G. Towne and Wakefield Baker.

Tourists' Rates

The President, Mr. Newhall, stated that jointly with the other commercial organizations of the city he had signed a petition requesting the Southern Pacific Company to meet with certain low rates to California those which had been given by the railroad lines to tourists and emigrants to the Northwest, reply being received from the Southern Pacific Company that the rates named would be granted. Resolution adopted by the Board of Trustees approving action of the President.

Letters of Introduction
The President, Mr. Newhall, reported that a letter of introducton had been given to a representative of the firm of Baker & Hamilton, who was about to visit Australia. Action of the President duly approved.

C. W. Burks, Stenographer
Resolution adopted by the Board of Trustees that the salary of Mr. C. W. Burks be made sixty dollars per month from January 1st, 1903.

Removal of Rooms of Chamber
The President, Mr. Newhall, stated that with the Secretary he had looked for rooms for the Chamber and the most available were at No. 307 Sansome Street, where two rooms could be had at $65.00 per month. Resolution adopted by the Board of Trustees that these rooms be engaged on the first of February, 1903.

Annual Meeting
Annual reports of the officers and committees presented at the Fifty-third Annual Meeting, January 20th, as published in the Annual Repart, including report of the election committee of the annual election for officers and trustees held January 13th, 1902.

Secretary, Treasurer, etc.
Mr. E. Scott unanimously elected by the Board of Trustees Secretary, Treasurer and Librarian of the Chamber.

Harbor Commissioners

The President, Mr. Newhall, stated that he had, on behalf of the Chamber, signed a joint dispatch to the Governor of the State of California urging that owing to the great importance of having the water front of this city under proper protection and management that he, in the appointment of members of the Board of State Harbor Commissioners endeavor to secure the services of those who through their business experience would be versed in the needs and necessities of the harbor and water front. Resolution adopted approving the action of the Chairman.

Harbor Improvements

A communication presented from a member of the Chamber containing various suggestions in regard to the improvement of the water front. The President, Mr. Newhall, stated that he had been requested to meet the Governor of the State and representatives of the mercantile interests of San Francisco in regard to this subject at Sacramento, January 21st, but it would be impossible for him to attend. Accordingly a resolution was adopted that Mr. Wm. H. Marston attend said meeting as a delegate from the Chamber of Commerce.

Cuban Reciprocity Treaty

The President, Mr. Newhall, stated that he had sent a dispatch on behalf of the Chamber to the Senators of California to oppose the ratification of the proposed Cuban Reciprocity Treaty as being inimical to the great agricultural and horticultural interests of this State, this telegram being in line with the resolution adopted by the Board of Trustees December 13th, 1901. Resolution adopted by the Board of Trustees approving the action of the chairman.

American Register

A communication presented from a member of the Chamber requesting its co-operation in securing American register for the British bark "Pyreenes," which had been burned and stranded in the South Pacific Ocean in December, 1900, and salved and brought into this harbor at considerable expense and under great difficulties, the owner intending to spend a large sum of money to place the vessel in a seaworthy condition. In view of these facts a resolution was adopted by the Board of Trustees that the California delegation in Washington be requested to induce the Congress to grant an American register to the British bark "Pyreenes."

Use of Rooms

The use of the rooms of the Chamber given to the American Institute of Bank Clerks, January 21st, at 7:30 P. M., 1903.

Standing Committees

The President, Mr. Newhall, reported that he had appointed the standing committees as published in the Annual Report.

FEBRUARY, 1903.

Louisiana Purchase Exposition

In compliance with a suggestion from the Los Angeles Chamber of Commerce and a committee of the Louisiana Purchase Exposition, a resolution was adopted by the Board of Trustees that the Legislature of the State of California be requested to appropriate adequate funds to defray the expense of a State exhibit at the Exposition in 1904.

Increase of the Navy

In compliance with a suggestion from the Maritime Association of the port of New York, a resolution was adopted that the California delegation at Washington be requested to endeavor to induce the National Congress to take proper steps for a large increase in the Navy and a corresponding increase of officers and men within as short a time as possible.

Harbor Commissioners

The President, Mr. Newhall, reported that he had, on behalf of the Chamber, signed a joint resolution urging upon the State Senate that they confirm no appointment of any man for the position of Harbor Commissioner who is not a business man doing business in San Francisco, and who is not a man of high character and broad intelligence, and who is not thoroughly conversant with the needs of the water front, and well qualified to perform the work that now confronts the Harbor Commission. Action of the President duly approved.

Harbor and Waterfront

A resolution adopted approving bill which was about to be presented to the State Legislature for favorable action to provide for the issuance and sale of State bonds to create a fund for the construction by the Board of State Harbor Commissioners of a sea wall and appurtenances in the City and County of San Francisco, and to create a sinking fund for the payment of said bonds, and providing for the submission of this act to a vote of the people.

State Irrigation Bill

Resolution adopted that the President of the Chamber of Commerce appoint three delegates to attend a meeting for the purpose of discussing a bill to be presented to the State Legislature prepared by the California Water and Forest Association and known as the "Irrigation Bill," the meeting to be held in Sacramento, February 17th, 1903, at 2 P. M. Mr. Wm. H. Marston being appointed to attend said meeting.

River Improvement and Drainage Association

A resolution adopted that the President, Mr. Newhall, appoint delegates from the Chamber of Commerce to attend a meeting of the River Improvement and Drainage Association of California, to be held in the Maple room of the Palace Hotel, February 12th, to discuss the subject of river improvement in this State, Messrs. Walter E. Dean, Byron Jackson and Edward Coleman being appointed as delegates.

Rebate Customs Duties and Tonnage Dues, United States Vessels

Resolution adopted by the Board of Trustees that the California delegation at Washington be respectfully requested to endeavor to induce the Congress to take prompt action to promote the commerce and foster the merchant marine of the United States by the allowance to United States vessels of rebates on customs duties and tonnage dues substantially as provided for in H. R. Bill No. 17,147, Fifty-seventh Congress, Second Session.

In Memoriam

The death announced of Louis Simon, of the firm of Stein, Simon & Co., members of the Chamber.

Proposed Chinese Treaty

Resolution adopted that a communication be sent to the Honorable the Secretary of State suggesting in effect that a conference be held by the representatives of the interested powers with a view of formulating a treaty with China arranged on lines acceptable to said parties and which would not discriminate against American productions.

Labeling California Manufactures

Resolution adopted by the Board of Trustees that the Chamber of Commerce co-operate with the Manufacturers' and Producers' Association in opposing the passage by the State Legislature of Senate Bill 254 now before that body, said bill requiring in effect that every article manufactured in this State shall be conspicuously labeled and stamped with the name and address of the manufacturer.

State Attachment Laws

The President, Mr. Newhall, reported that he had, on behalf of the Chamber, signed a joint petition to the State Assembly against the enactment of Assembly Bill 119 in regard to attachment laws of this State. Resolution adopted by the Board of Trustees approving the action of the President.

Governmental Transportation

The President, Mr. Newhall, reported that he had, on behalf of the Chamber, signed a telegram together with the presidents of the other commercial organizations to Senator Perkins as follows: "Reports that commercial bodies here oppose your amendment to lease transports is erroneous. After fully considering matter we unanimously endorse your amendment to army appropriation bill and urge you to use best endeavors to secure its passage. Wire if any further assistance can be given and by what means." Also, that he had signed a dispatch as follows: "We heartily approve your amendment army appropriation bill regarding Governmental transportation." Action of the President approved by the Board of Trustees.

Interstate Commerce and Department of Commerce

Mr. Newhall stated that he had, on behalf of the Chamber of Commerce, sent a telegram to Senators Perkins and Bard as follows: "We ask you to vigorously oppose and prevent the passage of that portion of Section 13 of House Amendment to Senate Bill 569 which provides for transfer of Inter-State Commerce Commission to a new Department of Commerce, Inter-State Commerce Commission being a quasi-judicial body, should be kept independent of all Departments." Action of the President approved by the Board of Trustees.

Use of Rooms

The Secretary announced that the use of the rooms of the Chamber had been given to the American Institute of Bank Clerks, Wednesday, February 18th, at 7:30 P. M.

City Sanitation

The Secretary announced for the information of the Board of Trustees the formation of a Mercantile Health Committee, composed of the President and Secretary of each commercial organization of this city and one other member, the object of this committee being to have proper steps taken for a thorough co-operation of the local health boards with the United States Marine Hospital Service for employing proper means of sanitation in this city.

Removal of Chamber

Notices of the removal of the Chamber sent to each member notifying them that the present location of the Chamber was 307 Sansome Street, Rooms 5 and 6.

Lewis & Clark Centennial Exposition

The Committee on Foreign Commerce and Revenue Laws, to whom the subject had been referred, recommended that the Board of Trustees approve and co-operate with the officers and members of the Lewis and Clark Centennial Exposition, to be held in Portland, Oregon, in 1905, for the purpose of assisting said exposition. Resolution adopted by the Board approving the recommendation of the committee.

Leasing Portion of Waterfront

Special meeting of the Board of Trustees held to consider bills now pending in the State Legislature conferring certain powers upon the Board of State Harbor Commissioners to lease portions of the harbor and water-front having special reference to suitable locations for terminal facilities for through transportation. A resolution adopted at this meeting in effect that the Chamber of Commerce of San Francisco endorse said Senate Bill 896 and Assembly Bill 925, Senate Bill 896 being identical with Assembly Bill 937, and Assembly Bill 925 being identical with Senate Bill 780, and requesting the Honorable the Senate and Assembly of the State of California to enact legislation substantially as provided for in said bills, and a resolution also adopted that copy of the preamble and resolution referred to be sent to each member of the State Senate and Assembly.

MARCH, 1903.

In Memoriam

Death announced of Mr. Jacob Hecht, of the firm of Hecht Bros. & Co., members of the Chamber.

California Polytechnic School

Communication presented to the Board of Trustees asking the co-operation of the Chamber in inducing the State Legislature to take favorable action on Assembly Bills 179 and 367 making certain appropriations for the California Polytechnic School. Resolution adopted that the matter be laid on the table.

Islais Creek

The special committee of the Chamber appointed to attend the meeting February 26th of the Water-Front Committee of the Board of Supervisors, the Board of State Harbor Commissioners and others in regard to improving Islais Creek, reported that it was the unanimous opinion of the meeting that Islais Creek should be improved, with a view of affording additional accommodations for the increasing shipping of the harbor; and that a resolution was adopted in effect that the Board of State

Harbor Commissioners and Board of Supervisors instruct their respective engineers to confer and devise some plan or plans of improvement of the creek which would be presented at a subsequent meeting of the general committees for examination. Resolution adopted approving the report of the committee.

Chief Bureau of Manufactures

The President, Mr. Newhall, reported that in compliance with telegrams received from Senators Perkins and Bard at Washington, he had conferred with the presidents of the commercial organizations of this city and also communicated with a number of commercial organizations of this State with a view of recommending some one from California as Chief, Bureau of Manufactures, in the new Department of Commerce and Labor. After a number of conferences the presidents of the commercial organizations had unanimously recommended Mr. Eugene Goodwin for the position and accordingly, he, Mr. Newhall, had notified the Senators and sent a letter to the President at Washington through the hands of Senator Perkins making this recommendation. Resolution adopted approving the action of the President.

Warehouse, Indian Supplies

The President, Mr. Newhall, reported that he had, on behalf of the Chamber, sent a telegram to Senators Perkins and Bard at Washington as follows: "Understand House conferees object to Indian Warehouse San Francisco. Kindly urge retaining it in bill." Resolution adopted approving action of the President.

Isthmian Canal Commission

The President, Mr. Newhall, reported that at a joint meeting of the presidents of the commercial organizations of this city, the name of a gentleman had been presented for endorsement as an applicant for the position as one of the Isthmian Canal Commissioners. Mr. Newhall also stated that inasmuch as the Board of Trustees had decided not to recommend any one in particular for that position, but had suggested to the President at Washington that some one from California be appointed, that he (Mr. Newhall) felt that he was not authorized to make a recommendation on behalf of the Chamber of any one in particular for this position. Resolution adopted approving action of the President.

Transfer Personal Property

The President, Mr. Newhall, stated that he had, on behalf of the Chamber, joined in a request to the Governor of California to give executive approval to a bill amending Section 3440 of the Civil Code of the State of California relating to certain transfers presumed fraudulent and regarding the recording of notice of intention to sell certain personal property. Resolution adopted approving action of the President.

Statistics, Electric Power

Owing to the increasing importance of electric power and power transmission in this State, suggestion was made to the Board of Trustees that a committee be appointed by the chairman for the purpose of gathering statistics in regard to these matters for the information of the members of the Chamber and the public in general. Resolution adopted that the matter be referred to the President, Mr. Newhall.

Use of Rooms

The use of the rooms of the Chamber given to the American Institute of Bank Clerks, March 4th, at 7:30 P. M.; also to the Brotherhood of St. Andrew, Monday, March 23rd, to 28th, inclusive.

Librarian

The Librarian reported to the Board of Trustees that there was a large accumulation of old Congressional Records and other public documents which occupied a great deal of room, and as space in the library was urgently needed for recent publications constantly being received, a resolution was adopted that the Librarian be authorized to sell or otherwise dispose of, as he deemed best, such publications as in his opinion were not required for reference.

Los Angeles Chamber of Commerce

The President, Mr. Newhall, reported to the Board of Trustees that the officers of the Chamber had been invited by the Los Angeles Chamber of Commerce to attend the ceremony of laying the corner-stone of its new building on March 28th; that he was conferring with the officers of the other commercial organizations of the city with a view of seeing if arrangements could be made for a delegation representing these organizations to attend the above-mentioned ceremony, which was duly approved.

APRIL, 1903.

In Memoriam

The death announced of Samuel Sachs, of the firm of Sachs Bros., and G. F. Swift, of Swift & Company, of Chicago, members of the Chamber.

Good Roads

Communication presented from the National Good Roads Association of St. Louis, Mo., inviting the Chamber to send representatives to the National Encampment of that body to be held at a subsequent date. Resolution adopted that the matter be laid on the table.

Synopsis of Transactions.

Report, Washington Bureau

The report of Mr. William M. Bunker, representative in Washington of the Chamber, presented to the Board of Trustees, giving an outline of the acts of the Fifty-seventh Congress, Second Session, affecting Pacific Coast interests. Resolution adopted that the report be presented at the next quarterly meeting of the Chamber, and that it be printed and sent to each member.

California Commissioner, Louisiana Purchase Exposition

Letter presented from a gentleman suggesting that the Board of Trustees endorse his application to the Governor of California for appointment as Commissioner from this State to the Louisiana Purchase Exposition. Resolution adopted that the matter be laid on the table.

State Board of Charities and Correction

The President, Mr. Newhall, stated that in compliance with a request of members of the Chamber he had petitioned the Governor to give executive approval to a bill providing for a State Board of Charities and Correction, and that the Governor had subsequently approved the bill. Resolution adopted approving the action of the President.

Harbor Police Boat

The President, Mr. Newhall, stated that in compliance with a request from members of the Chamber a petition had been sent to the Governor of California to give executive approval to a bill passed by the last Legislature providing for a Harbor Police Boat for San Francisco. Resolution adopted approving action of the President.

State Viticultural Interests

The President, Mr. Newhall, reported that he had, on behalf of the Chamber, petitioned the Governor of California to give executive approval to a bill passed by the last Legislature appropriating $10,000, to be given to the University of California for advancing the viticultural interests of this State. Resolution adopted approving action of the President.

Synopsis of Transactions.

Nome Sub-Port of Entry

The President, Mr. Newhall, reported that he had, at the request of members of the Chamber, suggested to the Secretary of the Treasury that Nome, Alaska, be made a sub-port of entry. Action of the President approved.

Official Vocabulary, International Cable Companies

The President, Mr. Newhall, stated that in compliance with a request from members of the Chamber and the recommendation of the Committee on Foreign Commerce and Revenue Laws, to whom he had referred the matter, he had sent a protest to the International Telegraph Convention of Berne, which was to meet in London in May, 1903, against the proposed adoption for compulsory use of the new so-called "Official Vocabulary," and that he had also requested and obtained the signature of the other commercial organizations of the city to this protest. Resolution adopted approving the action of the President.

Letter of Introduction

The Secretary reported that a general letter of introduction had been given to Mr. A. Mack, of the firm of A. Mack & Co., member of the Chamber, which was duly approved.

Merchants' Exchange Building

A letter was presented from the Secretary of the Merchants' Exchange requesting consideration of the subject of moving the rooms of the Chamber to the new building of the Merchants' Exchange when completed. Resolution adopted that the Secretary of the Chamber communicate with the Secretary of the Merchants' Exchange in regard to this matter.

Banquet, James W. Ragsdale

Banquet given to James W. Ragsdale, United States Consul at Tientsin, China, at the Palace Hotel, February 26th, by the Boards of Trustees of the commercial organizations of this city.

Use of Rooms	Use of rooms of the Chamber given to the American Institute of Bank Clerks, March 25th and April 8th, 1903.
Washington Bureau	Report of Mr. William M. Bunker, representative of the Chamber in Washington, D. C., reviewing the acts of the Fifty-seventh Congress, Second Session, affecting the interests of the Pacific Coast, presented at the quarterly meeting of the Chamber.
Gift, Marine Paintings	The family of the late Captain Oliver Eldridge, member of the Chamber of Commerce, presented the Chamber two handsome oil paintings, one being the ship "Roscius" and the other one of the famous "Blackball Line" of packet ships. Resolution adopted thanking the family of the late Captain Oliver Eldridge for their courtesy and consideration in presenting to the Chamber the above-named paintings.
California Delegation	A resolution was adopted at the quarterly meeting of the Chamber that the thanks of the Chamber of Commerce of San Francisco be and they are hereby respectfully tendered to the Senators and Representatives of the State of California for their able, energetic, conscientious and effective efforts on behalf of the interests of California during the last session of the Fifty-seventh Congress.
Address, J. P. Shanks	Mr. J. P. Shanks, of Manila, addressed the Chamber in quarterly meeting upon the commercial outlook of the Philippine Islands. He stated that in his opinion, besides the staple crops which had been raised there—such as hemp, cobra, sugar, tobacco, etc.—there were many others which in time could be produced in large quantities, such as coffee, rice, india rubber, gutta percha, indigo,

hardwoods, minerals, including coal, copper and gold. He stated that the system of agriculture was very crude and the natives were anxious to learn from Americans and to adopt modern methods.

Resolution of Thanks
At the conclusion of the address a resolution was adopted thanking Mr. Shanks for the able and instructive address which he had delivered.

MAY, 1903.

Special meeting held by the Chamber to consider the recommendation to the President at Washington for the appointment of a man from California as Chief of the Bureau of Manufactures. Resolution adopted confirming the previous action of the Board of Trustees and the President of the Chamber in recommending Mr. Eugene Goodwin for the position named.

JUNE, 1903.

Guatemala Earthquake Sufferers
Resolution adopted by the Board of Trustees that the balance of $4.39 remaining in the fund collected for the relief of the Guatemala earthquake sufferers be turned into the fund of the Chamber of Commerce, as the amount was too small to be of further use for the purpose for which it was collected.

In Memoriam
The death announced of Mr. R. G. Sneath, a former president of the Chamber, Mr. Irving M. Scott, of the Union Iron Works, and W. P. Thomas, of the New Zealand Insurance Company, members of the Chamber.

Synopsis of Transactions. 87

International Maritime Law

The Committee on Harbor and Shipping, to whom the communications of the Maritime Law Association of the United States had been referred, requested further time for considering, owing to the importance of the subject, which was duly granted.

Governmental Transportation

Communications and letters presented in reference to the action taken by the Joint Mercantile Committee May 4th at a conference with Mr. E. H. Harriman, President of the Southern Pacific Company, in regard to governmental transportation from this Coast to the Philippine Islands. The purport of the action of the conference being that the transportation interests there represented would present a bid to the Government in compliance with the circular issued by the War Department for army transportation, under date of April 24th, 1903.

Removal to Merchants' Exchange Building

Communications were presented from the Merchants' Exchange and Merchants' Association in reference to the removal of the rooms of the commercial organizations of this city to the new building of the Merchants' Exchange when completed. Resolution adopted that the matter be referred to the Finance Committee for consideration.

Banquet, Oakland Board of Trade

The President, Mr. Newhall, reported that in compliance with an invitation from the Oakland Board of Trade, he had appointed Messrs. Wm. E. Mighell, C. H. Bentley, Wm. H. Marston, J. W. Richards and Thomas Rickard to represent the Chamber of Commerce at the banquet given by the Oakland Board of Trade May 27th. Also that the thanks of the Chamber of Commerce had been tendered to the board of Trade for their kindness and courtesy in extending the invitation. Resolution adopted approving the action of the President.

Washington Bureau

Resolution adopted by the Board of Trustees that the thanks of the Chamber of Commerce of San Francisco be and they are hereby respectfully tendered to Mr. William M. Bunker, its representative in Washington, D. C., for his able, energetic and conscientious efforts on behalf of the interests of San Francisco and California at the National Capital; also that the Board deemed it of great importance to the welfare of our State and city that Mr. Bunker continue his labors there, and that the Washington Bureau be made a permanent work of the Chamber. Also, that Mr. Bunker be respectfully requested to visit San Francisco before the next session of Congress in the furtherance of this object.

Quarantine

The Secretary presented communication from Mr. Bunker and the Mercantile Joint Committee and others in reference to efforts made to have the Republic of Equador remove the quarantine at Guayaquil against San Francisco, which was duly approved by the Board of Trustees.

Leave of Absence

Leave of absence granted by the Board of Trustees to Mr. Geo. A. Newhall, President of the Chamber, as he desired to be absent from the city for about six months, to visit the Atlantic States and Europe.

Foreign Parcels Post

Communication presented from the Anglo-American Chamber of Commerce in Belgium, calling attention to the commercial importance of having a parcels post service established between Belgium and the United States, and requesting the co-operation of the Chamber in furthering this object. Resolution adopted by the Board of Trustees reiterating their previous action in requesting the California delegation at Washington to endeavor to have the postal service system established between the United States and all foreign countries with whom such service did not already exist.

Co-Operation of Chambers of Commerce

Communication presented from the Boise Chamber of Commerce suggesting joint co-operation between their organization and the Chamber of Commerce of San Francisco and other commercial organizations in furthering objects of mutual interest to the Western and the Pacific Coast States. Resolution adopted by the Board of Trustees thanking the Chamber of Commerce of Boise for their offer and that the Chamber of Commerce of San Francisco would be pleased to co-operate with them in efforts for the furtherance of objects of mutual interest.

Letters of Introduction

The Secretary reported that a special letter of introduction had been given Mr. S. C. Irving, of the Paraffine Paint Company, member of the Chamber, to Mr. William M. Bunker, and a general letter to whom it may concern, which was duly approved.

Use of Rooms

The use of the rooms of the Chamber given to the American Institute of Bank Clerks, Thursday, June 9th, 1903.

Damage in Grain Shipments

Communication presented from Mr. L. L. Lewis, of Australia, complaining of the torn condition of sacks in which wheat shipments had been arriving at Melbourne from San Francisco. Subject was referred to the Merchants' Exchange, as the handling and shipment of grain was a special feature of their work.

JULY, 1903.

Washington Bureau

Conference with Mr. William M. Bunker, representative in Washington, D. C., by the Board of Trustees in regard to conserving certain important interests of this city and State at the National Capital, and particularly during the next session of the Congress, and the importance being dwelt upon also of the outlined work of the new Department of Commerce and Labor, under the direction of Secretary Geo. B. Cortelyou.

The sentiment of the Board being that efforts should be made to obtain special subscriptions from the members of the Chamber to maintain the Washington Bureau for another year.

Tariff on Coffee

Petition presented from the Ponce Branch of the Porto Rico Chamber of Commerce requesting the co-operation of the Chamber of Commerce of San Francisco in endeavoring to induce the National Congress at the next session to impose an import duty on coffee as an aid to the coffee industry of Porto Rico. Resolution adopted by the Board of Trustees that the matter be laid on the table.

Stoppage, United States Transports at Honolulu

Mr. E. R. Dimond, Vice-President of the Chamber, stated that he had, on behalf of the Chamber, taken up the subject of the stoppage of the United States Transports at Honolulu on their way from San Francisco to Manila; that after a conference of the Secretary of the Chamber with Major Devol, Quartermaster in charge here, he had written to the Merchants' Association at Honolulu, informing them that the objection which the Quartermaster had to the transports stopping there was that no proper facilities were offered there for supplying them with coal at a reasonable price. The Vice-

President, Mr. Dimond, also stated that he had offered to co-operate with the Merchants' Association of Honolulu in endeavoring to assist them in any matters pertaining to our mutual benefit.

Letter of Introduction

A letter of introduction given to the President of the Chamber, Mr. Geo. A. Newhall, to the commercial organizations with whom he might be brought in contact on his trip to the Atlantic States.

Trans-Mississippi Commercial Congress

Invitation presented from the Trans-Mississippi Commercial Congress for the Chamber to send delegates to the annual session of this congress to be held at Seattle, Washington, August 18-21, 1903. Resolution adopted that the matter be referred to the Vice-President of the Chamber and the Secretary.

American Mining Congress

Invitation presented from the American Mining Congress for the Chamber to send delegates to the annual session of this congress to be held at Deadwood and Lead, South Dakota, September 7-12, 1903. Resolution adopted that the matter be referred to the Vice-President and the Secretary.

Pacific Cable

The Vice-President reported that cablegrams of congratulation had been received from and sent to the Chamber of Commerce and Merchants' Association of Honolulu upon the completion of the Pacific Cable, and also that in compliance with the invitation extended by Mr. Clarence H. Mackay, President of the Pacific Commercial Cable Company, messages of congratulation had been sent to and received from the American Chamber of Commerce of Manila, upon the completion of the cable to the Philippines.

Netherlands Chamber of Commerce in America

Letter presented from the Netherland Chamber of Commerce in America, New York, stating that they have been organized with the object of furthering the development of commercial interests between the United States and the Netherlands and their colonies, and requesting the co-operation of the Chamber in matters which might arise affecting our mutual interests. Resolution adopted that their courtesy be acknowledged and informing them that the Chamber would be pleased to co-operate with them.

Use of Rooms

The use of the rooms of the Chamber given to the American Institute of Bank Clerks, Wednesday, July 15th.

Washington Bureau

Report of Mr. William M. Bunker, representative of the Chamber of Commerce in Washington, D. C., presented at the quarterly meeting of the Chamber, the report dwelling upon the endeavors made and results accomplished in matters vitally affecting the commercial interests of San Francisco. Mr. Bunker also outlined the work of the new Department of Commerce and Labor, under the able leadership of Secretary Geo. B. Cortelyou, with particular reference to its influence upon the commercial development of the Pacific Coast.

Vote of Thanks

Vote of thanks tendered at the quarterly meeting to Mr. William M. Bunker for his able efforts on behalf of our commercial interests. Resolution adopted at the quarterly meeting that the Board of Trustees of the Chamber take such means as they deemed proper for the maintaining the Washington Bureau of the Chamber.

American Chamber of Commerce in Berlin

Letter presented from the American Chamber of Commerce in Berlin speaking of their organization and requesting the co-operation of the Chamber of Commerce of San Francisco in mutual endeavors to promote matters of interest common to Germany and the United States. Secretary instructed to reply to the communication thanking them for their courtesy and offering the co-operation of the Chamber in promoting matters of mutual interest.

In Memoriam

The death announced of Mr. William B. Hooper, an old member of the Chamber, who had served twice upon the Board of Trustees.

AUGUST, 1903.

Washington Bureau

Mr. William M. Bunker appointed representative of the Chamber of Commerce of San Francisco in Washington, D. C., for another year, commencing December 1st, 1903, with a salary of $500.00 per month.

Trans-Mississippi Commercial Congress

Messrs. Hugh Craig, A. L. Ehrman and J. C. Zellerbach appointed as delegates to represent the Chamber of Commerce at the Trans-Mississippi Commercial Congress, to meet in Seattle, Washington, August 18th, 1903.

American Bankers' Association

In compliance with invitation from the American Bankers' Association, Mr. Walter E. Dean was appointed to represent the Chamber of Commerce on the Reception Committee of this Association at their twenty-ninth annual convention, to meet in San Francisco, October 20th, 1903. The courtesy of the Chamber of Commerce was also extended to the members of this association, and they were invited to visit the rooms of the Chamber of Commerce during the convention.

Photographers' Association of America
The Vice-President, Mr. Dimond, reported that he had extended the compliments of the Chamber of Commerce to the Photographers' Association of America in convention at Indianapolis, Indiana, and expressed the hope that they would hold their next annual convention in San Francisco. Action of the Vice-President approved.

Arbitration Clause, Bills of Lading
The subject of having an arbitration clause inserted in bills of lading to cover disputes which might arise between parties in interest invclving nominal amounts being presented, the matter was referred to the Committe on Harbor and Shipping.

Pure Wine Meeting
Mr. William M. Bunker appointed as a delegate from the Chamber of Commerce to attend the Pure Wine Meeting, held at St. Helena, California, August 15th, the meeting having been called for the purpose of securing National legislation in favor of pure wines.

Mercantile Joint Committee
Pro rata of the Chamber of Commerce in the expense of the Mercantile Joint Committee ordered paid.

In Memoriam
The death announced of Alexander Hay, of the firm of Hay & Wright, member of the Chamber.

Use of Rooms
The use of the rooms of the Chamber given to those interested in the manufacture of wine in this State, August 6th, at 1 P. M., for the purpose of taking steps for making a proper exhibit at the St. Louis Exposition, 1904.

SEPTEMBER, 1903.

Removal of Chamber

The subject of the removal of the rooms of the Chamber of Commerce to the new building of the Merchants' Exchange when completed being presented to the Board of Trustees, the matter was laid over for future consideration.

Arbitration Clause, Bills of Lading

The Committee on Harbor and Shipping, to whom the subject had been referred, reported that they suggested to the Board that a resolution be adopted and afterwards confirmed by the Chamber, that an arbitration clause be recommended to be inserted in bills of lading. The recommendation of the committee was duly approved by the Board of Trustees. (For copy of clause see October transactions.)

Fire Insurance

Owing to the increase in the personal property of the Chamber, resolution adopted by the Board of Trustees that the amount of fire insurance carried on the personal property be increased from $1,000 to $1,500.

National Irrigation Congress

The Vice-President, Mr. E. R. Dimond, reported that in compliance with an invitation of the National Irrigation Congress, which met at Ogden, Utah, September 15-18, he had appointed Mr. H. D. Loveland a delegate of the Chamber of Commerce at said congress, which was duly approved.

Indian Bureau

The subject of the purchase of supplies in this market by the Italian Bureau being presented, resolved that the subject be referred to the Committee on Internal Trade and Improvements.

Interstate Commerce Commission

Communication presented from the Merchants' Association of New York, through the California Promotion Committee, requesting the co-operation of the Chamber of Commerce in endeavoring to increase the power of the Interstate Commerce Commission. The subject was referred by the Board to a special committee consisting of Messrs. A. G. Towne and Wakefield Baker having this matter in hand.

Cuban Treaty

Communication presented from the Merchants' Association of New York requesting the co-operation of the Chamber of Commerce in securing the Reciprocity Treaty with the Republic of Cuba. No action was taken on this subject, as the Board had previously opposed said reciprocity treaty as inimical to the agricultural and horticultural interests of California.

American Shipping

Communication presented from the Marine Association of the port of New York and the New York Board of Trade and Transportation, calling attention to the present lack of American shipping engaged in the foreign carrying trade, and suggesting that committees be formed of various commercial organizations, with a view of ascertaining by what means this branch of the American merchant marine could be re-established. Resolution adopted that the matter be referred to the Committee on Foreign Commerce and Revenue Laws.

State Board of Aribtration

The subject of the advisability of the appointing by the Legislature of a State Board of Arbitration to act in matters where differences arise between employer and employees being presented, resolution adopted that the subject be referred to an organization or committee making a specialty of this matter.

Electric Lights on Lightship

The Vice-President, Mr. E. R. Dimond, reported that a telegram had been received from the Lighthouse Inspector here from the Naval Secretary at Washington, stating in effect that they proposed to replace the electric lights on Lightship No. 70, at the entrance to this harbor, if the change met with the approval of the Chamber of Commerce, etc. He had presented the matter to the Committee of tne Chamber on Harbor and Shipping, and consulted with shipping men and pilots, and found them unanimous in their desire to have the electric lights replaced, and had accordingly informed the Lighthouse Inspector that the Chamber of Commerce was in favor of the change. Action of the Vice-President duly approved.

In Memoriam

The death announced of Isador Schwartz, member of the Chamber.

Parcels Post

Communication presented from the Anglo-American Chamber of Commerce, Belgium, acknowledging the receipt of the communication of the Chamber of the 24th of June, and stating that the Parcels Post Service between Belgium and the United States had been assured, and probably would be in effect early this winter; that the Belgian Minister had stated that the rate would be fixed at four pounds maximum, viz: two pounds for forty cents, four pounds for sixty cents.

Delay in Transportation

Communication presented from the merchants of Tacoma, Washington, stating that shipments of merchandise from San Francisco to Tacoma required as long a time, if not longer, than shipments made from St. Louis, Chicago and St. Paul. Resolution adopted that the matter be referred to the traffic managers of the railroads between this city and Tacoma.

Use of Rooms

The use of rooms of the Chamber given to the Naval League, October 14th, 1903, at 8 P. M.

OCTOBER, 1903.

Indian Supplies

The Committee on Internal Trade and Improvements, to whom the subject of Indian Supplies had been referred, reported that they thought it inadvisable to take any action in regard to this matter just at present. The Board of Trustees approved the report by the committee.

Restricting Immigration

Communication presented from the California Central Coast Counties Improvement Association requesting the co-operation of the Chamber in efforts towards restricting undesirable foreign immigration. Resolution adopted that the subject be referred to the Committee on Internal Trade and Improvement.

Conventions in San Francisco

Letter presented from the Denver Chamber of Commerce suggesting the co-operation of the Pacific Coast, Utah and Colorado Chambers of Commerce toward securing conventions in this section. Resolution adopted that the matter be referred to the California Promotion Committee.

California Promotion Committee

Second Vice-President Wm. E. Mighell reported that at a meeting of the presidents of the commercial organizations of this city, held September 23rd, a resolution had been adopted commending the work of the California Promotion Committee and suggesting to the California State Board of Trade that they take such action as would separate the California Promotion Committee from the said State Board of Trade. The California State Board of Trade having taken this action, a subsequent meeting of the presidents of the commercial organizations was held, when a resolution was adopted in effect reorganizing the California Promotion Committee, so that it would consist of five members—one from the Chamber of Commerce, one from Board of Trade of San Francisco, one from the Merchants' Association, one from the Manufacturers' and Producers' Association of California, and one from the Merchants' Exchange—the said California Promotion Committee to have full power to form sub-committees as it might deem necessary in its work. Also suggesting that an Advisory Board be formed and that the California State Board of Trade be invited to be represented on said Advisory Board.

He also stated that in the reorganization of the California Promotion Committee he had reappointed Mr. Rufus P. Jennings as the representative of the Chamber of Commerce on said committee. Resolution adopted by the Board of Trustees approving the above actions by the Second Vice-President.

San Francisco Exhibit, St. Louis Fair

Second Vice-President Wm. E. Mighell reported that a meeting of the presidents of the commercial organizations had been held for the purpose of considering the subject of a San Francisco exhibit at the St. Louis Fair in 1904. That in compliance with the resolution then adopted for the president of each commercial organization to appoint ten representatives of the organization to attend a subsequent meeting to consider the subject, he had appointed the following: Wakefield Baker, W. R. Wheeler, Rufus P. Jennings, C. L. Laumeister, Irving F. Moulton, James Rolph, Jr., C. H. Bentley, J. H. Speck, H. D. Morton and John Partridge.

Statistics, Annual Report — Resolution adopted that the same arrangements made last year be made with Mr. W. B. Thompson for preparing statistics for the fifty-fourth annual report.

Rules and Regulations, Commercial Matters — Resolution adopted by the Board of Trustees that the matter of revising the rates of commission and brokerage and regulations concerning the delivery of merchandise, payment of freight, etc., adopted by the Chamber of Commerce be referred to the Committee on Internal Trade and Improvements, with a view of presenting the matter for the consideration of the Chamber at the next annual meeting.

In Memoriam — The death announced of Mr. J. J. Smith, an old member of the Chamber.

Washington Correspondents — Suggestion was presented from Mr. Bunker that inasmuch as it had been customary for the Washington correspondents for the different newspapers in the United States to take trips each summer through different sections of the country by the courtesy of the different transcontinental companies, it might be well to suggest to the transcontinental railroad companies having terminals in San Francisco, that these correspondents be taken on a trip through California during the coming summer. Resolution adopted that the matter be referred to the California Promotion Committee.

River and Harbor Bill — Resolution adopted by the Board of Trustees that communications be sent to the commercial organizations located in that portion of the State adjacent to the navigable streams tributary to the Bay of San Francisco, with a view of obtaining united action in efforts to induce the National Congress to make appropriations in the River and Harbor Bill for the proper improvement of these waterways, as well as the Bay of San Francisco.

Arbitration Clause, Bills of Lading

Resolution adopted at the quarterly meeting of the Chamber that the following arbitration clause be recommended to all those in interest to be placed in bills of lading, said clause having been approved by the Board of Trustees September 22nd, 1903:

"Any disputed claim against the vessel not exceeding $100.00 to be settled by the Arbitration Committee of the Chamber of Commerce of the port in which dispute arises, or by arbitrators selected by the parties in interest, and to be binding on said parties, arbitration fees to be paid by the loser or losers."

Tube Works

Letter presented from Messrs. A. L. Parker & Co., of Boston, Mass., inquiring for information in regard to starting a 100-ton tube works in San Francisco. Resolution adopted at the puarterly meeting that the matter be referred to the Board of Trustees.

NOVEMBER, 1903.

American Merchant Marine

The Committee on Foreign Commerce and Revenue Laws, to whom the subject had been referred, reported that they suggested that the Board of Trustees take action in line with the request of the Maritime Association of New York and others having in view the revival of the American merchant marine engaged in the foreign carrying trade. The following resolution was accordingly adopted:

"That we recognize the urgent necessity of impressing upon the people of the United States a realization of the importance of immediate steps being taken which will result, after careful consideration of the interests involved, in such action by the national legislative and executive departments as will afford adequate encouragement for the building of American ships, manning them with Americans and enabling them to engage in competition with foreign ships in the carrying trade of the world, equivalent inducements being given to both sail and steam vessels."

Annual Report

The printing of the fifty-fourth annual report of the Chamber, to be issued about February, 1904, was awarded to the Commercial Publishing Company.

Lewis & Clark Centennial, Portland

Resolution adopted by the Board of Trustees respectfully requesting the California delegation at Washington to use their efforts towards having the National Congress appropriate adequate funds in aid of the Lewis and Clark Centennial and American Pacific Exposition and Oriental Fair, and also providing a Government exhibit thereat.

Customs Drawback Law

Resolution adopted that the action of the Board of Trustees taken December 9th, 1902, in favor of facilitating manufacturing for export substantially as provided for in the so-called "Lovering Bill," H. R., 15,368, Fifty-seventh Congress, Second Session, be reiterated.

Tube Plant

In compliance with the resolution previously passed, the Secretary reported that all information in his power had been furnished to Mr. Leonard Parker, of Boston, in regard to building a large manufactory of steel tubes in San Francisco.

River and Harbor Improvement

Letters presented from the commercial organizations of Oakland requesting the co-operation of the Chamber of Commerce in their endeavors to have the National Congress appropriate funds for the deepening of the channel of Oakland Harbor. Resolution adopted that the matter be referred to Mr. E. R. Dimond, Vice-President of the Chamber, with full power to act.

Towing Log Rafts

Resolution adopted by the Board of Trustees reiterating its previous action taken January 10th, 1899, October 16th, 1902, December 9th, 1902, in favor of inducing the National Congress to take such steps as would prevent the towing of logs and timber rafts on the Pacific Coast.

Calaveras Grove of Big Trees

Resolution adopted that the California delegation at Washington be respectfully requested to endeavor to induce the National Congress to appropriate adequate funds for the purchase of the Calaveras Grove of Big Trees.

Trade with Manchuria

Communication being presented in regard to the danger threatening American trade in Manchuria, China, resolution adopted that the subject be referred to the Committee on Foreign Commerce and Revenue Laws.

Pacific Cable

Communication presented from the North Australian League urging the importance of cable communication between the Pacific Coast of the United States and Australia. On motion, duly seconded, it was resolved that the matter be referred to Mr. Clarence H. Mackay, President of the Pacific Commercial Cable Company.

San Francisco Relics

Communication presented from the United States Consul-General at Auckland, New Zealand, in reference to some relics of the fire in San Francisco in 1851, being in possession of Sir John Logan Campbell, in Auckland, which he wishes to donate to the Golden Gate Park Museum or a similar institution. The Secretary was instructed to present the matter to the curator of the Park Museum, and to extend the thanks of the Chamber of Commerce to the Consul-General and Sir John Logan Campbell for his kind offer.

Use of Rooms

The use of the rooms of the Chamber given to the Committee of the San Francisco Exhibit at the St. Louis Fair, Thursday, November 4th, at 4 P. M.

DECEMBER, 1903.

Nominating and Election Committee

The Nominating and Election Committee appointed in compliance with the resolution adopted by the Board of Trustees, to select a ballot for the annual election of officers and trustees of the Chamber, to take place January 12th, 1904, and to preside at said election, the committee appointed being Messrs. Chas. Christensen, chairman, John O. Blanchard and John W. Mailliard.

Improvement Siuslaw Harbor

On motion, duly seconded, resolution adopted by the Board of Trustees that the matter of co-operating with the Senators and Representatives from Oregon for the improvement of the Siuslaw Harbor, Oregon, be referred to the Committee on Internal Trade and Improvements.

American Register

On motion, duly seconded, it was resolved that the previous action of the Board of Trustees taken January 20th, 1903, be reiterated in regard to requesting the California delegation to endeavor to induce the National Congress to grant an American register to the British bark "Pyrenees."

Restricting Undesirable Immigration

The Committee on Internal Trade and Improvements, to whom the matter had been referred, reported that they suggested that the question of restricting undesirable foreign immigration be laid on the table. Accordingly, resolution adopted in compliance with the suggestion of the committee.

Life-Saving Station, Halfmoon Bay

On motion, duly seconded, it was resolved that the California delegation be requested to have the National Congress make an adequate appropriation for establishing a Life-Saving Station at Halfmoon Bay, as provided for in S. B. 1748, Fifty-eighth Congress, First Session, introduced by Senator Perkins.

Parcels Post

On motion, duly seconded, it was resolved that the subject of Parcels Post, presented by the California Postal League, be referred to the Committee on Internal Trade and Improvements.

Hydrographic Office

On motion, duly seconded, it was resolved that Mr. William M. Bunker, at Washington, be requested to use his efforts towards having an appropriation made by the National Congress for the proper furnishing of the Branch Hydrographic Office in this city when it was moved into the new Merchants' Exchange Building.

Improvement, Oakland Harbor

The Vice-President, Mr. E. R. Dimond, to whom the matter had been referred, reported that in compliance with the request of the commercial associations of Oakland, a letter had been sent to the California delegation requesting their efforts to induce the National Congress to make an appropriation for dredging the channel of Oakland Harbor to a depth of twenty-five feet at low water. Action of Mr. Dimond duly approved.

American Trade in Manchuria

The President, Mr. Newhall, reported that in compliance with the request of the Committee on Foreign Commerce and Revenue Laws, to whom the matter had been referred, a letter had been sent to the Honorable the Secretary of State referring to a communication from the Manufacturers' and Producers' Association of California to the Secretary, and to a communication from Mr. J. B. Havre, in China, calling attention to the danger threatening American trade in Manchuria. On motion, duly seconded, the action of the President duly approved.

Isthmian Canal

On motion, duly seconded, the following resolution was adopted in regard to the action of President Roosevelt in regard to an Isthmian Canal:

"Whereas, We believe a canal joining the Atlantic and Pacific Oceans will be of great advantage to the United States, and particularly to that portion thereof on the Pacific Coast; therefore, the Chamber of Commerce of San Francisco have

"Resolved, That we hereby fully indorse the action taken by the President of the United States in his efforts towards securing the construction of an Isthmian Canal."

Wagon Road in Alaska

In compliance with the request of the Valdez Chamber of Commerce, Alaska, a resolution was adopted that the California delegation at Washington be requested to co-operate in efforts made towards securing an appropriation by the Congress for building a wagon road from Valdez to Eagle City, Alaska.

Philippine Commercial Commission

The President, Mr. Newhall, stated that Mr. Gustavo Neiderlein, a member of the Philippine Exposition Board, when in this city had suggested that the commercial organizations here extend some

Synopsis of Transactions. 107

courtesies to the commercial commission about to be appointed by Governor Taft when it arrived in San Francisco on its way to the St. Louis Fair. Mr. Newhall stated that he intended to call together the presidents of the commercial organizations to consider this matter, which was duly approved.

United States Consuls in South Africa

Resolution adopted that a letter be sent to the Honorable the Secretary of State at Washington, calling his attention to American trade relations with British South Africa, and requesting that the consular service there be extended and improved, to meet the demands in accordance with existing conditions and reasonable expectations.

Removing Rooms of Chamber

On motion, duly seconded, resolution adopted by the Board of Trustees that a committee be appointed by the President, Mr. Newhall, with full power to act, to arrange with the Merchants' Exchange for lease of rooms in their new building for the Chamber of Commerce of San Francisco on the best terms obtainable; the committee appointed being Messrs. E. R. Dimond, chairman, Henry Rosenfeld and A. B. Field.

National Exposition, Shanghai, China

A resolution adopted that the subject of establishing an American Exposition in Shanghai, China, under the auspices of the United States Government, as provided for in Senate Bill 195, Fifty-eighth Congress, First Session, be referred to the Pacific Commercial Museum.

Cornerstone Merchants' Exchange

Invitation presented from the Merchants' Exchange to the officers and members of the Chamber of Commerce to attend the ceremonies of laying the corner-stone of the new building of the Merchants' Exchange, Monday, December 14, 1903, at

12 m. Accordingly, the President, Mr. Newhall, appointed the members of the Board of Trustees as a special committee to represent the Chamber upon that occasion, and a resolution was adopted that the thanks of the Chamber of Commerce be extended to the Merchants' Exchange for their courtesy.

International Marine Association An invitation was presented from the International Marine Association of Paris for the Chamber to present any matter of international importance at the next meeting of their association, to be held in May, 1904, at Lisbon.

Rio Coffee Exchange Communication presented from the Rio Coffee Exchange informing the Chamber of the inauguration of the Exchange and desiring to co-operatae with the Chamber in the interchange of information bearing upon the commerce of Rio de Janeiro and San Francisco.

Use of Rooms The use of the rooms of the Chamber given to the La Carena Mining Company November 20th, to the Naval League December 9th, to the California Water and Forest Association December 10th, and to the Committee on California Wine Exhibit, St. Louis Fair, December 15th.

Load Line on American Ships The following resolution adopted by the Board of Trustees in regard to placing a load line on American ships:

"Resolved, That the Chamber of Commerce of San Francisco is opposed to the National Congress enacting legislation placing a load line on American vessels, which will injuriously affect the interests of Pacific Coast vessel owners."

Invitation to Governor Taft

The President, Mr. Newhall, stated that he was informed that Honorable Wm. H. Taft, Governor of the Philippine Islands, was expected to arrive in San Francisco about January 22nd, and that as January 19th was the time for the annual meeting of the Chamber, he suggested to the Board the advisability of combining the annual meeting with a banquet on the 23rd of January and inviting Governor Taft to be the guest of honor. Accordingly, the following cablegram was sent to Governor Taft at Manila:

"Chamber of Commerce invites you to their banquet January 23rd."

Use of Mails by Irresponsible Parties

The subject of preventing the use of mails by irresponsible parties being presented as outlined in S. B. 1261, Fifty-eighth Congress, First Session, resolution adopted that the matter be laid on the table.

Modification, Navigation Laws

A request was presented from the Honolulu Chamber of Commerce for the co-operation of the Chamber in efforts made to modify the existing navigation laws to the extent that passengers traveling between the port of Honolulu and the mainland of the Pacific Coast be not restricted to American vessels. It was the sentiment of the Board that while desiring to co-operate with the Honolulu Chamber of Commerce in efforts made for the mutual interests of the Islands and the mainland, the Board did not see its way clear to take the action suggested in this matter, as their previous efforts had been in favor of extending the coastwise laws between the Territory of Hawaii and the mainland.

Improvement Siuslaw Harbor

In compliance with the report of the Committee on Internal Trade and Improvements, to whom the matter had been referred, resolution adopted that the Senators and Representatives from California be requested to co-operate with the Senators and Representatives from Oregon in urging the National Congress to make an appropriation for the proper improvement of Siuslaw Harbor, Oregon.

Harbor Improvement

The subject presented of the desirability to have the submerged rocks in this harbor near the Pacific Mail S. S. Company's dock removed, as being a menace to navigation and particularly dangerous to vessels of deep draft, the subject was referred to the Committee on Harbor and Shipping.

Naval Officer Custom House

A request being made to the Board to recommend a gentleman for the position of Naval Officer of the Custom House, no action was taken. The Board of Trustees being of the opinion that it was not in their province to make such a recommendation.

Government of Hawaii

A request being presented from the Honolulu Chamber of Commerce for the co-operation of the Chamber in efforts to defeat certain proposed changes in the "Organic Act of the Territory of Hawaii," the subject was referred to the Committee on Internal Trade and Improvements.

Navigation Laws of Philippine Islands

The subject of changing the navigation laws affecting transportation between the Philippine Islands and the Pacific Coast being presented, resolution was adopted in effect that it was the urgent desire of the Chamber of Commerce that none but American vessels should be used in transportation between the ports of the Pacific Coast and the Philippine Islands and places and ports in the Philipine Islands, that the Senators and Representatives from California in the National Congress be requested to use their efforts to secure this result, and if to accomplish said result it is advisable to favor Senate Bill 2259, Fifty-eighth Congress, Second Session, permitting the temporary use of foreign bottoms in interisland transportation, the Senators and Representatives be urged to favor said bill.

American Vessels for Public Use

With a view of encouraging American shipping a resolution was adopted in effect that the Senators and Representatives from California in the National Congress be urged to use their efforts to obtain legislation substantially as provided for in Senate Bill 2263, Fifty-eighth Congress, Second Session, to require the employment of vessels of the United States for public purposes.

Removal of Rooms

The committee to whom the matter had been referred, reported that they had arranged with the Merchants' Exchange for lease of rooms for the Chamber of Commerce of San Francisco in the new Merchants' Exchange Building when completed.

National Civil Service Reform

The subject being presented of the Chamber appointing a delegate to attend the meeting of the National Civil Service Reform League in Washington, resolution adopted that the matter be laid on the table.

International Arbitration

The subject being presented of the Chamber appointing a delegate to attend a meeting in Washington in the interest of International Arbitration, resolution adopted that the matter be laid on the table.

ANNUAL STATISTICS

COMPILED FOR THE

Chamber of Commerce of San Francisco

For the Year ending December 31, 1903

A COMMERCIAL AND FINANCIAL RECORD WITH COMPARATIVE FIGURES.

THE TRADE OF SAN FRANCISCO AND ESTIMATED YIELD OF THE LEADING PRODUCTS OF CALIFORNIA.

BANK CLEARINGS.

The monthly Clearings at the San Francisco Clearing House during 1903, in comparison with the two preceding years, make the following showing:

Months.	1903	1902	1901
January............	$128,095,689 64	$105,569,792 78	$ 90,943,134 48
February..........	115,788,786 72	88,515,351 08	79,267,689 19
March.............	129,046,292 19	120,797,935 28	93,111,434 90
April..............	127,788,493 20	111,935,637 67	98,368,854 93
May...............	119,440,448 83	112,116,615 52	100,051,788 43
June...............	117,494,341 56	98,170,196 90	85,565,380 87
July...............	127,302,287 90	112,520,011 45	101,580,4 5 34
August.............	123,825,903 65	107,825,112 69	102,912,282 51
September.........	128,121,535 17	119,303,264 77	92,166,256 17
October............	142,358,567 68	134,814,471 94	118,288,132 23
November..........	126,495,422 28	125,221,938 19	109,875,359 71
December..........	134,442,913 25	136,571,697 04	106,038,767 54
Totals.........	$1,520,200,682 07	$1,373,362,025 31	$1,178,169,536 30

The total Clearings and Balances since the organization of the Clearing House and average daily Clearing for each year, is given in the following statement:

Year.	Clearings.	Balances.	Days	Average Daily Clearing.
1876	$ 476,123,237 97	$104,804,707		
1877	519,948,803 68	126,172,850		
1878	715,329,319 70	151,888,434		
1879	553,953,955 90	129,561,079 52	305	1,816,242 50
1880	486,725,953 77	118,046,934 94	304	1,601,072 20
1881	598,696,832 35	125,388,744 81	304	1,969,397 50
1882	629,114,119 81	108,487,872 15	303	2,076,284 20
1883	617,921,853 51	107,269,494 53	304	2,032,637 70
1884	556,857,691 03	95,275,201 49	304	1,831,768 72
1885	562,344,737 93	100,460,388 52	305	1,843,753 24
1886	642,221,391 21	105,832,828 47	301	2,133,625 88
1887	829,181,929 86	129,474,942 72	303	2,736,574 02
1888	836,735,954 39	123,271,533 66	305	2,743,396 57
1889	843,386,150 94	126,765,916 49	304	2,780,807 50
1890	851,066,172 60	118,824,559 86	302	2,818,099 91
1891	892,426,712 61	123,033,279 27	306	2,913,159 19
1892	815,368,724 41	110,364,511 10	304	2,682,133 96
1893	699,235,777 88	91,744,516 81	304	2,300,282 16
1894	658,526,806 13	88,426,316 52	303	2,173,355 79
1895	692,079,240 23	98,291,742 10	305	2,269,112 26
1896	683,229,599 26	90,491,491 73	304	2,247,465 79
1897	750,789,143 91	96,115,599 66	305	2,461,603 75
1898	813,153,024 00	103,329,265 56	303	2,683,673 35
1899	971,015,072 23	121,228,735 39	303	3,204,670 21
1900	1,029,582,594 78	118,157,405 71	303	3,397,962 36
1901	1,178,169,536 30	138,515,989 73	304	3,875,557 68
1902	1,373,362,025 31	166,234,644 08	303	4,532,547 94
1903	1,520,200,682 07	177,810,822 37	305	4,984,264 53

Bank Clearings.

The volume of San Francisco's bank clearings, in comparison with the clearings of all other Pacific and far western cities, where clearing houses are established, makes the following showing for the past two years:

Cities.	1903.	1902.
San Francisco	$1,520,200,682	$1,373,362,025
Los Angeles	306,376,837	245,516,095
Seattle	206,913,521	191,885,973
Salt Lake	156,085,394	175,114,600
Portland	175,742,510	154,741,110
Spokane	111,935,830	88,469,202
Tacoma	100,744,164	75,739,840
Helena	30,962,300	29,805,340
Fargo	29,243,006	24,613,705
Sioux Falls	13,272,409	13,675,283
Denver	237,324,959	230,369,178
Colorado Springs	22,090,595	30,541,500
Totals	$2,910,892,207	$2,633,833,851

San Francisco's total is larger than all the others combined. The aggregate increase for 1903 over the previous year for all the above named cities was $277,058,356 of which $146,838,657 or considerably more than one-half of the total is credited to San Francisco.

The position of San Francisco, with reference to bank clearings, among the leading cities of the United States is shown as follows:

Cities.	1903.	1902.
New York	$65,970,337,955	$76,328,189,165
Chicago	8,813,892,947	8,394,872,351
Boston	6,717,416,678	6,930,016,794
Philadelphia	5,841,630,726	5,875,328,360
St. Louis	2,510,479,245	2,506,804,320
Pittsburg	2,356,875,351	2,147,969,764
San Francisco	1,520,200,682	1,373,362,025
Baltimore	1,172,474,002	1,202,803,359
Cincinnati	1,154,647,600	1,080,902,000
Kansas City	1,074,878,589	988,294,998
New Orleans	827,710,850	672,360,577
Cleveland	802,198,631	762,604,187

In bank clearings San Francisco ranks seventh among the cities of the country.

SAN FRANCISCO COMMERCIAL BANKS.

The condition and affairs of the Commercial Banks in San Francisco, on the dates named, as reported to the Board of Bank Commissioners, make the following showing:

RESOURCES.	Jan. 23, 1904, 26 Banks.	Dec. 31, 1902, 19 Banks.
Bank Premises	$ 2,609,654 58	$ 2,223,685 11
Other Real Estate	2,381,145 92	2,452,108 22
Miscellaneous Bonds and Stocks	11,597,720 98	7,731,604 23
Loans on Real Estate	4,450,603 04	3,823,999 86
Loans on Stocks, Bonds and Warrants	23,149,995 31	23,531,576 82
Loans on other security (grain, etc.)	6,730,277 79	7,745,484 58
Loans on personal security	28,857,132 43	25,618,725 63
Money on hand	11,431,266 56	13,579,912 06
Due from Banks and Bankers	25,321,461 68	21,708,633 09
Other assets	946,933 96	879,136 36
Totals	$117,476,092 25	$109,294,865 96

Increase in Resources during 1903—$27,290,325.52.

LIABILITIES.	Jan. 23, 1904, 26 Banks.	Dec. 31, 1902, 19 Banks.
Capital paid in coin	$15,827,607 16	$12,997,236 57
Reserve Fund, Profit and Loss	22,609,669 32	17,526,744 88
Due Depositors	65,122,974 68	67,853,182 53
Due Banks and Bankers	12,445,345 15	8,512,477 70
State, County and City money	1,114 87	
Other liabilities	1,469,381 07	2,405,234 28
Totals	$117,476,092 25	$109,294,865 96

Increase in Deposits during 1903—$9,577,426.96.

Resources and deposits during the six preceding years, as shown by official statements were as follows:

DATE.	RESOURCES.	DEPOSITS.
1901—December 31	$90,185,766 73	$55,545,547 72
1900—December 31	76,543,241 09	46,270,737 20
1899—November 29	74,918,939 00	44,011,228 00
1898—December 31	64,122,154 00	34,516,310 00
1897—November 30	73,401,306 00	37,053,416 00
1896—November 30	68,339,005 00	30,178,548 00

SAN FRANCISCO SAVINGS BANKS.

Detailed statements of the condition and affairs of the Savings Banks in San Francisco on the dates named make the following showing:

RESOURCES.	Jan. 23, 1904, 9 Banks.	Dec. 31, 1902. 9 Banks.
Bank Premises	$ 2,235,551 98	$ 1,962,603 52
Real Estate taken for Debt	3,464,781 45	4,423,243 80
Miscellaneous Bonds and Stocks	69,237,473 82	67,769,346 33
Loans on Real Estate	79,427,746 52	67,150,286 70
Loans on Stocks, Bonds, Warrants, etc	6,300,203 03	7,298,335 36
Loans on other security	1,000 00	121,400 00
Loans on personal security		20,297 04
Money on hand	2,766,300 07	3,198,144 59
Due from Banks and Bankers	2,699,468 31	2,349,155 83
Other assests	334,248 47	469,977 31
Totals	$166,466,773 65	$154,762,790 48

Increase in resources during 1903—$11,703,983.17.

LIABILITIES.	Jan. 23, 1904, 9 Banks.	Dec. 31, 1902, 9 Banks.
Capital paid in Coin	$ 4,350,000 00	$ 4,050,000 00
Reserve Fund, Profit and Loss, etc	6,262,172 08	6,183,552 84
Due Depositors	154,906,701 98	144,295,034 57
Other liabilities	947,899 59	234,203 07
Totals	$166,466,773 65	$154,762,790 48

Increase in deposits during 1903, $10,611,667.41.

Resources and deposits during the six preceding years, as shown by official statements, were as follows:

DATE.	RESOURCES.	DEPOSITS.
1901—Dec. 31	$143,524,996 39	$133,430,482 77
1900—Dec. 31	134,498,940 61	124,580,434 81
1899—Nov. 29	127,317,067 00	115,688,396 00
1898—Dec. 31	119,548,502 00	110,001,652 00
1897—Nov. 30	113,882,945 00	102,119,990 00
1896—Nov. 30	112,877,677 00	100,851,482 00

NATIONAL BANKS.

The condition of the National Banks in San Francisco on the date named was as follows:

Resources.	Jan. 22, 1904. 7 Banks.
Loans and Discounts...............................	$25,902,527 68
Overdrafts...	124,488 06
U. S. Bonds for circulation	5,475,000 00
U. S. Bonds to secure deposits	1,624,000 00
U. S. Bonds on hand	5,237,500 00
Premium on U. S. Bonds...........................	477,624 64
Stocks, securities, claims, etc....................	2,491,689 53
Banking houses and fixtures......................	672,399 45
Other Real Estate, etc............................	....
Due from other National Banks...................	1,522,273 53
Due from State Banks.............................	3,106,707 93
Due from Reserve Agents	2,217,569 70
Internal Revenue Stamps.........................	....
Checks and other cash items.....................	34,376 54
Exchanges for clearing house....................	880,964 84
Bills of National Banks...........................	47,817 00
Fractional currency...............................	3,398 55
Specie..	7,022,323 35
Legal tender notes................................	11,368 00
Five per cent Redemption Fund	262,615 00
Due from U. S. Treasurer........................	11,500 00
Total Resources.............................	$57,126,141 80

Liabilities.	Jan. 22, 1904. 7 Banks.
Capital paid in....................................	$7,500,000 00
Surplus Fund......................................	3,901,000 00
Undivided profits..................................	745,362 09
Notes in circulation...............................	5,219,100 00
Due National Banks...............................	3,398,054 92
Due to State Banks................................	6,149,237 37
Due to trust companies...........................	3,499,331 72
Due to reserve agents	257,707 70
Dividends unpaid..................................	20,169 00
Individual deposits................................	21,314,531 67
United States deposits............................	1,639,386 01
Deposits U. S. disb. officers.....................	....
Miscellaneous.....................................	3,482,261 32
Total liabilities.............................	$57,126,141 80

INTERIOR COMMERCIAL BANKS.

The condition and affairs of the Commercial Banks in California, outside of San Francisco, on the dates named, is as follows:

RESOURCES.	Jan. 23, 1904 195 Banks.	Dec. 31, 1902 171 Banks.
Bank Premises	$2,594,008 98	$2,071,681 93
Other Real Estate	4,078,248 50	4,649,562 54
Stocks and Bonds	9,296,049 29	9,279,938 24
Loans on Real Estate	17,813,222 83	16,537,623 33
Loans on Stocks and Bonds	6,213,197 36	4,000,008 81
Loans on other securities	3,639,303 83	5,675,654 58
Loans on personal security	33,029,604 45	28,360,130 28
Money on hand	6,007,599 95	7,192,667 18
Due from Banks and Bankers	13,078,245 86	20,619,530 55
Other Assets	1,089,074 25	1,106,954 24
Totals	$96,838,555 30	$99,490,751 68

Decrease in Resources during 1903—$2,652,196.38.

LIABILITIES.	Jan. 23, 1904 195 Banks.	Dec. 31, 1902 171 Banks.
Capital paid up	$20,437,763 14	$18,962,634 22
Reserve Fund	8,258,011 65	8,795,502 67
Due Depositors	64,446,518 63	67,343,234 20
Due Banks	2,146,903 86	2,997,245 21
State and County Money	717,950 98	361,700 85
Other Liabilities	831,407 04	1,030,434 53
Totals	$96,838,555 30	$99,490,751 68

Decrease in Deposits during 1903—$2,896,715.57.

Resources and deposits during the six preceding years, as shown by official statements, were as follows:

DATE.	RESOURCES.	DEPOSITS.
1901—Dec. 31	$82,336,933 28	$52,943,472 16
1900—Dec. 31	75,680,459 00	46,570,773 00
1899—Nov. 29	71,225,438 00	42,932,631 00
1898—Dec. 31	62,996,189 00	34,928,569 00
1897—Nov. 30	62,973,135 00	34,482,929 00
1896—Nov. 30	57,132,803 00	28,395,729 00

INTERIOR SAVINGS BANKS

The condition and affairs of the Savings Banks in California, outside of San Francisco, on the dates named is as follows:

RESOURCES.	Jan. 23, 1904, 64 Banks.	Dec. 31, 1902, 53 Banks.
Bank Premises	$ 856,344 00	$ 809,905 15
Other Real Estate	1,715,623 31	2,127,371 83
Bonds and Stocks	15,149,188 22	12,236,235 71
Loans on Real Estate	40,531,262 68	33,092,589 77
Loans on Stocks, Bonds, etc	2,215,777 48	2,140,659 85
Loans on other securities	444,828 33	327,340 76
Loans on personal security	1,622,306 88	1,431,258 88
Money on hand	1,267,271 56	2,070,412 17
Due from other banks	7,463,173 51	5,588,828 18
Other Assets	408,464 66	398,511 90
Total Assets	$71,674,240 63	$60,223,114 20

Increase in Resources during 1903—$11,451,126.46.

LIABILITIES.	Jan. 23, 1904, 64 Banks.	Dec. 31, 1902, 53 Banks.
Capital paid up	$ 4,786,955 00	$ 4,029,480 00
Reserve Fund and Profit and Loss	2,511,490 66	2,007,247 79
Due Depositors	63,830,055 09	53,753,932 05
Due other Banks	161,911 80	38,542 25
State, City and County Money	12,173 59	13,800 00
Other Liabilities	371,654 49	380,112 11
Total Liabilities	$71,674,240 63	$60,223,114 20

Increase in Deposits during 1903—$10,076,123.04.

Resources and deposits during the six preceding years as shown by official statements were as follows:

DATE.	RESOURCES.	DEPOSITS.
1901—December 31	$52,356,564 62	$46,282,622 70
1900—December 31	45,510,762 00	39,925,483 00
1899—November 29	40,245,204 00	34,317,178 00
1898—December 31	36,730,611 00	31,178,317 00
1897—November 30	34,222,989 00	28,236,146 00
1896—November 30	32,690,001 00	26,474,526 00

PRIVATE BANKS.

The condition and affairs of the Private Banks in California, outside of San Francisco, is as follows:

RESOURCES.	Jan. 23, 1904, 20 Banks.	Dec. 31, 1902, 21 Banks.
Bank premises...........................	$ 64,828 29	$ 96,493 03
Other Real Estate........................	145,004 55	119,911 08
Bonds and Stocks........................	343,577 51	287,147 21
Loans on real estate.....................	641,888 86	575,659 56
Loans on stocks and bonds...............	64,692 57	47,274 08
Loans on other securities................	149,651 51	113,414 79
Loans on personal security..............	1,444,526 69	1,150,244 54
Money on hand..........................	231,250 19	241,528 24
Due from banks.........................	526,614 85	426,547 23
Other assets.............................	244,527 77	94,254 51
Total resources.....................	$3,856,832 79	$3,152,474 27

Increase in Resources during 1903—$704,358.52.

LIABILITIES.	Jan. 23, 1904, 20 Banks.	Dec. 31, 1902, 21 Banks.
Capital paid up.........................	$ 771,803 80	$ 696,802 80
Reserve fund, profit and loss............	350,507 88	256,866 93
Due depositors	2,597,920 65	2,170,438 95
Due banks..............................	67,838 41	13,737 92
Other liabilities.........................	68,764 05	14,627 67
Total liabilities.....................	$3,856,832 79	$3,152,474 27

Increase in Deposits during 1903—$427,481.70.

Resources and deposits during the six preceding years, as shown by official statements, were as follows:

DATE.	RESOURCES.	DEPOSITS.
1901—Dec. 31.	$3,143,711 05	$1,873,913 44
1900—Dec. 31.	2,611,868 00	1,580,710 00
1899—Nov. 29.	2,905,538 00	1,726,390 00
1898—Dec. 31.	2,849,223 00	1,546,109 00
1897—Nov. 30...........................	2,920,319 00	1,433,880 00
1896—Nov. 30...........................	2,649,736 00	1,074,035 00

BANKING IN CALIFORNIA.

The detailed aggregate condition of all the Savings, Commercial and Private banks in California under the supervision of the Bank Commission, was as follows on the dates named:

RESOURCES.	Jan. 23, 1904. 312 Banks.	Dec. 31, 1902. 277 Banks.
Bank premises	$ 8,360,387 83	$ 7,164,368 74
Real estate	11,784,703 73	13,772,197 47
Miscellaneous bonds and stocks	105,624,009 82	97,301,271 72
Loans on real estate	142,864,723 93	121,180,159 22
Loans on stocks, bonds and warrants	37,943,865 75	37,017,854 92
Loans on other securities	10,965,061 46	13,983,294 71
Loans on personal security	64,953,570 45	56,580,656 37
Money on hand	21,703,958 33	26,282,664 24
Due from banks and bankers	49,088,964 21	50,692,694 88
Other assets	3,023,249 11	2,948,834 32
Totals	$456,312,494 62	$426,923,996 59

Increase in resources during 1903—$29,388,498.03.

LIABILITIES.	Jan. 23, 1904. 312 Banks.	Dec. 31, 1902. 277 Banks.
Capital paid in coin	$ 46,174,128 10	$ 40,736,143 59
Reserve fund	39,991,850 59	34,769,915 11
Due depositors	350,904,171 03	335,415,822 30
Due banks and bankers	14,821,999 22	11,562,003 08
State, county or city Money	731,239 44	375,500 85
Other liabilities	3,689,106 24	4,064,611 66
Total liabilities	$456,312,494 62	$426,923,996 59

Increase in deposits during 1903, $15,488,348.73.

Resources and deposits during the six preceding years, as shown by official statements, were as follows:

DATE.	RESOURCES.	DEPOSITS.
1901—Dec. 31	$371,547,972 07	$290,076,038 79
1900—Dec. 31	338,845,271 40	258,928,138 28
1899—Nov. 29	316,612,186 00	238,675,823 00
1898—Dec. 31	286,246,679 00	212,170,957 00
1897—Nov. 30	287,400,694 00	203,326,361 00
1896—Nov. 30	273,689,222 00	186,974,320 00

NATIONAL BANKS.

The condition of the National Banks in California on the dates named was as follows:

RESOURCES	Jan. 22, 1904. 68 Banks.	Nov. 25, 1902. 51 Banks.
Loans and discounts	$65,368,849 81	$49,508,075 00
Overdrafts	1,178,374 09	1,346,607 00
U. S. bonds for circulation	10,492,000 00	7,719,000 00
U. S. bonds to secure deposits	2,584,000 00	2,284,000 00
U. S. bonds on hand	5,444,770 00	192,590 00
Premium on U. S. bonds	763,945 19	385,148 00
Stocks, securities, claims, etc	7,350,081 07	5,789,540 00
Banking houses and fixtures	2,326,779 79	1,343,459 00
Other real estate, etc	391,625 82	509,686 00
Due from other National Banks	3,724,100 25	4,203,707 00
Due from State Banks	5,982,566 68	5,829,780 00
Due from Reserve Agents	10,360,121 32	9,494,694 00
Internal revenue stamps	....	3,720 00
Checks and other cash items	623,882 25	698,482 00
Exchanges for Clearing House	1,313,830 93	1,235,979 00
Bills of National Banks	300,396 00	504,733 00
Fractional currency	20,068 05	11,931 00
Specie	13,221,991 05	9,081,928 00
Legal tender notes	429,795 00	264,303 00
Five per cent redemption fund	510,115 00	382,700 00
Due from U. S. Treasurer	40,100 00	2,800 00
Total resources	$132,437,392 30	$100,792,867 00

Increase in Resources during 1903—$31,644,525.30.

LIABILITIES	Jan. 22, 1904. 68 Banks.	Nov. 25, 1902. 51 Banks.
Capital paid in	$16,668,935 00	$12,712,800 00
Surplus fund	6,850,500 00	4,532,050 00
Undivided profits	2,978,490 33	2,968,580 00
Notes in circulation	10,104,575 00	7,469,395 00
Due National Banks	4,506,278 45	2,229,540 00
Due to State Banks	7,380,977 42	6,231,165 00
Due to trust companies	5,456,658 64	3,796,053 00
Due to reserve agents	418,614 15	146,996 00
Dividends unpaid	45,687 79	4,132 00
Individual deposits	70,994,557 93	58,175,686 00
United States deposits	2,505,297 52	2,184,628 00
Deposits U. S. disb. officers	100,963 85	113,967 00
Miscellaneous	4,425,856 22	227,876 00
Total liabilities	$132,437,392 30	$100,792,867 00

Increase in Deposits during 1903—$12,818,871.93.

PACIFIC OCEAN TRADE.

The value of all shipments of merchandise from San Francisco by sea to foreign countries and the Atlantic states, for each month of the past four years, is shown as follows:

Exports.	1903.	1902.	1901.	1900.
January	$ 4,179,551	$ 3,935,656	$ 3,575,510	$ 3,936,812
February	3,265,821	3,568,675	2,940,440	3,638,807
March	4,233,533	3,419,086	3,595,020	4,965,090
April	4,756,967	2,733,587	2,472,284	2,910,865
May	3,164,211	3,067,569	3,069,430	3,298,703
June	2,753,703	2,861,068	2,923,134	2,786,820
July	2,935,703	2,776,468	2,061,830	2,175,727
August	5,296,874	4,188,434	2,468,250	2,536,883
September	4,174,397	4,797,137	3,253,610	3,167,369
October	7,756,786	4,758,035	5,945,720	5,209,312
November	4,892,231	6,327,436	4,806,270	3,128,485
December	4,142,472	5,168,271	4,526,912	3,664,806
Totals	$51,552,249	$47,601,422	$41,638,410	$41,419,679

The monthly total values of all imports of foreign merchandise at San Francisco by sea, for four years past, are shown as follows:

Imports.	1903.	1902.	1901.	1900.
January	$ 2,879,178	$ 2,917,472	$ 2,398,408	$ 3,256,912
February	4,159,958	2,682,753	2,764,920	4,214,063
March	3,449,475	2,846,088	3,894,737	3,421,780
April	2,669,464	3,249,571	3,747,294	5,703,547
May	2,650,027	2,845,902	3,538,978	3,630,288
June	2,298,019	2,913,109	3,740,434	3,480,238
July	2,464,625	2,532,072	2,543,243	2,218,047
August	3,395,976	2,477,302	3,058,851	3,621,613
September	3,154,161	3,246,529	2,763,749	2,198,520
October	3,307,912	2,877,844	2,974,923	2,562,440
November	3,039,100	3,381,352	2,854,980	3,108,089
December	3,054,292	4,108,276	2,986,762	2,008,898
Totals	$36,522,187	$36,078,270	$37,267,279	$39,424,435

The aggregate ocean commerce of the port of San Francisco, exclusive of coastwise trade, during the past four years, is as follows:

	1903.	1902.	1901.	1900.
Exports	$51,552,249	$47,601,422	$41,638,410	$41,419,679
Imports	36,522,187	36,078,220	37,267,279	39,424,435
Total Trade	$88,074,436	$83,679,692	$78,905,689	$80,844,114

Note.—The exports for 1902 include the shipments from San Francisco to Hawaii from July 1 to December 31, aggregating $4,766,001. In 1901 Hawaiian shipments are omitted, and in 1900 exports to June 14 are included.

SAN FRANCISCO'S COMMERCE.

The annual valuations of merchandise traffic between San Francisco and foreign countries, the Atlantic States and non-contiguous territory for a series of years past are as follows:

EXPORTS.		IMPORTS.	
YEAR.	VALUE.	YEAR.	VALUE.
1855	$ 4,189,611	1855	$ 1,501,500
1856	4,270,516	1856	2,083,330
1857	4,369,758	1857	6,397,354
1858	4,770,163	1858	7,120,506
1859	5,553,411	1859	8,007,625
1860	8,532,439	1860	8,416,681
1861	9,888,072	1861	8,972,360
1862	10,565,294	1862	10,781,674
1863	12,877,399	1863	12,179,320
1864	13,271,752	1864	13,962,487
1865	14,554,496	1865	15,271,104
1866	17,303,818	1866	15,846,070
1867	22,465,903	1867	16,987,437
1868	22,943,340	1868	18,723,738
1869	20,888,981	1869	19,714,001
1870	17,848,160	1870	19,733,850
1871	13,951,149	1871	28,736,646
1872	23,793,530	1872	39,704,754
1873	31,160,208	1873	33,159,149
1874	28,425,248	1874	31,529,708
1875	33,554,081	1875	35,703,784
1876	31,314,782	1876	37,559,018
1877	29,992,393	1877	32,276,653
1878	34,155,394	1878	35,565,139
1879	36,564,328	1879	34,124,417
1880	35,563,286	1880	37,240,514
1881	53,664,352	1881	38,554,923
1882	51,752,428	1882	44,348,545
1883	45,767,373	1883	42,219,484
1884	37,244,639	1884	37,729,402
1885	36,102,842	1885	36,744,643
1886	40,201,727	1886	39,582,551
1887	35,964,882	1887	41,606,685
1888	40,825,062	1888	48,609,230
1889	41,250,921	1889	51,288,309
1890	39,969,591	1890	45,594,125
1891	53,887,459	1891	53,325,982
1892	40,246,608	1892	45,607,950
1893	33,853,345	1893	39,405,028
1894	26,410,672	1894	38,514,686
1895	33,264,861	1895	38,925,607
1896	43,513,996	1896	36,414,862
1897	44,280,000	1897	40,846,791
1898	35,852,544	1898	36,063,124
1899	38,924,908	1899	45,677,924
1900	41,419,679	1900	39,424,435
1901	41,638,410	1901	37,267,279
1902	47,601,422	1902	36,078,270
1903	51,552,249	1903	36,522,187

EXPORTS OF MERCHANDISE.

Comparative values of Domestic merchandise and produce exported to foreign countries from San Francisco by sea during the past year.

Destination	1903
France	$ 41,351
Germany	256,397
England	6,009,684
Ireland	3,543,374
Canada	133,517
British Columbia	1,027,915
Costa Rica	94,180
Guatemala	483,334
Honduras	128,884
Nicaragua	188,705
Salvador	332,685
Mexico	1,265,782
British West Indies	14,219
Chile	140,040
Colombia	161,070
Ecuador	113,093
Peru	432,361
China	2,423,985
Russian China	138,466
British East Indies	76,326
Dutch East Indies	59,375
Hongkong	3,683,798
Japan	3,460,687
Korea	83,153
Asiatic Russia	114,992
Australasia	4,794,019
Other British Oceanica	30,706
French Oceanica	381,450
German Oceanica	124,530
Philippines	772,747
British South Africa	658,759
Netherlands	43,826
Spain	6,854
Sweden	467
Belgium	539,316
Straits Settlements	22,702
Egypt	530
Italy	18,034
Total	$31,772,113

Exports of Merchandise.

The values of shipments of domestic merchandise forwarded in American vessels were as follows:

Months	Steam	Sail	Totals
January	$ 800,049	$ 19,600	$ 819,649
February	574,306	60,674	634,980
March	710,510	87,477	797,987
April	819,365	......	819,365
May	666,927	28,545	695,472
June	872,350	32,507	904,857
July	581,262	5,850	587,112
August	912,401	36,249	948,650
September	1,121,515	9,223	1,130,738
October	1,202,672	106,069	1,308,741
November	934,290	20,267	954,557
December	841,317	68,479	909,796
Totals	$10,036,964	$474,940	$10,511,904

The valuation of exports by foreign vessels for the year were as follows:

Months	Steam	Sail	Totals
January	$ 840,500	$ 1,480,776	$ 2,321,276
February	514,943	718,986	1,233,929
March	787,689	970,051	1,757,740
April	626,687	368,116	994,803
May	469,708	206,855	676,563
June	511,038	105,144	616,182
July	649,059	158,307	807,366
August	644,022	1,593,068	2,237,090
September	600,461	1,298,313	1,898,774
October	1,199,930	3,302,773	4,502,703
November	667,924	1,455,383	2,123,307
December	845,012	1,245,464	2,090,476
Totals	$8,356,973	$12,903,236	$21,260,209

The values of exports of Foreign merchandise from San Francisco by sea during 1903 were as follows:

Months	Free	Dutiable	Totals
January	$ 11,723	$ 42,585	$ 54,308
February	16,764	39,923	56,687
March	6,334	53,874	60,208
April	27,077	52,921	79,998
May	18,032	22,550	40,582
June	31,903	26,405	58,308
July	18,551	33,527	52,078
August	25,550	40,852	66,402
September	47,427	43,714	91,141
October	90,202	50,578	140,780
November	43,976	78,086	122,062
December	9,313	46,268	55,581
Totals	$530,883	$347,252	$878,135

Shipments of Domestic and Foreign merchandise combined make the following showing for the year:

Months	Domestic	Foreign	Totals
January	$ 3,140,925	$ 54,308	$ 3,195,233
February	1,868,909	56,687	1,925,596
March	2,555,727	60,208	2,615,935
April	1,814,168	79,998	1,894,166
May	1,372,035	40,582	1,412,617
June	1,521,039	58,308	1,579,347
July	1,394,478	52,078	1,446,556
August	3,185,740	66,402	3,252,142
September	3,029,512	91,141	3,120,653
October	5,811,444	140,780	5,952,224
November	3,077,864	122,062	3,199,926
December	3,000,272	55,581	3,055,853
Totals	$31,772,113	$878,135	$32,650,248

The shipments from San Francisco to the Atlantic States by sea during the year were as follows:

Months	1903
January	$ 177,642
February	495,666
March	587,205
April	290,520
May	453,111
June	178,984
July	452,862
August	753,209
September	246,997
October	866,066
November	727,751
December	138,239
Total	$5,368,252

The exports to Tutuila, Samoa, from San Francisco during the year were as follows:

Months	1903
January	$ 5,258
February	3,514
March	10,794
April	4,526
May	1,729
June	2,755
July	1,489
August	7,170
September	1,193
October	4 031
November	1,499
December	3,988
Totals	$47,946

The values of shipments of merchandise and produce from San Francisco to the Hawaiian Islands were as follows:

Months	1903
January	$ 792,090
February	832,514
March	884,892
April	732,105
May	1,004,899
June	760,579
July	919,271
August	1,102,740
September	672,320
October	921,560
November	957,185
December	938,400
Totals	$10,518,555

The values of exports to Alaska during the year were as follows:

Months	1903
January	$ 9,328
February	8,531
March	134,707
April	1,816,854
May	278,029
June	232,038
July	115,525
August	181,613
September	133,234
October	12,905
November	5,870
December	5,992
Totals	$2,934,626

The total monthly valuations of exports from San Francisco to non-contiguous territory of the United States, embracing Alaska, Hawaii, Tutuila, Guam and Midway Islands during the year were as follows:

MONTHS	1903
January	$ 806,676
February	844,559
March	1,030,393
April	2,572,281
May	1,298,483
June	995,372
July	1,036,285
August	1,291,523
September	806,747
October	938,496
November	964,554
December	948,380
Totals	$13,534,749

SUMMARY OF EXPORTS.

Classified the exports from San Francisco by sea during 1903 were as follows:

	1903
Domestic Merchandise	$31,772,113
Foreign Merchandise	878,135
To Hawaii	10,518,555
" Alaska	2,934,626
" Atlantic States	5,368,252
" Tutuila	47,946
" Guam	21,968
" Midway Island	10,654
Total	$51,552,249

IMPORTS OF FOREIGN MERCHANDISE.

The values of foreign merchandise imported at San Francisco by sea and rail during 1903 were as follows:

From	1903.
Belgium	$ 1,254,849
France	1,616,091
Germany	2,501,966
Greece	20,498
Italy	607,118
Netherlands	154,956
Spain	41,060
Sweden	106,123
Turkey	26,484
England	1,874,407
Scotland	291,003
Ireland	149,389
Canada	28,270
British Columbia	1,543,665
Costa Rica	254,111
Guatemala	1,732,762
Nicaragua	138,919
Salvador	729,586
Mexico	564,347
British West Indies	20,194
Cuba	267,220
Brazil	16,161
Chile	902,788
Ecuador	257,782
China	5,808,195
British East Indies	2,787,311
Dutch West Indies	74,540
Japan	10,182,218
Australasia	1,386,760
French Oceanica	507,435
Philippines	432,335
Honduras	15,456
Austria	19,714
Switzerland	79,491
Peru	55,251
Egypt	2,402
Colombia	2,539
British Oceanica	9,560
Portugal	12,499
German Oceanica	160
Dutch East Indies	4,433
Miscellaneous	42,239
Total	$36,522,187

The custom house classification of the imports during 1903 were as follows:

Months.	Free.	Dutiable.
January	$ 1,568,249	$ 1,310,929
February	2,758,152	1,401,806
March	2,090,347	1,359,128
April	1,382,532	1,286,932
May	1,389,784	1,260,243
June	1,099,571	1,198,448
July	1,441,992	1,022,633
August	1,655,095	1,740,881
September	2,145,850	1,008,311
October	1,704,460	1,603,452
November	1,659,423	1,379,677
December	1,676,836	1,377,456
Totals	$20,572,291	$15,949,896

The disposition of the imports received during the year, as entered at the custom house was as follows:

Months.	Immediate Use.	For Warehouse.
January	$ 2,563,788	$ 315,390
February	3,775,501	384,457
March	3,055,944	393,531
April	2,209,821	459,643
May	2,229,333	420,694
June	1,920,317	377,702
July	2,203,714	260,911
August	2,961,510	434,466
September	3,000,346	153,815
October	2,823,149	484,763
November	2,642,928	396,172
December	2,599,312	454,980
Totals	$31,985,663	$4,536,524

The imports of merchandise at San Francisco during each month of the year were as follows:

Months.	1903.
January	$ 2,879,178
February	4,159,958
March	3,449,475
April	2,669,464
May	2,650,027
June	2,298,019
July	2,464,625
August	3,395,976
September	3,154,161
October	3,307,912
November	3,039,100
December	3,054,292
Totals	$36,522,187

The method of receiving these importations is shown as follows:

Months.	By Sea.	By Rail.
January	$ 2,502,762	$ 376,416
February	3,874,770	285,188
March	3,188,718	260,757
April	2,360,024	309,440
May	2,403,304	246,723
June	1,994,494	303,525
July	2,100,103	364,522
August	3,079,614	316,362
September	2,870,882	283,279
October	2,937,114	370,798
November	2,706,598	332,502
December	2,633,267	421,025
Totals	$32,651,650	$3,870,537

EXPORT AND IMPORT SUMMARY.

COMBINED EXPORT VALUES.

The combined exports, treasure and merchandise, exclusive of merchandise by overland railroads, and treasure shipments by the United States Sub-Treasury during the past three years, were as follows:

VALUES.	1903.	1902.	1901.
Merchandise..................	$51,552,249	$47,601,422	$41,638,410
Treasure.....................	3,680,755	14,851,789	11,234,708
Totals.......................	$55,233,004	$62,453,211	$52,873,118

COMBINED VALUES OF IMPORTS.

The combined values of imports of merchandise and treasure from Foreign Countries during the last three years were as follows:

VALUES.	1903.	1902.	1901.
Merchandise..................	$36,522,187	$36,078,270	$37,267,279
Treasure.....................	13,975,718	10,692,232	20,768,638
Totals.......................	$50,497,905	$46,770,502	$58,035.917

SAN FRANCISCO'S TRADE SUMMARY.

The combined values of all exports of merchandise and treasure by sea and all imports of merchandise and treasure at San Francisco during the last three years make the following showing:

	1903.	1902.	1901.
Merchandise Exports............	$51,552,249	$47,601,422	$41,638,410
Treasure Exports...............	3,680,755	14,851,789	11,234,708
Merchandise Imports............	36.522,187	36,078,270	37,267,279
Treasure Imports...............	13,975,718	10,692,232	20,768,638
Total volume of trade..........	$105,730,909	$109,223,713	$110,909,035

NOTE. The exports of merchandise, commodities and supplies on United States Army Transports from San Francisco, which aggregates more than $1,450,000 per year are not included in the trade statistics, and the movement of treasure to and from non-contiguous territory of the United States is not included.

EXPORTS OF TREASURE.

The following is a statement of treasure shipments from San Francisco by sea during each month of the past three years:

Months.	1903.	1902.	1901.
January	$ 435,224	$ 484,218	$ 279,711
February	100,476	1,215,242	92,696
March	118,948	628,043	452,512
April	231,119	335,915	530,215
May	111,247	373,960	461,875
June	1,123,927	709,780	823,366
July	700,757	1,181,369	658,256
August	226,540	3,250,578	1,455,516
September	349,614	1,453,733	1,606,365
October	81,652	2,294,147	1,693,581
November	94,848	1,158,294	986,634
December	106,403	1,766,510	2,193,981
Totals	$3,680,755	$14,851,789	$11,234,708

The shipments of standard silver dollars and subsidiary silver coin by the United States Sub-Treasury in this city to the East during each month of the year 1903 were as follows:

Months.	Silver Dollars.	Subsidiary Silver.	Total.
January	$ 59,000	$ 49,865	$108,865
February	55,000	76,025	131,025
March	92,500	117,140	209,640
April	122,500	115,985	238,485
May	142,500	145,475	287,975
June	166,000	204,280	370,280
July	184,400	180,040	364,440
August	204,000	276,955	480,955
September	245,500	269,000	514,500
October	178,000	168,380	346,380
November	143,000	118,015	261,015
December	124,200	122,850	247,050
Totals	$1,716,600	$1,844,010	$3,560,610

The total shipments by sea and overland during the last three years compare as follows:

By	1903.	1902.	1901.
Sea	$3,680,755	$14,851,789	$11,234,708
Rail*	....	....	3,355,565
Sub-Treasury shipments	3,560,610	3,605,025	2,977,530
Totals	$7,241,365	$18,456,814	$17,556,803

*Per Wells, Fargo & Co.'s Express and not reported for 1902 and 1903.

During the past three years the treasure shipments by sea were destined as follows:

To	1903.	1902.	1901.
Costa Rica	$ 470		
Guatemala	3,080		$ 720
Hongkong	1,846,400	$9,289,003	11,040,479
China	21,829	464,200	48,755
French Oceanica	5,570	21,124	8,488
German Oceanica	955		
Salvador	13,442	3,705	
Philippine Islands	118,280	599,413	
Japan	1,646,600	2,795,232	2,280
Tutuila	2,000	38,000	400
Mexico	20,500	110,000	100,000
Nicaragua	1,000		
British Oceanica	629	3,000	
Elsewhere		1,528,112	33,586
Totals	$3,680,755	$14,851,789	$11,234,708

Classified, the shipments by sea for a series of years, are as follows:

Year.	Gold.	Silver.	Total.
1903	$1,818,737	$ 1,862,018	$ 3,680,755
1902	2,947,959	11,903,830	14,851,789
1901	246,182	10,988,526	11,234,708
1900	485,687	14,665,491	15,151,178
1899	2,775,754	7,884,477	10,660,231
1898	803,481	7,887,039	8,694,695
1897	1,088,333	17,668,003	18,756,336
1896	1,138,557	14,372,272	15,510,829
1895	558,570	18,241,101	18,799,671
1894	1,048,975	12,929,894	13,978,869
1893	1,153,509	11,899,433	13,052,942
1892	875,635	13,700,943	14,576,578
1891	1,318,287	7,756,019	9,074,306
1890	1,538,819	7,128,561	8,667,380
1889	1,679,636	18,586,221	20,265,857

IMPORTS OF TREASURE.

The treasure imports at San Francisco during the past three years were as follows:

From	1903.	1902.	1901.
British Columbia	$1,538,215	$ 42,348	$ 120,658
Costa Rica	19,059		
Salvador	25,844	105,640	94,698
Mexico	2,784,361	2,413,610	3,878,546
Japan	2,149,287	14,560	4,040,132
Ecuador	62,792	62,712	114,798
China	18,721	93,672	43,775
Australia	7,300,835	7,792,277	12,458,140
Peru	383		
Honduras	45,317		13,742
Colombia	1,800		
French Oceanica	8,704	12,413	4,149
Guatemala	20,400	2,000	
Manila		153,000	
Totals	$13,975,718	$10,692,232	$20,768,638

Classified, the imports during each month of 1903 were as follows:

Months.	Gold.	Silver.	Totals.
January	$ 63,395	$ 110,064	$ 173,459
February	128,618	104,610	233,228
March	99,023	144,222	243,245
April	40,383	179,217	219,600
May	75,265	317,194	392,459
June	112,502	74,097	186,599
July	1,594,292	360,490	1,954,782
August	2,640,802	202,482	2,843,284
September	1,774,226	221,305	1,995,531
October	1,713,617	522,376	2,235,993
November	262,719	358,524	621,243
December	2,521,134	355,161	2,876,295
Total	$11,025,976	$2,949,742	$13,975,718

TRADE WITH THE ORIENT.

EXPORTS

The monthly valuations of merchandise shipped from San Francisco to China, exclusive of Hongkong and Russian China, during 1903, makes the following showing:

Months.	Value.
January	$ 165,087
February	233,621
March	225,397
April	399,816
May	242,642
June	195,772
July	201,418
August	117,341
September	153,291
October	338,379
November	73,335
December	77,886
Total	$2,423,985

The monthly valuations of merchandise shipped from San Francisco to Hongkong during 1903 were as follows:

Months.	Value.
January	$ 168,953
February	197,049
March	326,746
April	102,827
May	160,996
June	263,197
July	177,348
August	323,411
September	655,060
October	591,745
November	371,895
December	344,571
Total	$3,683,798

The exports from San Francisco to Russian China during 1903 were as follows:

Months.	Value.
January	$ 4,776
February	6,686
March	18,210
April	10,460
May	6,199
June	8,930
July	15,653
August	25,792
September	15,507
October	14,972
November	5,205
December	6,076
Total	$138,466

The merchandise shipments from San Francisco to Siberia during 1903 were as follows:

Months.	Value.
January	$ 8,895
February	2,886
March	47,052
April	43,599
May	5,129
June	564
July	1,874
August	....
September	1,447
October	415
November	612
December	2,519
Totals	$114,992

The exports of merchandise from San Francisco to Japan during 1903 are as follows:

Months.	Value.
January	$ 583,154
February	227,671
March	402,997
April	245,037
May	167,346
June	204,068
July	225,086
August	179,206
September	182,118
October	355,049
November	302,163
December	386,792
Total	$3,460,687

The exports from San Francisco to the Philippine Islands during 1903, exclusive of shipments in United States Transports, were as follows:

Months.	Value.
January	$ 75,280
February	23,795
March	56,444
April	52,086
May	47,293
June	32,322
July	73,219
August	58,742
September	60,459
October	89,579
November	68,350
December	135,178
Total	$772,747

NOTE—Shipments by U. S. Army transports are not included in above valuations.

Shipments of merchandise from San Francisco to the East Indies during 1903 were as following:

Months.	Value.
January	$ 9,190
February	11,292
March	16,290
April	20,255
May	16,924
June	9,519
July	8,680
August	9,387
September	13,153
October	9,070
November	4,985
December	6,956
Total	$135,701

The exports from San Francisco to Korea during 1903 were as follows:

Months.	Value.
January	$ 2,041
February	1,802
March	10,279
April	7,028
May	5,093
June	4,273
July	8,325
August	4,772
September	14,956
October	13,203
November	8,107
December	3,274
Total	$83,153

The varieties of merchandise and commodities exported from San Francisco to China, including Hongkong, during 1903, in quantities were as follows:

Articles.		1903.
Agricultural Implements	pkgs.	31
Arms and Ammunition	pkgs.	191
Bagging	bales	22
	lbs.	279,972
	pkgs.	2,275
	lbs.	14
Biscuits	crates	280
Books and Stationery	pkgs.	361
Borax	lbs.	25
Boots and Shoes	pkgs.	1,185
Brandy	gals.	765
Bran	lbs.	73,466
	pkgs.	188
Candles	bxs.	66
Canned Goods	cs.	32,980
Cement and Plaster	lbs.	87
China Merchandise	pkgs.	15
Cider	cs.	19
Cigars and Cigarettes	cs.	1,560
Codfish	pkgs.	3,225
Coffee	lbs.	160,759
Cordage	coils.	71
Cotton	bales.	1,814
Drugs	pkgs.	1,505
Dry goods	pkgs.	1,770
Electric goods	pkgs.	178
Fertilizers	sks.	1.673
Fish	pkgs.	18,729
Flour	bbls.	547,811
Fruit, Fresh	bxs.	12,230
Fruit, Canned	cs.	16.570
Fruit, Dried	lbs.	276,729
Fruit, Dried	cs.	502
Fuse	cs.	16
Glassware	pkgs.	2,645
Groceries and Provisions	lbs.	380,800
Groceries and Provisions	pkgs.	32,596
Hardware	pkgs.	935
Harness	pkgs.	209
Hay	bales	1,751

Articles.		1903.
Honey	cs.	80
Hops	lbs.	26,157
Iron Manufactures	pkgs.	460
Lard	lbs.	56,608
Lead	pigs	15,790
Leather	pkgs.	329
Lime	bbls.	26
Liquor	cs.	736
Live Stock	No.	7
Lumber	ft.	182,479
Lumber Manufactures	pkgs.	698
Machinery	pkgs.	442
Malt	lbs.	8,420
Marble	pkgs.	12
Metal	pkgs.	125,082
Millstuffs	lbs.	524,587
Millstuffs	pkgs.	7,442
Miscellaneous	lbs.	1,272,072
Miscellaneous	pkgs.	60,894
Nails	kegs.	96
Nuts	sks.	161
Oats	ctls.	273
Oil and Kerosene	cs.	464
Oil and Kerosene	bbls.	55
Paint	cs.	575
Paper	rolls	519
Pipe	pcs.	225
Quicksilver	flasks	5,250
Raisins	bxs.	1,310
Rice	lbs.	18,113
Salmon	cs.	7,440
Salmon	bbls.	12
Salt	bales	223
Seed	lbs.	3,941
Ship Chandlery	pkgs.	13,595
Sewing Machines	cs.	773
Silk	cs.	3
Sugar	lbs.	774,993
Tallow	lbs.	5
Tea	lbs.	1,701
Tobacco	lbs.	22,735
Varnish	cs.	12
Vegetables	sks.	39,584
Wagon Material	pkgs.	90
Whisky	gals.	267
Whisky	cs.	618
Wine	gals.	31,354
Wine	cs.	3,441
Wire	bndls.	6,300
Wool	lbs.	70

Classified the merchandise and commodities shipped from San Francisco to Japan during 1903, in quantities, were as follows:

ARTICLES.	1903.
Agricultural Implements............................pkgs.	456
Alcohol..bbls.	47,222
Arms and Ammunition............................pkgs.	225
Asphaltum.......................................pkgs.	77
Bags and Bagging................................bales	100
Barley...ctls.	4,676
Beans..lbs.	13,446
Beer..pkgs.	648
Bicycles..crates	5,287
Books and Stationery.............................pkgs.	579
Borax..lbs.	640
Boots and Shoes..................................pkgs.	390
Brandy..gals.	11
Bread..lbs.	25,727
Candy...pkgs.	412
Candles..bxs.	31
Canned Goods.....................................cs.	29,476
Cement and Plaster...............................lbs.	55
China Merchandise................................pkgs.	1
Codfish...pkgs.	246
Coffee...lbs.	18,141
Corn..ctls.	51
Cotton..bales	21,053
Drugs...pkgs.	1,024
Dry Goods.......................................pkgs.	210
Electric Goods...................................pkgs.	1,146
Fish..pkgs.	1,091
Flour..bbls.	55,660
Fruit, fresh......................................bxs.	563
Fruit, canned.....................................cs.	2,500
Fruit, dried......................................lbs.	131,684
Fruit, dried......................................cs.	1,396
Fuse...cs.	89
Glassware.......................................pkgs.	43
Groceries and Provisions..........................lbs.	302,133
Groceries and Provisions.........................pkgs.	11,190
Hardware..pkgs.	1,488
Harness...pkgs.	241
Hay...bales	1,306
Honey..cs.	52

Articles.		1903.
Hops	lbs.	8,936
Iron, Manufactures	pkgs.	51,051
Lard	lbs.	470,946
Lead	pigs	16,846
Leather	pkgs.	7,389
Liquors	cs.	1,558
Live Stock	No.	37
Lumber	feet	23,841
Lumber, Manufactures	pkgs.	160
Machinery	pkgs.	1,732
Malt	lbs.	41,050
Marble	pkgs.	35
Metal	pkgs.	1,590
Millstuffs	lbs.	67,667
Millstuffs	pkgs.	495
Miscellaneous	lbs.	4,339,975
Miscellaneous	pkgs.	197,519
Nails	kegs	245
Nuts	sks.	387
Oats	sks.	471
Oil and Kerosene	cs.	390
Oil and Kerosene	bbls.	8
Paint	cs.	834
Paper	rolls	419
Pipe	pcs.	422
Poultry	coops	4
Quicksilver	flasks	1,270
Raisins	bxs.	1,247
Rice	lbs.	14,539
Salmon	cs.	39
Salmon	bbls.	39
Salt	bales	15,887
Seed	lbs.	5,439
Seed, Mustard	lbs.	2,167
Ship Chandlery	pkgs.	82
Sewing Machines	cs.	41
Sugar	lbs.	303,200
Tallow	lbs.	3,925
Tea	lbs.	2,503
Tobacco	lbs.	146,505
Varnish	cs.	189
Vegetables	sks.	421
Wagon Materials	pkgs.	2
Whisky	gals.	2,735
Whisky	cs.	320
Wheat	ctls	7,442
Wine	gals.	39,046
Wine	cs.	230
Wire	bndls.	1,101
Wool	lbs.	90

The monthly shipments of flour from San Francisco to China during the last two years, were as follows:

Month	1903	1902
January	14,070	137,170
February	29,665	37,040
March	49,618	22,533
April	48,782	9,410
May	24,580	12,015
June	48,495	31,700
July	24,547	38,901
August	58,156	79,998
September	101,691	63,258
October	69,808	49,225
November	34,829	52,140
December	43,570	93,030
Totals	547,811	616,420

The monthly shipments of Flour from San Francisco to Japan during the last two years were as follows:

Month	1903	1902
January	....	4,505
February	....	510
March	2,040	3,790
April	1,530	....
May	1,260	2,130
June	11,048	....
July	11,413	1,600
August	10,118	4,025
September	6,403	2,745
October	6,668	1,028
November	1,542	4,680
December	3,538	1,625
Totals	55,660	26,638

NOTE—The short wheat crop of California in 1903 caused a large reduction in the exports of flour and grain.

IMPORTS

The monthly valuations of the imports of merchandise at San Francisco from the Chinese Empire including Hongkong during 1903 were as follows:

Months.	Value.
January	$ 458,732
February	893,571
March	406,055
April	567,939
May	261,234
June	289,245
July	252,713
August	573,616
September	491,067
October	517,939
November	363,785
December	732,299
Total	$5,808,195

The imports of merchandise at San Francisco, from Japan during 1903 were as follows:

Months.	Value.
January	$ 732,490
February	1,336,859
March	767,209
April	327,746
May	251,705
June	452,825
July	577,238
August	1,001,859
September	1,340,380
October	1,075,179
November	1,294,825
December	1,023,903
Total	$10,182,218

The imports of merchandise at San Francisco from the Philippine Islands during 1903 were as follows:

Months.	Value.
January	$ 12,473
February	31,401
March	1,866
April	1,429
May	41,374
June	45,404
July	54,844
August	40,945
September	40,795
October	49,698
November	64,465
December	47,641
Total	$432,335

The imports of merchandise at San Francisco from the East Indies during 1903 were as follows:

Months.	Value.
January	$188,828
February	126,123
March	325,426
April	427,492
May	693,846
June	322,182
July	321,638
August	166,839
September	83,506
October	80,280
November	55,166
December	100,418
Total	$2,791,744

The values of San Francisco's merchandise exports to all the Oriental countries during 1903, were as follows:

To	Exports
China	$ 2,423,985
Hongkong	3,683,798
Russian China	138,466
Siberia	114,992
Japan	3,460,687
Philippine Islands	772,747
East Indies	135.701
Korea	83,153
Guam	21,968
Midway Island	10,654
Total	$10,846,151

The imports from all the countries at San Francisco during 1903 were as follows:

From	Imports
China and Hongkong	$ 5,808,195
Japan	10,182,218
Philippine Islands	432,335
East Indies	2,791,744
Total	$19,214,492

A comparative summary of the trade of San Francisco with China and Japan during 1903 makes the following showing:

Shipment	China Exports	China Imports	Japan Exports	Japan Imports
Merchandise	$6,246,249	$5,808,195	$3,460,687	$10,182,218
Treasure	1,868,229	18,721	1,646,600	2,149,287
Totals	$8,114,478	$5,826,916	$5,107,287	$12,331,505

TONNAGE MOVEMENT.

The following shows the registered net tonnage entered at the San Francisco Custom House during the year 1903 from foreign and Atlantic ports, the actual carrying capacity being largely in excess of the given figures:

ARRIVALS FROM	STEAM No.	STEAM Tons.	SAIL No.	SAIL Tons.
Great Britain	2	4,866	43	85,511
Germany	10	31,918	14	24,130
Belgium	4	12,260	12	21,012
Sweden			2	2,791
France	5	14,870	21	38,610
Italy	1	2,746	1	1,921
Australia	18	69,509	84	171,406
Hawaii	54	113,758	178	164,724
Mexico	4	9,888	1	1,702
Hongkong	62	166,980	6	8,814
Japan	2	4,916	2	3,440
China	15	88,680		
Alaska	12	17,251	31	55,161
Pacific Islands	10	21,828	3	8,816
British Columbia	135	245,832	10	9,230
Philippine Islands	20	52,972	1	1,778
Siberia			1	870
Central America			2	2,960
Chile	12	39,862	2	4,088
Peru	6	14,534	3	6,130
Brazil	3	10,112		
Colombia	10	35,914	1	1,223
South Africa			4	7,680
India	2	2,084	1	1,483
Russia			1	2,380
Atlantic States	36	95,984	12	19,586
Elsewhere	6	14,250	9	11,630
Totals	422	1,019,959	445	652,021
Coasting		1,423,330		273,414
Grand Total Tonnage		2,443,289		925,435

The total annual inward tonnage movement at San Francisco, exclusive of the coasting trade, for a series of years past is as follows:

YEARS	STEAM No.	STEAM Tons.	SAIL No.	SAIL Tons.	TOTAL No.	TOTAL Tonnage.
1889	304	453,803	678	706,529	982	1,160,332
1890	309	470,348	582	610,129	891	1,280,447
1891	358	573,673	783	898,753	1141	1,472,426
1892	312	488,511	684	776,827	996	1,265,338
1893	337	530,463	565	642,188	902	1,172,651
1894	323	541,348	606	685,312	929	1,226,660
1895	324	568,442	583	709,183	907	1,277,625
1896	338	612,580	625	768,187	963	1,380,767
1897	285	520,394	535	634,073	820	1,154,467
1898	330	592,865	494	530,092	824	1,122,957
1899	438	802,085	444	479,919	882	1,282,004
1900	473	914,897	479	572,919	952	1,487,816
1901	484	993,739	479	568,311	963	1,562,050
1902	430	923,757	488	674,081	918	1,597,838
1903	422	1,019,959	445	652,021	867	1,671,980

The clearances from San Francisco during 1903 were as follows:

Sailing for	Steam No.	Steam Tons.	Sail No.	Sail Tons.
Great Britain			82	147,889
Germany	12	87,235	3	5,230
Belgium			5	8,702
Sweden			1	1,616
France	7	20,826	3	4,820
Italy	3	9,174	1	1,834
Australia	24	69,768	43	78,907
Hawaii	52	127,497	136	134,047
Mexico	5	11,185	2	2,828
Hong Kong	44	148,720	1	1,458
Japan	16	36,383	1	1,235
China	3	7,860		
Alaska	10	19,964	41	57,609
Pacific Islands	10	19,390	4	4,865
British Columbia	146	273,587	18	30,456
Philippine Islands	18	58,466		
Siberia			1	870
Central America	1	2,298		
Chile	14	32,405	1	2,236
Peru	12	29,284	5	9,302
Brazil	5	12,143		
Colombia	11	24,324	1	2,122
South Africa	1	1,843	8	12,296
India	1	1,120		
Russia			1	377
Atlantic States	26	61,712	8	11,918
Elsewhere	16	31,020	19	38,462
Totals	437	1,036,112	385	560,209
Coasting		1,434,599		376,644
Grand Total Tonnage		2,470,711		936,853

The total amount outward tonnage movement from San Francisco, exclusive of the coasting trade, for a series of years past, is as follows:

Year.	Steam No.	Steam Tons.	Sail No.	Sail Tons.	Total No.	Total Tons.
1889	289	448,292	625	654,011	914	1,102,303
1890	296	459,635	572	617,223	868	1,076,858
1891	338	559,273	670	736,149	1,008	1,295,422
1892	312	498,415	615	692,330	937	1,180,745
1893	361	572,980	662	752,649	1,023	1,325,629
1894	335	548,416	551	617,389	886	1,165,805
1895	321	560,622	530	638,364	851	1,198,986
1896	331	607,119	574	683,603	905	1,290,722
1897	301	537,902	558	689,970	859	1,227,872
1898	313	567,542	419	464,153	732	1,031,695
1899	431	790,463	442	459,996	873	1,250,459
1900	471	903,986	443	504,466	914	1,408,452
1901	473	873,053	428	524,000	901	1,497,053
1902	428	907,800	429	560,247	857	1,468,047
1903	437	1,036,112	385	560,209	822	1,596,231

TONNAGE ACCORDING TO NATIONALITY.

Combining the arrivals and departures, sail and steam, for 1903, the total registered tonnage according to nationality, was as follows:

NATIONALITY.	ARRIVALS. No.	ARRIVALS. Tons.	DEPARTURES. No.	DEPARTURES. Tons.
American	516	918,924	497	875,494
British	166	358,346	143	324,110
Norwegian	32	67,679	24	60,072
French	69	123,640	74	135,368
Italian	2	4,339	2	4,331
Austrian	1	1,520	1	1,520
German	55	125,967	57	131,287
Japanese	16	51,670	15	48,120
Mexican	1	350	1	350
Danish	7	16,754	6	12,878
Swedish	2	2,791	2	2,791
Totals	867	1,671,980	822	1,596,321

The arrivals and departures of deep-water tonnage at and from San Francisco during each month of 1903 was as follows:

MONTH.	ARRIVALS. No.	ARRIVALS. Tons.	DEPARTURES. No.	DEPARTURES. Tons.
January	64	127,612	60	118,928
February	69	146,198	62	120,477
March	78	151,114	79	146,860
April	67	141,607	68	135,214
May	59	95,222	52	106,953
June	76	147,959	71	131,635
July	68	145,122	64	122,314
August	88	176,516	79	156,640
September	72	134,733	70	134,090
October	89	160,315	84	162,632
November	74	135,036	71	138,718
December	63	110,546	62	121,860
Totals	867	1,671.980	822	1,596,321

Vessels to and from domestic Coast ports are not included in the foregoing figures.

EXPORTS OF FLOUR, WHEAT AND BARLEY

The shipments of each year for the last four cereal years, ending June 30, respectively, are as follows:

WHEAT.

DESTINATION.	1902–1903. CENTALS.	1901–1902 CENTALS.	1900–1901. CENTALS.	1899–1900. CENTALS
Ports of Call	2,352,438	8,447,826	6,858,148	5,750,295
United Kingdom	349,346	630,525	458,007	303,149
Continent	23,610	227,426	113 699	....
South America	19,481	182,197	547,354	244,651
Australia	1,726,315	18,257	....	....
Africa	740,489	144,443	....	189 935
Miscellaneous	41,172	20,433	12,978	31,741
Totals	5,252,851	9,671,107	7,990.186	6,519,771

FLOUR.

DESTINATION.	BARRELS.	BARRELS.	BARRELS.	BARRELS.
China	547,811	590,044	451,907	598,225
Japan	55,660	34,544	61,878	79,729
Hawaii and Pacific Islands	128,822	28,244	11,690	131,406
East Indies	....	85,665	129,082	116,779
Siberia	4,628	2,617	3,611	6,657
Mexico	8,934	5,867	6,885	7,421
Central America & Panama	105,545	211,913	189,947	161,721
South America	48,929	101,833	181,520	39,406
United Kingdom	24,325	76,789	51,010	50,638
Australia	60,800	39,644	1,420	2,551
Africa	....	....	....	260
Miscellaneous	3,410	1,025	2,634	990
Totals	988,864	1,178 215	1,091,684	1,195.783

BARLEY.

DESTINATION.	CENTALS.	CENTALS.	CENTALS.	CENTALS.
United Kingdom	2,359,403	3,286,844	1,880,303	3,549,538
Continent	280,792	....	....	68,768
Australia	348,681	231,107	9,195	....
China	....	....	68 935	....
New York	....	552,331	154,693	....
Railroad, to East	....	....	227,840	248,100
Africa	....	....	....	....
Miscellaneous	501,922	9,020	6,166	384,830
Totals	3,544,859	4,281,182	2,347,132	4,251,236

WHEAT AND FLOUR.

Receipts of Flour and Wheat at San Francisco for the year ending December 31, 1903, and the preceding year were as follows:

FLOUR.			WHEAT.		
—BARRELS—			—CENTALS—		
	1902	1903		1902	1903
California	1,379,256	1,000,778	California	8,902,646	2,807,221
Oregon, etc.	364,293	366,199	Oregon, etc.	217,897	1,082,756
Totals	1,743,549	1,366,977	Totals	9,120,543	3,889,977

Receipts of Flour and Wheat from January 1, 1903, to December 31, 1903, inclusive, reduced to Wheat centals.

Flour*—California, barrels.....................3,002,334	}	5,809,555
Wheat—California, centals......................2,807,221		
Flour*—Oregon, barrels.........................1,098,597	}	2,18!,353
Wheat—Oregon, centals 1,082,756		

Total receipts, centals................	7,990,908
Receipts of flour and wheat combined from January 1, 1902, to December 31, 1902, inclusive........................	14,351,190
Decrease in receipts for 1903, centals............	6,360,282

Exports of flour and wheat from January 1, 1903, to December 31, 1903, inclusive, reduced to Wheat centals.

Flour*, barrels.......................... 2,619,570	}	5,379,095
Wheat, centals 2,759,525		

Exports from January 1, 1902, to December 31, 1902, inclusive:

Flour*, barrels........ 3,566,652	}	12,861,190
Wheat, centals 9,294,538		

Decrease in exports for 1903, centals.....	7,482,095

Value of flour and wheat shipments from January 1, 1903, to December 31, 1903, inclusive:

Flour $3,929,355	
Wheat.. 3,863,335	
	$7,792,690

Value of shipments from January 1, 1902, to December 31, 1902, inclusive:

Flour..$4,161,094	
Wheat..10,297,227	
	$14,458,321

Decrease in value of shipments for 1903....	$6,665,631

*Flour is reduced to wheat at the rate of three centals of wheat to one barrel of flour.

Wheat and Flour.

The receipts of Wheat and Flour, at San Francisco, from all sources, for a series of years were as follows:

Harvest Years	Receipts. Flour Barrels.	Wheat Centals.	Equal to Ctls. Wheat.
July 1, 1857, to June 30, 1858	35,966	243,052	350,920
July 1, 1858, to June 30, 1859	68,554	433,002	638,664
July 1, 1859, to June 30, 1860	91,407	985,026	1,259,247
July 1, 1860, to June 30, 1861	113,779	2,160,723	2,502,060
July 1, 1861, to June 30, 1862	106,565	1,361,218	1,680,913
July 1, 1862, to June 30, 1863	159,588	1,864,652	2,343,416
July 1, 1863, to June 30, 1864	100,602	1,846,118	2,147,924
July 1, 1864, to June 30, 1865	134,735	527,881	932,086
July 1, 1865, to June 30, 1866	181,498	2,207,158	2,751,652
July 1, 1866, to June 30, 1867	300,749	4,999,346	5,901,593
July 1, 1867, to June 30, 1868	201,186	5,031,966	5,635,524
July 1, 1868, to June 30, 1869	223,350	6,046,350	6,716,400
July 1, 1869, to June 30, 1870	181,517	6,172,635	6,716,186
July 1, 1870, to June 30, 1871	123,513	4,422,729	4,793,268
July 1, 1871, to June 30, 1872	139,982	2,391,666	2,811,612
July 1, 1872, to June 30, 1873	222,279	10,780,895	11,447,732
July 1, 1873, to June 30, 1874	469,533	7,829,821	9,238,420
July 1, 1874, to June 30, 1875	461,845	9,807,776	11,193,311
July 1, 1875, to June 30, 1876	457,365	6,597,288	7,969,383
July 1, 1876, to June 30, 1877	514,298	10,803,776	12,346,670
July 1, 1877, to June 30, 1878	382,697	4,454,838	5,602,929
July 1, 1878, to June 30, 1879	472,155	10,101,075	11,517,540
July 1, 1879, to June 30, 1880	492,911	10,887,604	12,366,337
July 1, 1880, to June 30, 1881	594,876	16,217,284	18,001,912
July 1, 1881, to June 30, 1882	810,844	20,883,788	23,316,320
July 1, 1882, to June 30, 1883	1,031,499	15,337,207	18,431,704
July 1, 1883, to June 30, 1884	1,289,591	12,817,069	16,685,842
July 1, 1884, to June 30, 1885	1,301,019	17,298,686	19,201,743
July 1, 1885, to June 30, 1886	1,181,002	12,604,635	16,147,641
July 1, 1886, to June 30, 1887	1,123,489	14,140,355	17,510,822
July 1, 1887, to June 30, 1888	1,149,578	9,710,625	13,159,359
July 1, 1888, to June 30, 1889	1,208,745	14,238,096	17,864,331
July 1, 1889, to June 30, 1890	1,454,537	14,758,497	19,122,108
July 1, 1890, to June 30, 1891	1,502,730	15,220,844	19,729,034
July 1, 1891, to June 30, 1892	1,329,585	13,879,305	17,868,060
July 1, 1892, to June 30, 1893	1,391,461	11,531,702	15,706,085
July 1, 1893, to June 30, 1894	1,061,015	10,806,736	13,989,781
July 1, 1894, to June 30, 1895	1,345,529	10,889,037	14,925,624
July 1, 1895, to June 30, 1896	1,410,886	10,355,285	14,587,943
July 1, 1896, to June 30, 1897	1,484,572	10,789,299	15,243,015
July 1, 1897, to June 30, 1898	1,334,513	10,313,379	14,316,918
July 1, 1898, to June 30, 1899	1,426,019	3,213,083	7,491,140
July 1, 1899, to June 30, 1900	1,633,806	7,157,027	12,058,445
July 1, 1900, to June 30, 1901	1,656,873	8,918,523	13,889,142
July 1, 1901, to June 30, 1902	1,697,846	10,310,905	15,404,543
July 1, 1902, to June 30, 1903	1,515,701	6,242,859	10,789,962

by sea during the past twenty-eight years were as follows:

Calendar Years.	Wheat. Centals.	Wheat. Value.	Flour. Barrels.	Flour. Value.
1903	2,759,525	$3,890,930	873,190	$3,929,355
1902	8,237,782	10,297,227	1,188,884	4,161,093
1901	9,294,538	9,526,812	1,169,184	3,624,470
1900	7,733,667	7,923,347	1,130,353	3,671,963
1899	3,245,434	3,576,329	970,396	3,276,430
1898	3,964,817	5,694,448	810,516	3,383,755
1897	9,250,591	13,884,158	869,767	3,900,004
1896	12,208,241	14,455,656	1,171,528	4,214,396
1895	11,051,002	10,418,012	948,762	2,762,501
1894	7,200,816	6,648,095	787,457	2,372,012
1893	10,675,268	12,725,413	882,580	3,185,498
1892	9,762,816	14,254,905	1,115,267	4,680,704
1891	16,947,917	27,323,251	1,231,993	5,781,590
1890	13,014,306	17,277,604	1,190,262	4,835,539
1889	12,115,075	16,641,194	1,130,950	4,754,859
1888	11,720,100	18,318,477	822,347	3,392,182
1887	9,064,145	14,714,321	797,232	3,409,963
1886	15,832,155	21,443,167	1,124,615	4,372,965
1885	11,842,242	16,428,985	1,298,169	5,326,258
1884	12,158,714	17,329,448	1,201,761	5,288,575
1883	12,960,540	22,978,530	1,246,218	6,220,627
1882	18,756,239	31,355,452	959,889	4,808,291
1881	20,006,540	30,821,996	785,078	3,569,190
1880	9,452,099	15,243,378	560,770	2,754,267
1879	10,540,197	19,258,457	511,600	2,548,486
1878	8,062,287	14,462,182	489,462	2,614,764
1877	4,931,437	11,020,343	434,684	2,691,691
1876	9,967,941	17,034,758	508,143	2,560,759

WHEAT CROPS AND DISTRIBUTION.

The following table shows the rainfall at San Francisco for a series of years and the wheat crop of California and distribution, in centals.

Season.	Rainfall.	Crop Year.	Crop.	Exports.	Local Consumption.	Carry over Stock.	Imports.
1887-88	16.74	1888	18,643,080	15,138,800	6,315,000	2,394,020	1,067,020
1888-89	23.86	1889	25,174,940	17,161,280	6,340,000	5,036,220	768,540
1889-90	45.84	1890	18,889,680	17,388,400	6,300,000	1,977,940	1,740,440
1890-91	17.58	1891	21,095,440	16,586,380	6,000,000	2,451,000	1,964,000
1891-92	18.53	1892	20,445,960	13,489,480	6,300,000	5,727,580	1,520,100
1892-93	21.75	1893	19,904,640	11,883,540	6,500,000	7,878,980	1,630,300
1893-94	18.47	1894	14,335,844	11,095,480	7,200,000	6,456,000	768,540
1894-95	27.29	1895	15,730,004	13,613,980	6,800,000	2,930,700	1,168,560
1895-96	21.25	1896	17,452,041	13,452,693	7,000,000	1,990,272	2,060,224
1896-97	23.43	1897	18,351,786	12,907,953	6,800,000	3,388,606	2,754,501
1897-98	9.38	1898	7,341,220	4,259,913	7,000,000	3,585,606	4,115,693
1898-99	16.87	1899	19,462,047	9,455,737	6,860,000	8,615,583	1,883,667
1899-1900	18.47	1900	12,230,516	11,211,648	7,190,000	4,218,718	1,774,267
1900-01	21.17	1901	18,620,263	13,710,220	7,270,000	2,984,147	1,125,386
1901-02	18.98	1902	11,255,698	8,576,530	6,785,000	1,401,910	2,523,595

Wheat and Flour.

The exports of Wheat and Flour from San Francisco by sea, from July 1, 1857, to June 30, 1903, were as follows:

From.	Flour Barrels.	Wheat Centals.	Equal to Ctls. Wheat.
July 1, 1857, to June 30, 1858.........	5,387	3,801	19,962
July 1, 1858, to June 30, 1859.........	20,577	123	61,854
July 1, 1859, to June 30, 1860.........	58,926	381,768	558,546
July 1, 1860, to June 30, 1861.........	197,181	1,529,924	2,121,467
July 1, 1861, to June 30, 1862.........	101,652	851,844	1,156,800
July 1, 1862, to June 30, 1863.........	144,883	1,043,652	1,478,301
July 1, 1863, to June 30, 1864.........	152,633	1,074,292	1,529,191
July 1, 1864, to June 30, 1865.........	91,479	25,369	299,806
July 1, 1865, to June 30, 1866.........	279,554	1,039,515	1,877,177
July 1, 1866, to June 30, 1867.........	465,337	3,636,190	5,032,201
July 1, 1867, to June 30, 1868.........	423,189	3,803,778	5,073,345
July 1, 1868, to June 30, 1869.........	453,920	4,374,524	5,736,284
July 1, 1869, to June 30, 1870.........	352,962	4,863,891	5,922,776
July 1, 1870, to June 30, 1871.........	196,219	3,571,846	4,160,503
July 1, 1871, to June 30, 1872.........	270,079	1,404,382	2,214,619
July 1, 1872, to June 30, 1873.........	263,645	9,822,688	10,613,623
July 1, 1873, to June 30, 1874.........	644,710	7,273,241	9,207,371
July 1, 1874, to June 30, 1875.........	485,551	8,793,354	10,241,007
July 1, 1875, to June 30, 1876.........	445,143	6,135,460	7,571,889
July 1, 1876, to June 30, 1877.........	524,885	10,513,104	12,087,759
July 1, 1877, to June 30, 1878.........	442,061	3,969,728	5,295,911
July 1, 1878, to June 30, 1879.........	530,549	10,012,220	11,603,867
July 1, 1879, to June 30, 1880.........	496,572	10,626,692	12,116,408
July 1, 1880, to June 30, 1881.........	660,763	13,371,603	15,353,892
July 1, 1881, to June 30, 1882.........	860,850	22,279,545	24,862,095
July 1, 1882, to June 30, 1883.........	1,099,652	14,601,796	17,900,752
July 1, 1883, to June 30, 1884.........	1,262,351	11,368,267	15,155,320
July 1, 1884, to June 30, 1885.........	1,304,412	16,113,924	20,027,160
July 1, 1885, to June 30, 1886.........	1,087,191	11,322,325	14,583,898
July 1, 1886, to June 30, 1887.........	998,312	12,334,114	15,329,050
July 1, 1887, to June 30, 1888.........	852,687	8,773,887	11,331,948
July 1, 1888, to June 30, 1889.........	909,032	13,385,095	16,112,191
July 1, 1889, to June 30, 1890.........	1,189,629	13,702,191	17,271,078
July 1, 1890, to June 30, 1891.........	1,185,410	13,836,467	17,392,697
July 1, 1891, to June 30, 1892.........	1,083,577	12,945,956	16,196,687
July 1, 1892, to June 30, 1893.........	1,113,291	10,555,242	13,895,115
July 1, 1893, to June 30, 1894.........	800,026	9,014,228	11,414,306
July 1, 1894, to June 30, 1895.........	922,476	9,602,661	12,370,098
July 1, 1895, to June 30, 1896.........	961,331	10,359,414	13,243,407
July 1, 1896, to June 30, 1897.........	1,120,027	10,103,775	13,463,856
July 1, 1897, to June 30, 1898.........	824,266	10,056,558	12,529,356
July 1, 1898, to June 30, 1899.........	1,309,416	2,285,862	5,314,110
July 1, 1899, to June 30, 1900.........	1,195,783	6,519,771	10,107,120
July 1, 1900, to June 30, 1901.........	1,091,684	7,990,186	11,265,238
July 1, 1901, to June 30, 1902.........	1,178,235	9,671,107	13,205,812
July 1, 1902, to June 30, 1903.........	988,864	5,252,851	8,219,443

WHEAT QUOTATIONS.

The following prices are for No. 1 White Wheat per cental, based on actual transactions in the San Francisco market during each month of the last cereal year.

MONTH.	AVERAGE.	HIGHEST.	LOWEST.
July 1902	$1 14$	$1 16$¼	$1 13$¾
August	1 13⅝	1 15	1 12½
September	1 16½	1 20	1 12¼
October	1 25¼	1 35	1 18¾
November	1 37½	1 45	1 32¼
December	1 40¼	1 43¾	1 37½
January 1903	1 42¾	1 50	1 36¼
February	1 49⅝	1 55	1 43¾
March	1 42¼	1 52½	1 35
April	1 36¼	1 38¾	1 35
May	1 35	1 40	1 32½
June	1 36	1 40	1 32½

The ruling prices for No. 1 White Wheat per cental for a series of years past are as follows:

YEAR.	AVERAGE.	HIGHEST.	LOWEST.	YEAR.	AVERAGE.	HIGHEST.	LOWEST.
1902–03	$1 32½	$1 55	$1 12½	1883–84	$1 64¾	$1 90	$1 42½
1901–02	1 05	1 16¼	0 95	1882–83	1 73½	2 05	1 60
1900–01	1 00	1 06¼	0 97	1881–82	1 60	1 75	1 30
1899–00	1 01	1 12¼	0 90	1880–81	1 42⅞	1 62½	1 25
1898–99	1 14½	1 25	1 05	1879–80	1 82	2 15	1 45
1897–98	1 47⅛	1 82¼	1 20	1878–79	1 67¾	1 77½	1 57½
1896–97	1 26¾	1 57½	90	1877–78	2 18	2 45	1 32½
1895–96	1 01⅛	1 17½	88¾	1876–77	1 92½	3 00	1 45
1894–95	87½	95	76¼	1875–76	1 93½	2 32½	1 67½
1893–94	1 01⅛	1 16¼	90	1874–75	1 62	1 85	1 52½
1892–93	1 27⅛	1 37½	1 17⅜	1873–74	2 05¼	2 35	1 70
1891–92	1 63⅞	1 90	1 38¾	1872–73	1 76½	2 05	1 50
1890–91	1 46¼	1 85	1 27½	1871–72	2 34	2 82¼	1 87½
1889–90	1 28⅞	1 38¾	1 25	1870–71	2 20½	3 10	1 65
1888–89	1 34¼	1 65	1 26¼	1869–70	1 69	1 82½	1 55
1887–88	1 40¼	2 00	1 22¼	1868–69	1 87	2 12½	1 55
1886–87	1 52¾	1 87½	1 20	1867–68	2 36	3 05	1 67½
1885–86	1 43½	1 52½	1 17½	1866–67	1 73	2 15	1 35
1884–85	1 31⅛	1 50	1 15	1865–66	2 11	4 75	1 62½

BARLEY QUOTATIONS.

Average, highest and lowest prices of No. 1 Feed Barley for each month of the last cereal year. Quotations based on actual transactions in the San Francisco market.

MONTH.	AVERAGE.	HIGHEST.	LOWEST.
July, 1902	$0 92½	$0 95	$0 90
August	93⅞	98¾	90
September	1 06⅛	1 12½	95
October	1 17½	1 22½	1 10
November	1 20½	1 25	1 16¼
December	1 22⅛	1 26¼	1 17½
January, 1903	1 18	1 21¼	1 15
February	1 18⅞	1 22½	1 15
March	1 15½	1 20	1 11¼
April	1 11⅜	1 16¼	1 05
May	1 08¼	1 12½	1 05
June	1 01¼	1 12½	90

BARLEY QUOTATIONS FOR A SERIES OF YEARS.

Average Highest and Lowest Price No. 1 Feed Barley, Spot, per cental.

YEAR.	AVERAGE.	HIGHEST.		LOWEST.	
1902-03	$1 10½	$1 26¼	December	$0 90	July, Aug., June
1901-02	83⅓	1 02½	May	70	July, Sept., Oct.
1900-01	74⅛	82½	April	70	July, Sept., Nov.
1899-1900	79	1 00	July	67½	June
1898-99	1 19	1 35	December	87½	June
1897-98	1 01	1 45	April	70	July
1896-97	75	92½	November	66¼	July
1895-96	66¾	73¾	June	53¾	September
1894-95	77⅛	87½	July, August	57½	June
1893-94	79⅔	1 12½	May	65	Aug., Sept.
1892-93	85¾	93¾	August	78¾	June
1891-92	1 05¼	1 20	July	92½	June
1890-91	1 39⅛	1 65	June	1 00	July
1889-90	81⅛	1 06¼	May	63¾	July
1888-89	75⅝	85	Sept., Nov., Feb.	57½	May, June
1887-88	86⅛	1 08¾	July	75	Jan., March, April
1886-87	1 00½	1 20	May	80	August
1885-86	1 28	1 50	October	76¼	June

CEREAL EXPORTS.

The clearances of flour and grain cargoes from San Francisco, by sea, during 1903, and the totals for a series of years, are as follows:

1903	FLOUR Bbls.	WHEAT Ctls.	BARLEY Ctls.	OATS Ctls.	CORN Ctls.	RYE Ctls.
January.....	36,112	849,695	149,638	2,572	1,500	167
February....	43,866	426,461	92,935	9,181	2,571	....
March.......	75,707	595,154	75,381	1,929	9,217	2,240
April........	36,971	189,360	32,581	1,506	2,310	....
May.........	52,379	142,766	41,830	3,279	3,857	200
June.........	88,158	5,529	77,347	1,963	2,715	....
July.........	64,737	14,382	80,942	11,740	1,486	203
August......	100,730	111,430	704,668	10,916	1,909	....
September...	132,099	53.618	707,294	1,487	1,445	....
October......	106,253	160,005	1,080,331	1,461	1,661	....
November ..	67,492	49,252	331,775	1,204	1,442	....
December ...	68,686	161,873	532,305	2,349	2,294	....
Totals, 1903..	873,190	2,759,525	3,907,027	49,587	32,407	2,810
Totals, 1902..	1,188,884	8,237,782	3,937,894	38,416	35,349	301,232
Totals, 1901..	1,169,184	9,294,538	4,072,241	151,704	10,792	144,446
Totals, 1900..	1,260,202	7,752,722	2,489,826	234,613	13,002	49,240
Totals, 1899..	1,077,580	3,247,102	3,167,383	31,033	21,389	54,215
Totals, 1898..	831,083	3,973,536	786,303	28,308	31,633	29
Totals, 1897.	869,437	9,508,591	3,405,832	23,362	78,483	69,792
Totals, 1896..	1,172,733	12,182,706	3,856,394	32,312	30,351	152,437
Totals, 1895..	949,981	11,047,414	1,622,567	16,204	46,011	....
Totals, 1894..	787,432	7,144,017	1,058,172	21,430	178,320	12
Totals, 1893..	872,506	10,880,219	2,817,151	19,856	95,867	33,739
Totals, 1892..	1,077,956	9,726,697	1,323,495	21,982	70,648	32 420
Totals, 1891..	1,225,183	16,823,743	929,216	12,392	123,998	93,615
Totals, 1890..	1,182,111	13,019,910	318,313	28,447	78,337	96,012
Totals, 1889..	1,109,126	12,257,046	830,331	59,323	26,486	....
Totals, 1888..	808,439	11,708,261	1,029,361	35,985	51,041	....
Totals, 1887..	788,180	9,140,689	416,583	....	....	....
Totals, 1886..	1,104,335	15,874,268	760,606	....	....	....

GRAIN FREIGHTS.

The following tabulation shows the highest and lowest rates paid per ton for iron ships during each month of the harvest year, 1902-1903, based on the prices paid for spot engagement to Cork for orders to U. K., Havre or Antwerp.

Months.	Average. £ s. d.	Highest. £ s. d.	Lowest. £ s. d.
July, 1902	1 6 5	1 8 0	1 5 0
August	1 4 7	1 7 6	1 3 0
September	1 2 6	1 4 0	1 1 3
October	1 0 3	1 1 3	1 0 0
November	0 12 6	0 13 9	0 11 3
December	0 11 6	0 11 9	0 10 6
January, 1903	0 11 2	0 11 3	0 11 0
February	0 11 3	0 11 3	0 11 3
March	.. .. ..	.. .. ..	.. .. ..
April	0 13 6	0 14 6	0 12 6
May	.. .. ..	.. .. ..	.. .. ..
June	0 18 6	0 19 6	0 17 6

The average rates during the past twenty-three years were as follows:

Years.	Grain Ships Cleared. Am.	Foreign.	Total.	Rates. Wood. £ s. d.	Iron. £ s. d.
1902-1903	2	135	137	.. .. ..	0 17 3
1901-1902	8	208	216	.. .. ..	1 10 0
1900-1901	10	149	159	.. .. ..	1 18 6
1899-1900	3	159	162	.. .. ..	1 17 5
1898-99	12	54	66	.. .. ..	1 6 0
1897-98	8	207	215	.. .. ..	1 8 0
1896-97	24	226	250	1 6 3	1 3 9
1895-96	13	195	208	1 7 0	1 6 6
1894-95	13	150	163	1 5 6	1 7 0
1893-94	26	163	189	1 5 3	1 7 7
1892-93	29	201	230	0 19 6	1 2 8
1891-92	39	234	273	1 11 11	1 11 1
1890-91	52	213	265	1 18 10	2 1 11
1889-90	55	229	284	1 13 5	1 17 3
1888-89	60	229	289	1 8 3	1 12 7
1887-88	33	165	198	1 5 6	1 6 2
1886-87	55	227	282	1 6 1	1 8 2
1885-86	88	161	249	1 9 3	1 12 6
1884-85	116	255	371	1 14 2	1 18 0
1883-84	81	210	291	1 5 8	1 14 8
1882-83	169	202	371	2 3 6	2 6 9
1881-82	154	405	559	3 5 7	3 7 3
1880-81	132	224	356	3 6 9	3 13 0
Highest, 1880-1881				3 6 9	3 13 0
Lowest, 1902-1903				.. .. ..	0 17 3

GRAIN OPTIONS.

WHEAT.

The monthly record of sales of Wheat contracts in the San Francisco Call Board during the last five years of its existence was as follows:

Month.	1902.	1901.	1900.	1899.	1898.
January	102,700	49,300	120,700	124,000	207,200
February	84,100	82,400	92,500	108,000	165,800
March	53,500	91,700	131,700	215,800	217,900
April	76,800	88,600	111,100	183,500	275,100
May	73,600	63,500	87,500	101,200	347,700
June	45,000	70,800	155,100	137,800	262,500
July	53,600	81,700	100,700	101,200	93,300
August	49,800	31,400	126,800	125,900	166,400
September	....	27,800	84,900	115,400	186,900
October	....	83,500	123,800	136,500	202,700
November	....	70,200	90,900	204,600	171,300
December	....	82,700	53,200	104,700	31,700
Total tons	539,100	823,600	1,279,900	1,658,600	2,328,400

BARLEY.

The monthly sales of Barley contracts during the last five years of the Call Board were as follows:

Month.	1902.	1901.	1900.	1899.	1898.
January	25,000	3,500	3,500	14,300	42,400
February	44,200	6,100	2,500	47,000	70,300
March	21,200	6,100	500	159,800	119,800
April	16,000	33,400	5,100	48,400	113,100
May	35,300	13,900	11,900	37,500	62,400
June	16,500	16,000	11,000	40,800	52,200
July	26,800	5,500	14,900	48,100	17,700
August	36,000	1,800	15,000	39,900	20,300
September	....	3,000	5,700	14,800	18,300
October	....	6,900	7,100	8,800	12,600
November	....	6,200	11,000	7,600	20,000
December	....	8,150	5,800	8,200	10,000
Total tons	221,000	110,550	94,000	475,000	551,000

Note.—The San Francisco Call Board discontinued operations on September 1, 1902, and became merged into the grain department of the Merchants Exchange, since which date no record of sales has been kept.

The Call Board was organized February 27, 1882, and the sales during each cereal year until the Board was closed were as follows:

YEAR	WHEAT Tons	BARLEY Tons	TOTAL Tons
Feb. 27, 1882-June 30, 1884	686,500	2,614,103	3,300,513
1884-85	871,800	1,564,600	2,436,400
1885-86	2,228,700	590,000	2,818,700
1886-87	3,386,000	1,385,300	5,271,300
1887-88	973,400	1,083,300	2,056,700
1888-89	1,979,600	706,700	2,686,300
1889-90	1,416,400	515,700	1,932,100
1890-91	1,656,500	587,800*	2,244,300
1891-92	1,717,500	859,200	2,576,700
1892-93	1,427,000	585,400	2,012,400
1893-94	2,111,500	694,800	2,806,300
1894-95	3,342,900	612,600	3,955,100
1895-96	1,860,800	279,200	2,140,000
1896-97	2,324,500	210,200	2,534,700
1897-98	3,378,700	577,200	3,955,900
1898-99	1,845,900	436,700	2,282,600
1899-1900	1,497,900	161,900	1,659,800
1900-01	1,016,600	138,500	1,155,100
1901-02	813,000	189,700	1,002,700
July 1, to Aug. 31, 1902	103,400	62,800	166,200

CALIFORNIA CANNED FRUITS.

Trade estimates of the annual pack of Canned Fruits in 2½-lb. tins and 2 dozen tins to the case, for a series of years past, are as follows:

YEAR.	CASES.	YEAR.	CASES.
1863	7,500	1884	576,900
1864	10,000	1885	565,750
1865	14,000	1886	675,000
1866	19,000	1887	772,500
1867	35,000	1888	1,360,400
1868	43,000	1889	1,420,600
1869	82,000	1890	1,495,300
1870	132,600	1891	1,571,250
1871	187,490	1892	1,602,370
1872	228,140	1893	1,418,700
1873	216,230	1894	1,528,830
1874	248,500	1895	1,639,807
1875	264,320	1896	1,602,450
1876	270,833	1897	1,942,982
1877	206,250	1898	2,085,166
1878	235,324	1899	3,003,170
1879	298,356	1900	2,775,896
1880	236,458	1901	2,677,072
1881	472,916	1902	2,252,790
1882	541,665	1903	2,570,000
1883	593,750		

CUSTOMS RECEIPTS.

The monthly receipts of Customs duties paid into the United States Treasury at San Francisco during each month of 1903 compare with the seven preceding years as follows:

MONTHS.	1903	1902	1901	1900	1899	1898	1897	1896
January	$677,441 60	$736,246 31	$606,396 20	$754,582 84	$536,100 28	$516,789 12	$505,896 90	$500 01
February	694,807 97	508,299 00	472,861 43	500,313 41	519,902 95	490,597 87	308,415 00	463,192 32
March	686,363 87	568,626 59	518,488 34	552,544 95	631,104 89	448,769 93	539,276 21	457,750 15
April	626,211 34	717,753 94	586,721 52	706,337 95	570,945 17	455,988 92	558,690 59	423,888 57
May	570,816 75	643,121 63	575,359 75	543,740 14	585,407 47	598,789 59	320,278 61	369,745 96
June	625,488 05	594,193 10	585,360 82	567,902 43	655,677 57	522,275 28	543,193 78	355,836 55
July	572,971 28	680,197 77	657,026 63	653,927 73	556,860 99	559,258 33	461,158 44	411,363 01
August	720,714 24	593,578 07	577,945 03	630,641 81	747,385 81	560,453 51	331,371 02	419,482 07
September	549,364 64	710,139 17	595,835 43	562,285 40	522,202 11	463,805 39	284,376 40	421,067 90
October	667,216 10	656,086 92	695,251 74	778,744 25	603,644 63	478,879 63	426,059 68	446,766 04
November	575,058 87	553,369 33	564,122 03	790,651 79	508,560 23	481,644 00	419,468 78	8,951 12
December	654,702 34	686,822 00	609,003 43	591,639 41	424,759 65	487,534 40	366,303 31	374,494 14
Totals	$7,621,157 05	$7,648,433 83	$7,044,372 35	$7,693,342 11	$6,862,551 75	$6,064,785 97	$5,064,488 72	$5,059,737 84

INTERNAL REVENUE COLLECTIONS.

During the year ending December 31, 1903, and for the two preceding years, the monthly collections of Internal Revenue in the San Francisco District were as follows:

Months.	1903	1902	1901
January	$207,860 84	$242,885 25	$288,556 29
February	182,489 55	213,973 47	286,272 08
March	208,726 22	242,365 67	339,655 60
April	203,744 28	239,108 51	332,897 93
May	198,688 68	245,838 38	301,801 35
June	227,586 11	249,447 26	252,974 57
July	425,321 02	449,056 75	646,226 12
August	194,645 24	201,331 87	236,410 40
September	233,013 27	223,506 60	224,236 55
October	248,941 36	228,652 49	290,700 21
November	220,927 54	178,413 92	244,750 28
December	242,653 10	178,180 16	232,611 08
Totals	$2,794,597 21	$2,892,760 33	$3,677,092 46

The total collections for several previous years were as follows: 1900, $4,019,086.30; 1899, $3,686,417.20; 1898, $3,023,902.20; 1897, $2,490,471.20; 1896, $2,410,019 46; 1895, $2,067,946.28; 1894, $1,692,796.07 1893, $1,686,592.23; 1892, $1,818,351.43; 1891, $1,887,561.23; 1890, $1,858,852.48.

Classified, the collections in 1903 and the two preceding years were as follows:

For	1903	1902	1901
Lists	$ 109,085 57	$ 104,957 16	$ 273,117 11
Beer	823,127 75	945,774 30	1,179,904 45
Spirits	1,231,903 66	1,040,861 36	1,001,684 46
Cigars and Cigarettes	269,187 05	242,709 07	243,587 74
Snuff	303 68	406 63	442 43
Tobacco	21,911 35	30,691 19	44,294 86
Specials	327,264 07	323,262 99	343,169 19
Playing Cards	674 90	1,113 80	1,323 94
Export Stamps	70 40	56 60	1 10
Documentary	1,068 78	170,095 80	489,995 90
Proprietary	....	22,831 43	94,567 78
Mixed Flour	....	....	3 50
Totals	$2,794,597 21	$2,892,760 33	$3,677,092 46

THE SILVER MARKET.

The fluctuations in the price of refined Silver in the American and English markets for the twelve months ending December 31, 1903, were as follows:

Months.	New York.		London	
	High.	Low.	High	Low.
	Cents.	Cents.	Pence.	Pence.
January	$47\frac{5}{8}$	47	$22\frac{5}{8}$	$21\frac{11}{16}$
February	$48\frac{3}{8}$	$47\frac{3}{8}$	$22\frac{5}{16}$	$21\frac{7}{8}$
March	$49\frac{1}{2}$	48	$22\frac{7}{8}$	$22\frac{1}{8}$
April	$54\frac{3}{8}$	49	$25\frac{1}{16}$	$22\frac{5}{8}$
May	$54\frac{7}{8}$	$52\frac{3}{4}$	$25\frac{1}{4}$	$24\frac{5}{16}$
June	$53\frac{5}{8}$	$52\frac{5}{8}$	$24\frac{9}{16}$	$24\frac{1}{16}$
July	$55\frac{1}{4}$	$52\frac{5}{8}$	$25\frac{1}{2}$	$24\frac{1}{4}$
August	$56\frac{3}{4}$	$54\frac{3}{4}$	$26\frac{1}{4}$	$25\frac{5}{16}$
September	59	$56\frac{7}{8}$	$27\frac{9}{16}$	$26\frac{5}{16}$
October	$61\frac{3}{4}$	$59\frac{3}{8}$	$28\frac{1}{2}$	$27\frac{7}{16}$
November	$59\frac{5}{8}$	$56\frac{1}{4}$	$27\frac{5}{8}$	$26\frac{1}{4}$
December	$56\frac{7}{8}$	$54\frac{1}{8}$	$26\frac{7}{16}$	$25\frac{3}{16}$
Highest	$61\frac{3}{4}$	.....	$28\frac{1}{2}$	.....
Lowest	.....	47	.....	$21\frac{11}{16}$

The New York prices are per ounce of 1000 fine, and the London rates are per ounce 925 fine.

The extremes of fluctuation in the respective markets during the preceding nine years were as follows:

Year.	New York.		London.	
	High.	Low.	High.	Low.
	Cents.	Cents.	Pence.	Pence.
1894	69	$58\frac{3}{8}$	$31\frac{3}{4}$	27
1895	$68\frac{5}{8}$	$59\frac{3}{8}$	$31\frac{3}{8}$	$27\frac{3}{16}$
1896	$69\frac{1}{8}$	$64\frac{3}{8}$	$31\frac{9}{16}$	$29\frac{3}{4}$
1897	65	$51\frac{1}{4}$	$29\frac{13}{16}$	$23\frac{3}{4}$
1898	$61\frac{7}{16}$	54	$28\frac{5}{16}$	25
1899	$63\frac{1}{4}$	$57\frac{5}{8}$	29	$26\frac{5}{8}$
1900	65	$58\frac{5}{8}$	$30\frac{3}{16}$	27
1901	64	54	$29\frac{9}{16}$	$24\frac{15}{16}$
1902	$56\frac{1}{8}$	$46\frac{5}{8}$	$25\frac{15}{16}$	$21\frac{11}{16}$

On November 28, 1902, Silver touched the lowest point on record, being $46\frac{5}{8}$c in New York and $21\frac{11}{16}$d in London, the latter, however, was duplicated in January, 1903.

NEW MONEY MINTED.

The United States Mint at San Francisco is the largest mint in the world and the coinage during the last three calendar years was as follows:

Description.	1903.	1902.	1901.
Double Eagles	$19,080,000 00	$35,072,500 00	$31,920,000 00
Eagles	5,380,000 00	4,695,000 00	28,127,500 00
Half Eagles	9,275,000 00	4,695,000 00	18,240,000 00
Standard Silver Dollars	1,241,000 00	1,530,000 00	2,284,000 00
Half Dollars	960,386 00	730,335 00	423,522 00
Quarter Dollars	259,000 00	381,153 00	18,166 00
Dimes	61,330 00	207,000 00	59,302 20
Pesos	11,361,000 00		
20 Centimes	30,316 00		
10 Centimes	120,000 00		
Totals	$47,767,732 00	$47,310,988 00	$81,072,490 20

The Pesos and Centimes were for the Philippine Islands.

The monthly coinage during the last three years was as follows:

Month.	1903.	1902.	1901.
January	$ 4,976,000 00	$ 7,885,637 00	$4,488,000 00
February	4,240,000 00	6,676,000 00	2,473,160 00
March	5,132,386 00		6,631,933 00
April	1,732,000 00	3,638,153 00	11,665,000 00
May	2,032,000 00	4,486,000 00	9,535,000 00
June	1,994,000 00	850,000 00	5,947,500 00
July	1,281,000 00	2,320,000 00	4,225,000 00
August	2,548,000 00	8,040,000 00	7,030,000 00
September	2,842,330 00	2,960,000 00	4,413,369 00
October	3,185,000 00	1,750,000 00	6,023,522 00
November	8,597,000 00	3,195,000 00	5,565,000 00
December	9,158,016 00	5,510,198 00	12,065,000 20
Totals	$47,767,732 00	$47,310,988 00	$81,072,490 20

The United States Mint was established in San Francisco in April, 1854, and the total coinage to December 31, 1903, is $1,476,494,753.75, divided as follows:

Double Eagles	$1,064,337,520 00	Quarter Dollars	$ 9,445,534 25
Eagles	113,134,560 00	Double Dimes	231,000 00
Half Eagles	112,099,540 00	Dimes	5,643,188 00
Three Dollars	186,300 00	Half Dimes	119,100 00
Quarter Eagles	1,861,255 00	Pesos	11,361,000 00
Dollars (gold)	90,232 00	20 Centimes	30,316 00
Standard Dollars	107,219,073 00	10 Centimes	120,000 00
Trade Dollars	26,647,000 00		
Half Dollars	23,969,435 50	Total	$1,476,494,753 75

The annual coinage of the U. S. Mint at San Francisco, since its establishment, is as follows:

CALENDAR YEARS	COINAGE Gold	COINAGE Silver	TOTAL VALUE
1854	$ 4,084,207	$............	$ 4,084,207 00
1855	18,008,300	164,075 00	18,172,375 00
1856	25,306,400	184,000 00	25,490,400 00
1857	20,327,000	99,500 00	20,426,500 00
1858	17,158,200	274,250 00	17,432,450 00
1859	12,918,000	329,000 00	13,247,000 00
1860	11,178,000	264,000 00	11,442,000 00
1861	15,665,000	511,000 00	16,176,000 00
1862	17,275,960	710,825 00	17,986,785 00
1863	19,543,400	478,750 00	20,022,150 00
1864	15,917,640	361,500 00	16,279,140 00
1865	21,213,500	371,250 00	21,584,750 00
1866	17,362,000	553,500 00	17,915,500 00
1867	18,720,000	630,000 00	19,350,000 00
1868	17,230,000	644,000 00	17,874,000 00
1869	14,028,050	403,500 00	14,431,550 00
1870	19,848,000	507,000 00	20,355,000 00
1871	18,905,000	1,136,775 00	20,041,775 00
1872	16,000,000	380,600 00	16,380,600 00
1873	21,154,500	920,900 00	22,075,400 00
1874	24,460,000	2,868,000 00	27,328,000 00
1875	24,674,000	7,395,000 00	32,069,000 00
1876	32,022,500	10,682,000 00	42,704,500 00
1877	35,092,000	14,680,000 00	49,772,000 00
1878	36,209,500	13,977,000 00	50,186,500 00
1879	28,955,750	9,110,000 00	38,065,750 00
1880	28,527,000	8,900,000 00	37,427,000 00
1881	29,085,000	12,760,000 00	41,845,000 00
1882	28,665,000	9,250,000 00	37,915,000 00
1883	24,576,000	6,250,000 00	30,826,000 00
1884	20,447,500	3,256,496 90	23,703,996 90
1885	22,007,500	1,501,369 00	23,508,869 00
1886	24,600,000	770,652 40	25,370,652 40
1887	23,390,000	2,216,445 00	25,606,445 00
1888	25,148,500	1,133,000 00	26,281,500 00
1889	19,748,000	797,267 80	20,545,267 80
1890	16,055,000	8,372,680 60	24,427,680 60
1891	25,762,500	6,169,611 60	31,932,111 60
1892	21,250,000	2,054,604 75	23,304,604 75
1893	22,457,000	1,082,773 85	23,539,773 85
1894	21,500,500	3,946,552 65	25,447,052 65
1895	23,920,000	1,507,213 25	25,427,213 25
1896	30,093,000	5,674,989 35	35,767,989 35
1897	33,522,500	6,561,791 65	40,084,291 65
1898	63,226,500	5,706,673 70	68,933,173 70
1899	56,341,000	3,768,954 80	60,109,954 80
1900	61,645,000	5,801,634 25	57,446,634 25
1901	78,287,500	2,784,990 20	81,072,490 20
1902	44,462,500	2,848,488 00	47,310,988 00
1903	33,735,000	14,032,732 00	47,767,732 00
Totals	$1,291,709,407	$184,785,346 75	$1,476,494,753 75

FRUIT AND CANNED GOODS SHIPMENTS.

The shipments of canned goods, exclusive of salmon, from San Francisco, by sea during 1903 and for the three preceding years were as follows:

Months.	1903 Cases.	1902 Cases.	1901 Cases.	1900 Cases.
January	21,455	24,696	91,989	19,378
February	15,983	19,750	10,243	16,773
March	42,067	20,726	15,973	36,536
April	20,468	18,744	10,607	13,801
May	19,704	15,825	11,658	17,750
June	18,899	16,456	13,356	15,491
July	19,466	13,601	10,259	18,574
August	209,901	12,708	11,944	122,070
September	158,722	116,558	16,468	187,458
October	235,669	121,647	73,660	241,572
November	86,934	187,548	100,403	84,051
December	88,790	71,612	59,269	118,058
Totals	938,058	639,871	425,829	891,512

DRIED FRUITS.

The shipments of Dried Fruit from San Francisco by sea during 1903 and for the preceding year were as follows:

Months.	1903 Pounds.	1903 Cases.	1902 Pounds.	1902 Cases.
January	826,946	3,139	506,978	82
February	401,786	36	252,116	140
March	948,483	467	136,613	10
April	1,107,237	136	191,483	59
May	558,786	1,180	228,240	38,153
June	661,702	352	162,078	125
July	875,503	1,396	158,369	125
August	1,019,096	1,226	642,573	84
September	2,625,249	1,126	631,154	503
October	2,168,241	4,989	758,692	43
November	6,006,982	2,793	2,302,495	387
December	3,165,490	174	4,060,189	153
Totals	20,365,501	17,014	10,030,980	39,864

FRESH FRUIT SHIPMENTS.

The number of cars of Deciduous Fruits forwarded by rail from California during the past seven years were as follows:

DESTINATION.	1897	1898	1899	1900	1901	1902	1903
Chicago	1,410	1,203	1,060	1 101	1,273	1,301	1,256
New York	1,456	1,429	1,694	1,527	1,482	1,475	1,680½
Boston	543	536	710	649	639	745	846
Philadelphia	202	176	339	212	257	295	384
Minneapolis	180	167	247	302	275	419	203
Baltimore	16	16	67	34	23	63	84
Cincinnati	20	15	89	35	29	51	64
Kansas City	86	116	165	129	85	101	109
Montreal	98	96	128	126	128	102	107
New Orleans	81	62	126	136	118	165	240½
Denver	98	229	269	233	246	104	109
St. Louis	59	27	115	79	64	94	142
St. Paul	121	67	125	131	108	267	217
Omaha	165	156	194	240	205	165	129
Cleveland	37	25	83	63	58	101	106
Pittsburg	40	47	137	144	167	278	297
Buffalo	15	5	34	10	32	28	25
Milwaukee	52	19	60	68	62	68	41
England	58	42	117	192	93	156	90
Scotland	....	....	4	7	16	9	4
Germany	....	....	2	....	....	....	....
Mexico	....	1	1	....	1	1	1¼
Minor points—Canada	....	....	52	71	55	143	122
" U. S.	586	572	1,051	946	1,043	1,010	1,410¼
Wrecked	....	....	....	....	....	....	2
Totals	5,323	5,007	6,869	6,435	6,459	7,141	7,670

The varieties of the annual shipments are shown as follows:

VARIETIES.	1897	1898	1899	1900	1901	1902	1903
Pears	1,640	1,595	1,684	2,115	1,535	2,011	1,719
Peaches	1,316	1,103	2,625	1,361	1,901	1,777	1,857
Grapes	1,100	734	847	825	966	1,033	1,804
Plums and Prunes	742	542	885	1,158	936	1,478	1,145
Apricots	177	123	90	152	201	222	241
Cherries	239	297	85	238	110	245	211
Apples	61	596	490	512	739	359	671
Quinces	24	1	19	10	13	10	19
Figs	3	....	....	....	....	....	....
Nectarines	10	....	2	....	2	....	2
Persimmons	2	1	1	3	2	....	1
Mixed	9	15	24	27	23	6	....
Cars not reported	....	....	117	34	31	....	....
Totals	5,323	5,007	6,869	6,435	6,459	7,141	7,670

WINES AND BRANDIES.

The receipts of California Wines at San Francisco during each month of 1903 and the three previous years were as follows:

Months.	1903. Gallons.	1902. Gallons.	1901. Gallons.	1900. Gallons.
January	1,245,250	1,796,270	2,041,450	1,360,470
February	1,683,400	1,543,130	2,864,820	1,384,225
March	1,515,700	1,809,230	1,631,810	1,230,055
April	1,153,200	1,242,760	1,680,120	842,825
May	1,158,650	1,774,080	1,385,720	1,370,244
June	1,120,948	1,518,970	812,580	1,279,375
July	1,622,390	751,200	592,400	966,665
August	1,089,581	670,840	311,950	1,030,775
September	1,154,150	645,120	592,100	825,780
October	1,475,200	1,236,480	983,736	959,175
November	1,458,060	1,728,210	1,363,406	1,851,872
December	1,585,950	1,694,200	1,554,690	1,442,140
Totals	16,262,479	16,410,540	15,814,782	14,546,601

MONTHLY RECEIPTS OF CALIFORNIA BRANDIES.

Months.	1903. Gallons.	1902. Gallons.	1901. Gallons.	1900. Gallons.
January	95,785	68,320	53,300	99,950
February	30,950	23,670	9,100	16,250
March	48,600	14,700	11,770	6,525
April	25,950	8,050	13,485	9,350
May	16,125	1,200	29,400	14,300
June	25,950	3,480	17,150	700
July	4,050	1,300	5,300	8,250
August	20,375	1,960	2,500	3,375
September	18,690	2,550	3,200	5,000
October	29,000	84,300	28,700	21,133
November	93,050	172,530	135,800	77,060
December	105,950	176,950	107,500	63,600
Totals	514,475	559,010	417,205	325,493

Receipts for a series of years, in gallons, are as follows:

Year.	Wine.	Brandy.	Year.	Wine.	Brandy.
1881	4,937,876	157,083	1891	12,576,665	712,472
1882	4,452,386	136,883	1892	9,474,353	636,080
1883	4,838,623	131,711	1893	11,836,750	693,059
1884	4,858,458	112,265	1894	11,626,710	764,130
1885	5,895,100	157,752	1895	15,387,216	276,380
1886	6,209,131	180,324	1896	13,840,726	201,305
1887	8,496,344	256,104	1897	12,350,728	229,210
1888	8,882,394	242,196	1898	15,498,229	485,398
1889	10,563,864	514,593	1899	13,662,491	472,938

WINE EXPORTS BY SEA.

During the year 1903 the exports of California Wine from San Francisco by sea were, as follows:

To	Cases.	Gallons.	Values.
Atlantic States	169	5,690,640	$2,105,536
Europe	22	81,372	30,107
Mexico	711	86,190	31,890
Central America	1,180	120,930	44,744
South America	152	94,172	34,843
Hawaii	1,928	607,327	224,710
England	30	56,410	20,871
Pacific Islands	34	12,796	4,734
Tahiti	14	37,840	13,942
Philippine Islands	240	6,912	2,558
Japan	224	42,780	15,828
China	256	36,174	13,385
Far East	48	9,864	3,649
Australia	55	870	291
British Columbia	528	24,342	9,006
Siberia	18	8,171	3,013
South Africa	12	1,724	637
Elsewhere	72	20,232	7,486
Total	5,693	6,938,746	$2,567,228

The totals of exports and values for a series of years past are as follows:

Year.	Gallons.	Cases.	Value.
1902	6,636,186	4,360	$2,478,659
1901	5,839,447	11,237	1,993,327
1900	5,790,786	8,358	1,755,923
1899	3,518,631	7,073	1,157,965
1898	5,145,003	7,895	1,824,259
1897	5,462,686	13,585	1,988,197
1896	4,202,869	16,567	1,496,366
1895	4,015,126	15,793	1,323,223
1894	2,440,024	11,507	1,017,027
1893	3,666,412	22,618	1,527,678
1892	4,797,172	13,347	2,031,405
1891	4,918,222	11,552	2,160,516
1890	4,162,068	8,975	1,662,128

EXPORTS OF BRANDY BY SEA.

The exports of California Brandy from San Francisco by sea during 1903, were as follows:

To	Gallons.	Cases.	Value.
Eastern States	1,798	12	$2,013
Europe	48,226	24	52,860
Mexico	194	40	333
Central America	725	8	821
South America	105	4	127
Hawaii	1,008	12	1,144
Pacific Islands	18	....	19
Philippine Islands	754	96	1,117
Japan	9	2	16
China	758	32	897
East Indies	136	....	149
Australia	173	2	195
British Columbia	123	8	157
Siberia	12	....	13
Elsewhere	267	14	328
Totals	54,168	254	$60,189

The totals of exports and values for a series of years past are as follows:

Year.	Gallons.	Cases.	Value.
1902	24,349	643	$36,423
1901	29,512	352	28,746
1900	56,776	1,816	54,536
1899	126,572	4,190	106,413
1898	120,046	694	117,149
1897	18,058	231	26,806
1896	72,998	580	78,871
1895	91,953	422	76,845
1894	357,103	311	374,153
1893	309,353	242	265,975
1892	532,347	250	495,368
1891	432,821	289	395,396
1890	303,425	434	324,462

CALIFORNIA WINES AND BRANDY.

The production of each vintage season, for a series of fiscal years past, is as follows:

WINE.		BRANDY.	
YEAR.	GALLONS.	YEAR.	GALLONS.
1864-65	2,000,000	1864-65	20,415
1865-66	2,250,000	1865-66	74,773
1866-67	2,500,000	1866-67	47,303
1867-68	4,000,000	1867-68	152,418
1868-69	3,000,000	1868-69	286,753
1869-70	3,800,000	1869-70	169,791
1870-71	4,500,000	1870-71	157,107
1871-72	3,000,000	1871-72	211,916
1872-73	2,500,000	1872-73	118,605
1873-74	4,000,000	1873-74	99,680
1874-75	4,000,000	1874-75	297,147
1875-76	4,000,000	1875-76	142,799
1876-77	4,000,000	1876-77	157,159
1877-78	5,000,000	1877-78	318,071
1878-79	7,000,000	1878-79	158,393
1879-80	10,200,000	1879-80	238,928
1880-81	8,000,000	1880-81	351,206
1881-82	9,000,000	1881-82	502,513
1882-83	8,500,000	1882-83	324,717
1883-84	10,000,000	1883-84	295,039
1884-85	11,000,000	1884-85	383,756
1885-86	18,000,000	1885-86	402,121
1886-87	15,000,000	1886-87	742,445
1887-88	17,000,000	1887-88	953,580
1888-89	15,500,000	1888-89	915,573
1889-90	17,500,000	1889-90	1,072,957
1890-91	20,000,000	1890-91	1,245,698
1891-92	15,000,000	1891-92	1,475,525
1892-93	24,700,000	1892-93	2,209,617
1893-94	14,000,000	1893-94	2,007,965
1894-95	18,000,000	1894-95	1,754,062
1895-96	17,000,000	1895-96	2,090,000
1896-97	16,400,000	1896-97	1,442,468
1897-98	31,500,000	1897-98	1,250,000
1898-99	19,000,000	1898-99	1,690,000
1899-00	23,500,000	1899-00	3,256,513
1900-01	22,500,000	1900-01	1,688,482
1901-02	43,000,000	1901-02	3,564,172
1902-03	32,000,000	1902-03	5,776,571

SALMON.

The receipts of canned salmon at San Francisco during the past three years were as follows:

Months.	1903. Cases.	1902. Cases.	1901. Cases.
January	4,104	7,653	3,248
February	650	9,474	89
March	3,484	7,887	293
April	3,133	7,784	862
May	1,579	5,268	2,675
June	12,171	4,907	2,364
July	1,449	9,515	8,076
August	42,329	101,079	94,686
September	1,182,500	996,938	801,345
October	227,606	275,870	477,877
November	166,372	192,436	172,506
December	20,677	25,680	72,175
Totals*	1,666,054	1,644,491	1,635,596

* Includes 4,754 cases Californian in 1903 and 1,661,300 cases from Oregon, Alaska and British Columbia. In addition to the above there were received in the past year 28,799 barrels of salt salmon.

In 1900 the receipts of canned salmon were 1,434,965 cases.

PACIFIC COAST SALMON PACK.

The total pack of the Pacific Coast Canneries for 1903 and the two preceding years, was as follows:

Location.	1903 Cases.	1902 Cases.	1901 Cases.
Alaska Companies	2,444,994	2,554,423	2,034,895
British Columbia	473,547	625,982	1,236,156
Puget Sound	480,258	569,307	1,380,590
Columbia River	334,811	367,241	248,494
Sacramento River	8,500	14,043	17,500
Various Rivers	71,996	134,190	123,326
Totals	3,814,106	4,259,186	5,040,961

EXPORTS BY SEA.

The exports of packed Salmon from San Francisco by sea during 1903 were as follows:

To	CASES.	BARRELS.	VALUES.
Eastern States	212,515	4,038	$ 898,516
Australia	59,802	2,027	263,532
New Zealand	7,987	226	34,660
England	392,650		1,570,600
China	7,439	10	29,876
East Indies	10,330	38	41,776
Tahiti	1,587	110	7,668
Japan	139	39	1,034
Samoan Islands	3,722	54	15,536
Central America	1,450	2	5,824
Philippines	1,935		7,640
Mexico	1,373	1	7,904
Colombia	1,823	2	7,316
Europe	5,731		22,924
South Africa	907		3,628
Hawaii	12,971	5,227	114,608
Siberia	19		76
Chile	16,420	3	65,716
Peru	2,446	6	9,836
Ecuador	1,480		5,920
Venezuela	2,962	1	11,860
Java	652	5	2,668
Ceylon	78	3	348
Barbadoes	126		504
West Indies	118		472
British Guiana	428		1,712
Argentine	285		1,140
Pacific Islands	615	23	2,736
Elsewhere	116	4	512
Totals	748,706	11,819	$3,136,542
1902	793,156	11,845	3,048,268
1901	804,347	9,839	3,623,746
1900	856,594	15,734	3,602,562
1899	694,866	27,146	2,946,028
1898	703,442	16,727	2,921,178
1897	789,252	17,066	3,338,331
1896	707,903	10,693	3,026,888
1895	902,089	11,072	3,711,686
1894	640,163	7,753	2,704,728
1893	203,316	7,373	1,027,051
1892	758,517	5,946	3,490,877
1891	464,291	11,982	2,091,292
1890	480,006	9,751	2,229,313
1889	475,317	7,011	2,636,361

The following statement shows the product of the Pacific Coast for a series of years, in cases:

Year.	Columbia River	Sacramento River.	Outside Rivers.	Puget Sound.	British Columbia.	Alaska.	Totals.
1866	4,000						4,000
1867	18,000						18,000
1868	28,000						28,000
1869	100,000						100,000
1870	150,000						150,000
1871	200,000						200,000
1872	250,000		3,000				253,000
1873	250,000	1,000	6,000				257,000
1874	350,000	2,500	9,750				362,250
1875	375,000	3,000	16,800		6,270		401,070
1876	450,000	8,300	25,600		9,847	2,800	496,547
1877	460,000	21,500	24,800		67,387	5,200	578,887
1878	460,000	36,500	30,000		113,601	8,159	648,260
1879	480,000	31,000	30,000		57,394	12,530	610,924
1880	630,000	51,000	37,200		61,300	6,539	786,039
1881	551,000	181,200	48,500		175,675	8,977	965,352
1882	541,300	200,300	49,000		255,061	10,244	1,055,905
1883	629,400	160,000	38,000		243,000	36,000	1,106,400
1884	656,179	81,450	41,350		138,945	54,000	971,924
1885	524,530	48,500	51,750		106,865	74,850	806,495
1886	454,943	39,300	131,100		163,004	120,700	909,047
1887	373,800	36,500	195,400	2,200	201,990	190,200	1,000,090
1888	367,750	58,000	154,000	4,000	135,600	427,372	1,146,722
1889	325,500	66,666	199,062	5,000	414,400	709,347	1,719,981
1890	433,500	35,006	67,117	8,000	409,464	688,332	1,641,419
1891	390,183	4,142	66,805	11,500	314,813	789,294	1,576,737
1892	481,900	4,600	144,200	15,000	221,797	461,482	1,325,979
1893	425,200	23,336	119,660	66,500	590,229	645,545	1,870,470
1894	511,000	28,463	118,500	67,933	494,470	678,501	1,898,867
1895	617,460	24,000	264,300	52,000	512,877	619,379	2,090,016
1896	463,621	13,387	115,400	248,200	598,300	958,700	2,397,608
1897	552,721	42,500	68,683	423,500	1,015,477	969,850	3,072,731
1898	473,230	28,000	78,600	417,700	454,500	956,979	2,409,009
1899	340,125	33,550	82,432	871,500	711,600	1,098,833	3,138,040
1900	313,417	34,000	106,300	478,742	527,281	1,534,745	2,994,485
1901	248,494	17,500	123,326	1,380,590	1,236,156	2,034,895	5,040,961
1902	367,241	14,043	134,190	563,307	625,982	2,554,423	4,259,186
1903	334,811	8,500	71,996	480,258	473,547	2,444,994	3,814,106

IMPORTS OF TEA.

The following shows all the imports of Tea at San Francisco from China and Japan from 1860 to 1883, both years inclusive; and the quantities credited to San Francisco since 1883, during which latter period in transit shipments to the East were not included in the statistics of the Custom House at San San Francisco:

YEAR.	CHINA. POUNDS.	CHINA. VALUE.	JAPAN. POUNDS.	JAPAN. VALUE.	TOTALS. POUNDS.	TOTALS. VALUE.
1860	965,543	$ 265,292	179,287	$ 35,474	1,144,830	$ 300,766
1861	1,233,381	307,903	124,236	25,067	1,357,616	322,970
1862	1,430,163	423,734	204,015	46,305	1,634,178	470,039
1863	1,822,585	439,435	382,633	105,678	2,205,218	545,113
1864	1,388,408	364,820	464,796	127,545	1,853,204	492,365
1865	700,760	178,333	923,456	236,737	1,624,216	415,070
1866	1,042,499	291,389	1,293,650	435,188	2,336,149	726,577
1867	1,331,660	445,686	552,070	188,560	1,886,730	634,246
1868	876,282	241,492	1,277,862	447,686	2,154,144	689,178
1869	725,430	201,264	1,283,023	440,106	2,008,453	641,870
1870	981,919	313,969	2,137,144	746,043	3,119,063	1,060,012
1871	8,215,439	3,633,221	7,710,389	3,136,827	15,925,828	6,770,148
1672	5,709,895	2,512,660	6,881,628	2,768,507	12,581,523	5,281,167
1873	4,104,972	1,529,130	8,431,804	3,276,557	12,536,776	4,805,687
1874	2,828,570	1,096,480	10,386,331	4,066,758	13,214,901	5,163,238
1875	1,881,651	518,926	17,990,578	6,491,368	19,872,229	7,010,294
1876	1,095,800	340,391	17,556,236	5,904,400	18,652,036	6,244,871
1877	4,721,858	1,550,014	13,507,258	3,906,085	18,229,116	5,456,099
1878	3,249,082	1,148,464	13,867,586	3,384,630	17,116,668	4,533,094
1879	5,884,856	2,035,813	14,092,816	4,289,169	19,977,672	6,324,982
1880	4,997,527	1,513,583	17,081,997	4,674,437	22,079,524	6,188,020
1881	5,278,766	1,526,907	12,704,741	4,257,461	17,983,507	5,784,368
1882	4,701,588	1,209,870	19,469,028	4,444,458	24,170,616	5,654,328
1883	4,775,129	1,098,209	17,194,448	3,048,575	21,969,577	4,146,784
1884	2,039,691	467,546	8,536,660	1,287,971	10,576,371	1,755,517
1885	1,581,186	305,773	5,205,178	737,476	6,786,784	1,043,249
1886	2,035,023	411,134	6,904,729	888,901	8,939,752	1,300,035
1887	2,307,186	394,632	5,759,475	746,895	8,066,661	1,141,527
1888	1,951,672	349,210	5,743,389	642,305	7,695,061	991,515
1889	1,598,767	272,934	5,860,289	656,851	7,459,106	929,785
1890	2,001,252	350,055	4,264,663	572,970	6,265,915	923,025
1891	2,206,840	390,549	5,033,333	752,259	7,240,173	1,142,808
1892	1,872,198	315,040	4,209,835	608,822	6,082,033	923,862
1893	2,358,745	384,178	3,721,566	540,419	6,080,311	924,597
1894	1,820,606	264,804	3,508,815	431,254	5,329,421	696,058
1895	2,330,366	341,222	3,491,695	459,529	5,822,061	800,751
1896	1,913,863	283,512	3,601,522	422,313	5,515,385	705,825
1897	5,149,896	779,621	9,022,804	1,211,390	14,172,700	1,991,011
1898	3,175,071	399,903	4,746,872	659,593	7,921,943	1,059,496
1899	4,238,862	468,600	7,494,735	917,698	11,733,597	1,386,298
1900	4,435,220	506,757	10,127,267	1,346,596	14,562,487	1,853,353
1901	1,891,637	228,970	6,606,152	838,692	8,497,789	1,067,662
1902	2,226,584	287,530	3,554,620	581,215	5,781,204	868,745
1903	2,956,468	406,822	5,968,805	1,106,347	8,925,277	1,513,169

TEA.

The imports during each month of the last four years, in pounds, are as follows:

Month.	1903.	1902.	1901.	1900.
January	248,909	56,830	252,767	242,657
February	124,647	88,730	155,818	65,608
March	128,481	69,779	108,886	52,840
April	56,201	46,715	70,650	190,952
May	176,131	41,387	16,435	52,930
June	1,330,413	447,942	1,461,196	1,086,311
July	1,570,960	974,928	3,133,455	2,928,159
August	2,210,913	997,443	1,619,606	4,350,019
September	1,666,827	828,592	1,000,985	2,461,222
October	1,199,111	1,174,789	593,856	1,987,272
November	566,894	597,092	241,524	1,200,591
December	316,473	721,579	168,883	236,935
Totals	9,595,960	6,045,806	8,824,061	14,855,496

The sources of imports during 1903 were as follows:

Sources.	Pounds.	Value.
China	2,956,468	$ 406,822
Japan	5,968,809	1,106,347
British East Indies	437,275	77,089
Elsewhere	233,408	38,280
Totals	9,595,960	$1,628,538

Exports by sea during 1903 were as follows:

To	Pounds.	Values.
Atlantic States	720	$ 126
Mexico	31,588	5,372
Central America	14,489	2,467
South America	2,183	374
Hawaii	57,247	9,742
Pacific Islands	2,545	435
Japan	2,508	429
China	1,710	291
British Columbia	350	60
Elsewhere	2,680	458
Totals	116,020	$19,754
1902	101,905	$11,323
1901	87,697	7,875
1900	197,127	30,268
1899	122,646	15,698

SUGAR.

The imports during each month of the last four years, in pounds, are as follows:

Month.	1903	1902*	1901*	1900
January	484,868	911,248	487,053	7,955,976
February	992,807	1,620,549	266,372	19,967,379
March	628,545	660,070	376,542	29,066,549
April	718,797	1,750,317	1,595,377	31,927,154
May	207,167	1,080,210	1,108,478	33,123,169
June	792,955	599,436	1,456,343	11,848,772
July	2,087,526	777,331	2,471,585	85,059
August	364,382	732,797	955,252	694,278
September	3,376,134	1,399,731	205,216	1,471,985
October	1,017,303	176,166	76,884	11,906,185
November	324,746	32,166	9,065,127	12,023,472
December	2,620,020	97,357	1,759,153	1,187,666
Totals	14,212,255	9,837,878	10,824,280	161,257,644

* Does not include Hawaiian Island sugar.

The sources of imports during 1903 were as follows:

Source.	Pounds.	Values.
China	1,860,276	$ 35,183
Guatemala	4,979,421	94,388
Salvador	2,314,860	42,286
Nicaragua	3,791,718	73,434
Peru	487,269	8,645
Chile	623,340	11,466
Elsewhere	155,371	2,917
Totals	14,212,255	$268,319

Exports by sea during 1903 were as follows:

To	Pounds.	Values.
Atlantic States	170,280	$ 3,407
Mexico	486,341	9,728
Central America	10,048	202
South America	82,945	1,659
Hawaii	1,515,605	30,314
Pacific Islands	122,229	2,446
Japan	313,201	6,265
China	776,993	15,540
Far East	9,445	189
Australasia	1,400,483	28,010
British Columbia	87,187	1,745
South Africa	4,012	82
Elsewhere	12,460	250
Totals	4,991,229	$99,837
1902	1,809,271	$50,527

COFFEE.

The imports during each month of the past four years, in pounds, are as follows:

Month.	1903	1902	1901	1900
January	3,814,276	518,759	1,270,519	2,370,522
February	4,604,392	2,727,854	2,485,522	3,185,836
March	5,764,474	3,055,525	6,328,087	4,994,875
April	5,083,246	4,813,997	12,087,124	4,993,205
May	5,070,507	4,391,157	8,811,019	2,497,747
June	2,951,276	4,102,531	5,589,264	2,170,761
July	3,600,956	2,667,329	2,758,871	716,857
August	846,981	1,496,237	2,348,794	665,925
September	695,964	859,749	595,768	542,620
October	397,757	746,564	440,604	249,157
November	408,731	768,247	247,607	206,204
December	780,505	1,408,643	651,171	594,905
Totals	34,019,565	27,556,592	43,614,350	23,188,614

The sources of imports during 1903 were as follows:

Source.	Pounds.	Values.
Central America	28,517,062	$2,632,014
Ecuador	1,374,830	109,226
East Indies	1,116,084	113,214
Mexico	1,538,725	122,103
Elsewhere	472,864	33,126
Totals	34,019,565	$3,009,683

Exports by sea during 1903 were as follows:

To	Pounds.	Values.
Atlantic States	2,110	$ 230
Europe	4,920	542
Mexico	127,500	14,071
Central America	165	18
South America	7,250	797
Hawaii	133,484	14,687
Pacific Islands	20,205	2,198
Philippine Islands	39,826	4,382
Japan	18,151	1,996
China	160,759	17,684
Far East	6,267	690
Australasia	695,382	76,498
British Columbia	121,661	13,385
Asiatic Russia	1,200	135
Totals	1,338,880	$147,313
1902	161,907	26,854
1901	1,501,070	168,867
1900	1,359,748	183,265
1899	1,194,607	143,172

RICE.

The imports during each month of the last four years, in pounds, are as follows:

Month.	1903.	1902.	1901.	1900.
January	4,590,207	5,218.846	4,186,689	4,419,906
February	5,621,489	5.790,578	5,260.013	3,748,523
March	8,293,141	4,759,047	3,842,396	7,048,050
April	3,839,559	6,311,475	6,137,571	6,838,200
May	2,706,064	1,276,914	1,524,020	2,764,007
June	465,650	1,165,097	3,545,890	2,546,230
July	1,009,511	748,179	1,515,131	1,290,039
August	707,695	524,585	554,063	2,076,767
September	285,380	408,790	295,594	865,573
October	555,255	179,954	556,052	791,784
November	452,878	394,544	1,148,585	1,129,354
December	2,166,697	2,648,150	1,337,647	1,484,683
Totals	30,694,826	29,426,059	29.903,651	35,003,116

The sources of imports during 1903 were as follows:

Source.	Pounds.	Values.
China	23,509,472	$514,474
Japan	6,897,614	139,989
Italy	165,293	4,727
Elsewhere	122,447	3,582
Totals	30,694.826	$662,772

Exports by sea during 1903 were as follows:

To	Pounds.	Values.
Atlantic States	33,917	$ 1,017
Europe	4,700	141
Mexico	543,334	16,302
Central America	945,015	28,353
South America	59,950	1,799
Hawaii	4,474,621	134,240
Pacific Islands	376,076	11,284
Japan	14,539	438
China	18,323	551
Far East	17,869	538
Australasia	12,221	363
British Columbia	21,690	652
Elsewhere	37,282	1,120
Totals	6,559,541	$196,803
1902	3,405,749	$ 58,269
1901	2,422,497	42,390
1900	10,725,888	382,790
1899	3,748,539	86,013

WHALEBONE AND OIL.

The receipts of Oil, Bone and Ivory at San Francisco from the Arctic for the season of 1903 were as follows:

Received Per	Arrived.	Oil, bbls.	Bone, lbs.	Ivory lbs.
St. Paul	July 7...	......	2,860	......
St. Paul	July 20...	......	180	......
Umatilla	July 21...	......	3,000	200
C. W. Morgan	Oct. 27...	1,750	......	......
Gayhead	Oct. 30...	500	3,000	......
Jeanette	Oct. 30...	......	4,350	400
Gotoma	Nov. 1...	......	......	35
Beluga	Nov. 1...	290	30,000	401
Belvedere	Nov. 3...	107	......	......
California	Nov. 3...	1,160	......	......
A. Knowles	Nov. 4...	1,870	......	......
Karluk	Nov. 5...	......	1,600	......
Monterey	Nov. 7...	......	3,500	......
Alexander	Nov. 7...	......	12,000	......
And. Hicks	Nov. 8...	800	......	......
Morning Star	Nov. 9...	......	3,000	500
John & Win	Nov. 10...	10	150	......
W. Baylies	Nov. 16..	......	50	......
Umatilla	Nov. 18...	......	1,100	......
Totals	....	6,487	64,790	1,536

San Francisco is the leading whaling port of the world, and the product of the industry for the past thirty years has been as follows:

Years.	Vessels.	Oil, bbls.	Bone, lbs.	Ivory, lbs.
1874	11	10,300	86,300	7,600
1875	12	16,300	157,000	25,400
1876	7	2,800	8,800	7,000
1877	20	13,900	139,600	74,000
1878	21	9,600	73,300	30,000
1879	22	17,400	127,500	32,900
1880	20	23,200	339,000	15,300
1881	26	21,800	354,500	15,400
1882	30	21,100	316,600	17,800
1883	37	13,300	160,200	23,100
1884	40	20,373	295,700	5,421
1885	43	30,143	448,075	7,066
1886	43	20,661	332,931	5,273
1887	41	32,884	603,400	550
1888	42	16,083	275,700	14,700
1889	48	12,019	216,775	1,130
1890	44	14,985	247,360	4,000
1891	46	12,124	220,650	1,300
1892	42	12,700	416,850	15,800
1893	50	6,935	310,200	8,600
1894	18	8,409	240,050	7,367
1895	15	4,147	104,595	4,415
1896	23	6,052	189,212	6,470
1897	18	5,280	141,470	5,500
1898	20	7,603	225,225	9,510
1899	18	6,221	306,125	6,430
1900	19	4.910	177,700	580
1901	16	6,745	76,680	1,139
1902	21	10,976	110,662	15,566
1903	19	6,487	64,790	1,536
Totals	828	474,287	5,958,930	370,853

COAL, COKE AND IRON.

The annual receipts of Coal and the various sources of supply during the last four years, were as follows:

SOURCES.	1903 Tons.	1902 Tons.	1901 Tons.	1900 Tons.
British Columbia	289,890	591,732	710,330	766,917
Australia	276,186	197,328	175,959	178,563
English and Welsh	61,580	95,621	52,270	54,099
Scotch	3,495	3,600	......	......
Eastern (Cumberland and Anthracite)	13,262	24,133	27,370	17,319
Seattle (Washington)	127,819	165,237	240,574	250,590
Tacoma (Washington)	256,826	209,358	433,817	418,052
Mt. Diablo, Coos Bay and Tesla	84,277	111,209	143,318	160,915
Japan, and Rocky Mountains by rail	102,219	47,380	51,147	42,673
Totals	1,215,554	1,445,598	1,834,785	1,889,128

The quantity of coal imported during 1903 was 230,044 tons less than for 1902, but this cannot be accepted as the amount of fuel to fill our requirements, as the quantity of fuel oil which was produced this year was 60 per cent in excess of the product of 1902, hence the showing made for the coal consumption cannot be accepted as being a discouraging one for manufacturing interests locally. In the early portion of the year, labor disturbances developed in the British Columbia Collieries and they were not amicably compromised for some considerable time, as the Manager of the Wellington Collieries showed a disposition to maintain his rights rather than make concessions, although at a serious loss to himself. The laborers, however, finally acceded to his demands. The abrogation of the duty of 67 cents per ton on Australian and British Columbia coals, has proved for the year a marked advantage and has aided in giving large consumers here a pronounced benefit.

COKE.

The total deliveries here by water, foot up 68,090 tons, as against 64,916 tons last year. Fully 75% of this amount was shipped from England, and Germany, the balance principally from Belgium and Australia.

PIG IRON.

The total importations by water aggregate 29,845 tons, about half of which was shipped from Great Britain. This would demonstrate an increase of manufacturing interests during the year, as the total amount received in 1891 was 8,478 tons.

CRUDE OIL PRODUCTION.

The output of petroleum oil in California during 1903 and the number of wells in operation at the close of the year are shown as follows:

Producing Fields.	Producing Wells.	Production, Bbls.
Fullerton...........................	138	250.000
Puente.............................	80	100,000
Whittier............................	103	50,000
Los Angeles........................	984	900,000
Newhall............................	25 }	900,000
Ventura............................	300 }	
Summerland.........................	190	100,000
Santa Maria........................	24	1,000,000
Kern River.........................	750	15,750,000
Sunset and Midway..................	120	250,000
McKittrick.........................	76	1,700,000
Coalinga...........................	115	2,600,000
Sargents...........................	4	1,000
Half Moon Bay......................	5	1,000
Totals.............................	2,914	23,602,000

Average daily production for the year, 64,663 barrels.

In consequence of the insufficiency of transportation facilities and the want of a market at prices at which the oil could be laid down at tide water, a number of wells were shut down during several months of the year.

Stocks of oil in tankage and reservoirs, 7,000,000 barrels.

The production of the State varies in gravity from 9° Beaume, the lowest gravity in the Sunset field, to 38° B., the highest gravity in the Newhall field.

The depth of the producing wells ranges from 200 feet at Summerland to 2,500 feet at Fullerton.

The bulk of the kerosine used on the Pacific Coast is now being refined from California oil.

THE YIELD OF OIL.

The annual output in California for a series of years is as follows:

Year.	Barrels.	Value.
1870	3,600	$ 5,125
1871	5,200	7,370
1872	6,500	9,876
1873	7,200	10,920
1874	7,700	11,540
1875	8,400	12,090
1876	9,600	15,410
1877	12,750	18,140
1878	15,227	22,780
1879	19,858	29,672
1880	42,399	68,450
1881	99,862	130,678
1882	128,636	172,730
1883	142,857	207,540
1884	262,000	428,600
1885	325,000	613,920
1886	377,145	642,785
1887	678,572	1,357,144
1888	690,333	1,380,666
1889	303,220	368,048
1890	307,360	384,200
1891	323,600	401,264
1892	385,049	561,333
1893	470,179	608,092
1894	783,078	1,064,521
1895	1,245,339	1,000,235
1896	1,257,780	1,180,793
1897	1,911,569	1,918,269
1898	2,249,088	2,376,420
1899	2,677,875	2,660,793
1900	4,329,950	4,152,928
1901	8,754,500	7,487,600
1902	13,692,514	10,269,385
1903	23,602,000	16,521,400

Valuations are based on selling prices at tidewater.

ELECTRIC POWER.

The leading facts and statistics relative to the electric power stations in California on July 1, 1902, are shown as follows:

ITEMS.	PRIVATE.	MUNICIPAL.	TOTALS.
Number of plants	105	10	115
Cost of Construction	$36,161,996	$415,478	$36,577,474
Yearly earnings from operation			
Arc Lights—			
Private use	$509,375	$714	$510,089
Public use	456,708	33,269	489,977
Incandescent Lights—			
Private use	2,172,206	55,135	2,227,341
Public use	58,190	19,721	77,911
Electric Railway service	181,494	2,492	183,986
Motor service	1,217,379	10,720	1,228,099
Other electric service	228,687		228,687
All other sources	113,405	6,922	120,327
Total earnings	$4,937,444	$128,973	$5,066,417
Yearly expenses for operation—			
Salaries and wages	$1,144,447	$32,294	$1,176,741
Supplies, materials and fuel	1,323,325	42,807	1,366,132
Rents, taxes and sundries	669,058	7,491	676,549
Interest on bonds	691,701	7,852	699,553
Total expenses	$3,828,531	$90,444	$3,918,975
Horse Power—			
Steam engines, No	139	11	150
Horse power	52,565	1,660	54,225
Water wheels, No	130	3	133
Horse power	78,483	450	78,933
Gas engines, No	6		6
Horse power	618		618
Auxiliary engines, No.	44		44
Horse power	1,012		1,012
Total Horse power	132,678	2,110	134,788
Dynamo Capacity—			
Number in use	377	23	400
Horse power	110,381	1,973	112,354
Direct current constant voltage, No.	124	7	131
Horse power	16,433	66	16,499
Direct current constant amperage, No.	77	5	82
Horse power	5,150	180	5,330
Alternating and polyphase current, No.	176	11	187
Horse power	88,798	1,727	90,525
Transmission wire, miles	4,799	281	5,080
No. of arc lights in use	15,357	407	15,764
No. of incandescent lights in use	977,384	29,491	1,006,879
Employes and salaries—			
Officials and clerks	335	16	351
Annual salaries	$385,769	$9,818	$395,587
Wage earners	976	33	1,009
Annual wages	$758,678	$22,476	$781,154

Electric power statistics in operation in the Pacific Coast States on July 1, 1902, were as follows:

STATES.	PRIVATE.	MUNICIPAL.	TOTAL.	Horse Power. Engine and Waterwheel.	Dynamo Capacity.
California	105	10	115	134,788	112,354
Oregon	33	6	39	17,798	14,967
Washington	33	7	40	22,894	18,337
Nevada	5	......	5	1,720	1,024
Arizona Ter	13	......	13	2,540	2,428
Totals	189	23	212	179,740	149,110

The magnitude of the industry in the Pacific Coast States is shown by the following statement with annual earnings and expenses:

STATES.	Stations.	COST.	EXPENSES.	EARNINGS.
California	115	$36,547.474	$3,918,975	$5,066,417
Oregon	39	5,157,651	499,632	691,582
Washington	40	3,537,022	651,495	783,651
Nevada	5	301,785	39,687	44,549
Arizona Ter	13	810,341	240,953	293,066
Totals	212	$46,354,273	$5,350,742	$6,879,265

There were 3,620 electric light and power stations in the United States on July 1, 1902, of which 2,805 were operated by private owners and 815 were operated under municipal control. California stands prominent among the leading States as shown by the following:

STATES.	Private.	Municipal.	Total.	Horsepower.
California	105	10	115	134,788
Illinois	264	82	346	126,866
Indiana	118	62	180	54,237
Iowa	131	38	169	39,504
Massachusetts	97	17	114	124,213
Michigan	120	81	201	64,883
Minnesota	68	70	138	34,823
Missouri	80	43	123	45,318
New York	228	28	256	323,413
Ohio	145	88	233	103,745
Pennsylvania	243	36	279	175,510
Texas	130	7	137	34,887
Wisconsin	124	28	152	35,715
Totals	1,853	590	2,443	1,297,902

QUICKSILVER.

The receipts at San Francisco from California mines during the past four years were as follows.:

MONTHS.	1903. FLASKS.	1902. FLASKS.	1901. FLASKS.	1900. FLASKS.
January	1,559	1,751	1,827	1,985
February	2,755	1,536	2,203	1,728
March	1,708	1,658	2,040	2,465
April	1,464	1,821	1,941	1,745
May	2,056	2,054	1,667	1,738
June	2,344	1,380	1,373	1,758
July	1,966	1,676	1,698	1,364
August	1,841	2,245	1,712	1,330
September	2,453	1,379	1,679	1,352
October	2,966	1,794	1,614	1,735
November	2,139	1,282	1,594	1,654
December	3,283	1,752	1,876	2,393
Totals	26,534	20,328	21,224	21,247

EXPORTS BY SEA

TO	1903. FLASKS.	1903. VALUES.	1902. FLASKS.	1902. VALUES.
Mexico	3,087	$135,828	3,332	$148,782
China	5,250	231,000	1,500	186,250
Central America	915	41,580	1,000	44,044
British Columbia	42	1,848	28	1,263
New York	6,065	266,860	942	42,397
Japan	1,270	55,880	....	....
Siberia	15	660	....	....
Chile	16	704	....	....
Korea	28	1,232	....	....
Panama	4	176	21	953
Ecuador	16	704	1	45
Hawaii	3	132	2	96
Totals	16,741	$736,604	9,826	$423.830

Quicksilver Production and Exports.

The annual production of Quicksilver in California and the exports from San Francisco for a series of years are as follows:

| PRODUCTION. || EXPORTS. ||
YEAR.	FLASKS.	YEAR.	FLASKS.
1850	7,223	1850	165
1851	27,779	1851	1,080
1852	20,000	1852	900
1853	22,284	1853	12,737
1854	30,004	1854	20,963
1855	33,000	1855	27,165
1856	30,000	1856	23,740
1857	28,204	1857	27,262
1858	31,000	1858	24,142
1859	13,000	1859	3,399
1860	10,000	1860	9,448
1861	35,000	1861	35,995
1862	42,000	1862	33,747
1863	40,531	1863	26,014
1864	47,489	1864	36,927
1865	53,000	1865	42,469
1866	46,550	1866	30,287
1867	47,000	1867	28,853
1868	47,728	1868	44,506
1869	33,811	1869	24,415
1870	30,077	1870	13,788
1871	31,686	1871	15,205
1872	31,621	1872	13,089
1873	27,642	1873	6,395
1874	27,756	1874	6,770
1875	50,250	1875	28,960
1876	75,074	1876	41,140
1877	79,396	1877	46,280
1878	63,880	1878	34,250
1879	73,684	1879	52,180
1880	59,926	1880	34,648
1881	60,851	1881	35,269
1882	52,732	1882	40,166
1883	46,725	1883	37,873
1884	31,913	1884	21,896
1885	32,073	1885	25,495
1886	29,981	1886	10,030
1887	33,760	1887	21,137
1888	33,250	1888	16,620
1889	26,464	1889	12,078
1890	22,926	1890	5,640
1891	22,904	1891	13,654
1892	27,993	1892	27,108
1893	30,164	1893	28,326
1894	30,416	1894	28,884
1895	36,104	1895	30,687
1896	30,765	1896	27,048
1897	26,648	1897	24,864
1898	31,092	1898*	6,077
1899	29,454	1899	10,155
1900	26,317	1900	7,294
1901	25,492	1901	5,337
1902	26,184	1902	9,826

RECEIPTS OF DAIRY PRODUCE.

The monthly receipts of butter at San Francisco during 1903 and the three preceding years, were as follows:

MONTHS.	1903. Pounds.	1902. Pounds.	1901. Pounds.	1900. Pounds.
January	760,700	798,700	936,700	1,108,800
February	992,000	828,800	1,028,900	1,056,400
March	1,303,300	1,387,000	1,400,400	1,098,200
April	2,007,000	2,074,400	2,286,560	1,604,600
May	2,251,300	2,418,800	1,752,420	1,999,300
June	2,244,300	2,175,400	1,684,640	1,386,300
July	1,188,300	1,494,800	1,593,100	1,328,900
August	567,800	1,016,700	883,080	1,241,000
September	524,800	788,300	902,600	945,700
October	516,400	707,100	730,280	1,132,000
November	423,400	660,800	772,100	964,700
December	790,300	449,700	1,001,000	898,200
Totals	13,569,600	14,801,150	14,971,780	14,564,100

The monthly receipts of cheese for four years are shown as follows:

MONTHS.	1903. Pounds.	1902. Pounds.	1901. Pounds.	1900. Pounds
January	289,800	277,900	190,180	438,100
February	350,500	273,800	230,870	342,200
March	469,900	449,000	339,785	460,600
April	628,500	603,100	536,700	493,500
May	767,300	730,800	435,825	618,100
June	720,200	597,900	389,120	515,200
July	765,300	551,700	429,665	495,400
August	548,800	578,600	273,870	474,800
September	483,300	555,900	340,625	412,100
October	477,900	374,800	253,970	502,400
November	372,800	293,200	259,960	387,200
December	330,400	275,600	300,300	269,555
Totals	6,204,700	5,562,300	3,980,870	5,409,155

The monthly receipts of eggs is shown as follows:

Months	1903 Dozens	1902 Dozens	1901 Dozens	1900 Dozens
January	482,960	356,580	438,210	339,420
February	796,240	869,790	801,430	383,742
March	1,291,320	1,295,390	1,136,280	513,534
April	1,474,320	1,456,179	1,354,110	557,682
May	1,392,180	1,140,870	1,181,810	756,762
June	1,222,590	882,210	781,470	463,302
July	877,950	758,420	776,550	428,610
August	588,890	563,460	460,410	504,081
September	505,970	398,465	453,810	398,373
October	478,380	334,420	270,810	530,250
November	442,290	224,590	311,040	397,734
December	503,740	311,380	359,060	233,406
Totals	10,056,830	8,551,754	8,324,990	5,506,896

The receipts of butter, cheese and eggs at San Francisco for a series of years past, were as follows:

YEARS.	BUTTER, Lbs.	CHEESE, Lbs.	EGGS, Doz.
1899	13,807,300	6,092,840	7,120,654
1898	15,606,050	4,777,300	6,101,405
1897	14,634,000	6,036,420	5,442,202
1896	13,769,850	5,124,660	4,941,967
1895	14,344,300	5,257,900	4,932,204
1894	17,257,100	6,689,620	4,881,375
1893	17,037,900	6,750,000	4,715,711
1892	14,677,300	7,497,900	5,308,908
1891	12,881,950	6,637,600	5,070,668
1890	12,583,400	6,835,700	6,122,776
1889	12,123,200	5,889,000	5,836,203

HOPS.

The monthly shipments from San Francisco by sea during the last two years were as follows:

Month.	1903. Pounds.	1903. Value.	1902. Pounds.	1902. Value.
January	13,756	$ 2,840	40,215	$ 5,260
February	10.305	2,117	3,000	605
March	3,092	639	20,230	3,293
April	58,763	12,724	8,470	1,340
May	21,113	4,070	57,520	8,972
June	4 806	1,012	2,450	320
July	19,490	3,964	1,040	187
August	27,416	5,618	1,387	291
September	81,207	17,725	40,732	10,189
October	142,927	35,108	50,181	12,632
November	100,889	25,317	127,818	37,584
December	60,898	17,436	75,386	21,160
Totals	544,662	$128,570	428,329	$101,824

The destinations of the exports during the last two years were as follows:

To	1903. Pounds.	1903. Value.	1902. Pounds.	1902. Value.
New Zealand	31,264	$ 7,379	29,420	$ 7,569
Australia	332,625	79,178	207,092	70,162
Hawaiian Islands*	22,563	4,964	10,655	2,500
China	26,156	5,955	7,035	1,079
Mexico	1,927	364	890	196
Central America	8,089	1,779	8,764	1,897
Japan	8,936	1,966	5,672	1,107
India	73,481	17,866	12,187	3,248
British Columbia	24,945	5,688	8,436	1,392
England	273	61	740	175
South America	8,263	1,918	827	160
Pacific Islands	259	57	1,000	181
Manila	3,318	729	2,743	704
Siberia	923	204	380	90
Siam	....	....	195	40
Eastern States	1,220	369	68,265	11,130
Elsewhere	420	93	1,028	194
Totals	544,662	$128,570	428,329	$101,824

* Domestic since June 14, 1900, and figures for 1902 are from June 1 to December 31, only. Figures for 1903 are for the full year.

LUMBER.

The receipts of Pine, Spruce and Fir lumber in feet, at San Francisco, from California, Oregon and Washington during 1903 and the two preceding years were as follows:

Months.	1903.	1902.	1901.
January	27,991,000	30,359,000	22,992,000
February	21,694,794	9,938,000	6,811,599
March	27,417,939	41,899,500	25,365,000
April	33,701,000	20,667,000	17,053,000
May	28,483,000	30,393,000	22,100,700
June	33,250,000	25,497,000	17,371,942
July	31,515,000	27,799,974	22,980,993
August	18,317,000	30,530,000	14,529,859
September	41,555,000	21,755,000	8,277,200
October	31,912,409	24,298,664	17,176,600
November	25,772,000	27,637,636	12,556,786
December	45,044,000	19,276,000	33,522,000
Totals	366,653,142	310,050,774	220,737,679

The total domestic and foreign shipments of Redwood lumber from all the mills in California during 1903 and the preceding year, in feet, were as follows:

Months.	1903.	1902.
January	22,083,459	21,035,886
February	20,091,229	15,956,254
March	23,822,095	21,735,879
April	21,588,305	22,343,626
May	24,478,915	24,396,295
June	21,985,050	18,945,062
July	28,449,281	21,542,527
August	26,969,961	23,915,025
September	27,296,068	21,397,652
October	29,286,753	23,628,073
November	27,455,381	23,782,344
December	27,837,456	23,918,392
Totals	301,343,953	262,597,015
Other Lumber	28,511,603	20,451,594
Total mill cut	329,855,556	283,048,609

Lumber.

The exports from San Francisco by sea during the past two years, were as follows:

To	1903. Feet.	1903. Value.	1902. Feet.	1902. Value.
Australia	9,666,736	$336,177	4,648,603	$166,591
Central America	924,937	24,622	2,060,370	52,056
England	2,282,069	65,559	4,997,821	91,156
Mexico	4,816,759	102,379	3,053,607	63,654
Tahiti	761,969	21,334	1,376,199	34,680
Samoa	616,817	16,965	738,736	15,306
Panama	144,166	4,261		
Japan	23,841	858	30,000	450
Siberia	14,739	735	47,490	1,032
Ecuador	5,000	55	10,133	240
Marshall Islands	4,500	50	65,926	1,535
Marquesas Islands	56,990	1,566	20,000	400
New Zealand	31,144	1,132	56,548	1,660
Germany	153,983	4,024	133,628	3,720
British Columbia	6,000	240	7,200	345
China	275,979	7,800	30,000	450
Fanning Island	18,980	762	153,000	4,688
South Africa	282,266	6,737	160,732	3,920
Caroline Islands	145,534	3,880	115,152	3,243
Manila	465,002	11,007	5,520	300
Peru	1,462,427	47,438	404,520	9,508
Chile	60,888	3,450	22,965	755
Colombia	183,381	4,903	386,751	9,844
Gilbert Islands			2,420	57
South Sea Islands	20,720	860	305,246	4,900
South America	16,500	720	47,000	1,175
Philippine Islands	10,000	370	398,759	6,797
Miscellaneous	334,259	6,158	280,473	5,488
Total Foreign	22,785,486	$674,042	19,558,849	$493,945
New York	43,688	1,944	16,321	760
Hawaii	659,729	17,929	574,262	15,724
Guam			398,759	6,797
Dunnage	2,410,975	40,490		
Totals	25,899,878	$734,405	20,548,191	$517,226

Dunnage for 1902 is included in enumerated shipments.

The record of exports from San Francisco by sea for a series of years past is shown as follows:

Year.	Feet.	Value.	Year.	Feet.	Value.
1893	14,124,601	$283,772	1898	22,080,922	$413,195
1894	18,427,812	354,362	1899	20,827,884	483,017
1895	17,671,082	300,031	1900	26,208,541	564,249
1896	33,620,005	650,448	1901	29,861,299	714,171
1897	26,057,484	476,813			

The shipments of lumber from San Francisco by sea during each month of the last two years, were as follows:

Months	1903. Feet.	1903. Value.	1902. Feet.	1902. Value.
January	3,265,129	$ 61,356	1,071,758	$ 19,042
February	818,404	17,288	1,648,504	39,718
March	812,699	22,004	1,467,936	37,863
April	2,078,894	61,373	2,510,240	64,570
May	784,396	23,241	3,307,096	80,845
June	1,046,909	32,627	1,360,174	31,380
July	2,797,083	88,706	910,428	18,435
August	3,847,725	123,596	1,430,374	33,247
September	2,195,829	63,465	1,304,920	26,731
October	3,111,008	101,657	1,921,237	47,437
November	527,487	14,152	1,725,682	45,978
December	4,614,315	124,940	1,989,842	59,832
Totals	25,899,878	$734,405	20,548.191	$505,078

LUMBER RECEIPTS.

The monthly receipts of Redwood Lumber at San Francisco during 1903 and the two preceding years, in feet, were as follows:

Month.	1903.	1902.	1901.
January	11,379,701	12,418,641	9,077,399
February	13,674,840	11,364,363	12,596,588
March	13,579,649	15,516,187	14,132,899
April	13,847,119	15,293,435	14,489,905
May	15,435,943	14,119,462	13,690,427
June	12,971,894	13,085,570	10,405,894
July	14,131,364	12,228,776	10,419,455
August	12,901,812	14,429,293	4,054,098
September	15,687,891	14,403,712	7,970,889
October	18,829,490	13,217,333	11,827,750
November	15,339,350	12,730,177	15,965,343
December	15,223,989	13,905,908	17,658,431
Totals	173,003,042	162,712,857	142,289,078

The total annual receipts for the seven preceding years were as follows:

Year.	Feet.	Year.	Feet.
1894	92,741,008	1898	118,148,890
1895	135,578,205	1899	141,465,146
1896	109,613,151	1900	136,760,974
1897	132,579,056		

THE WOOL TRADE.

Comparatively little wool is exported from California by the water routes, the bulk being shipped East by the overland railroads. Records of the latter, however, are no longer furnished for publication.

PRODUCTION.

The estimated production annually in this State since 1854 has been as follows:

YEAR.	POUNDS.	YEAR.	POUNDS.
1854	175,000	1879	46,903,360
1855	300,000	1880	46,074,154
1856	600,000	1881	42,204,769
1857	1,100,000	1882	32,448,349
1858	1,428,351	1883	40,484,690
1859	2,378,250	1884	37,415,330
1860	3,055,325	1885	36,561,390
1861	3,721,998	1886	38,509,160
1862	5,990,300	1887	31,564,231
1863	6,268,480	1888	32,567,972
1864	7,923,670	1889	34,008,770
1865	8,949,931	1890	34,917,320
1866	8,532,047	1891	33,183,475
1867	10,288,600	1892	35,802,930
1868	14,232,657	1893	33,169,375
1869	15,413,970	1894	36,968,400
1870	20,072,660	1895	35,356,690
1871	22,187,188	1896	27,195,550
1872	24,255,468	1897	32,534,230
1873	32,455,169	1898	28,063,240
1874	39,356,781	1899	22,000,000
1875	43,532,223	1900	21,360,000
1876	56,550,970	1901	22,040,500
1877	53,110,742	1902	25,835,700
1878	40,842,061	1903	22,500,000

BONDS AND STOCKS.

The monthly valuation record of sales of bonds at the San Francisco Stock and Bond Exchange during the past five years, is as follows:

Month.	1903.	1902.	1901.	1900.	1899.
January	$895,700	$800,600	$754,000	$500,850	$714,040
February	955,500	597,000	786,700	268,200	710,360
March	730,200	808,000	476,400	546,500	457,200
April	582,500	811,860	536,700	464,000	627,700
May	419,000	436,000	640,560	455,400	534,900
June	219,100	373,000	426,100	264,900	529,500
July	281,040	609,000	294,120	211,500	295,500
August	346,000	500,000	735,540	616,020	293,000
September	479,000	437,200	429,000	514,600	460,200
October	474,000	544,700	664,000	657,900	547,200
November	360,500	610,500	488,500	592,000	557,160
December	540,600	732,000	574,500	651,100	358,380
Totals	$6,283,140	$7,259,860	$6,806,120	$5,742,970	$6,085,140

The monthly totals of shares of miscellaneous stocks sold at the San Francisco Stock and Bond Exchange during the past five years, are as follows:

Month.	1903.	1902.	1901.	1900.	1899.
January	21,781	12,421	29,404	37,151	61,522
February	33,428	16,582	58,003	42,174	62,472
March	38,535	16,250	44,366	59,258	65,577
April	13,440	14,234	40,818	40,212	84,589
May	20,828	12,862	40,665	41,760	86,918
June	18,914	6,666	26,506	21,680	46,682
July	19,027	8,146	26,359	23,635	33,239
August	15,663	12,189	33,029	33,681	43,806
September	14,378	13,178	18,183	19,091	35,840
October	9,880	20,411	29,764	20,040	44,004
November	12,101	19,578	20,965	32,196	57,735
December	8,872	40,027	14,055	27,411	46,019
Total shares	226,847	192,544	382,117	398,289	669,403

SALES OF STOCKS.

The monthly record of sales of oil and miscellaneous shares at the California Stock and Oil Exchange during 1903 and the previous year is as follows:

Month.	1903. Shares.	1903. Value.	1902. Shares.	1902. Value.
January	267,019	$ 255,202	187,584	$ 81,633
February	322,445	219,358	288,562	76,447
March	190,908	151,982	214,293	109,364
April	236,268	115,571	442,231	239,938
May	401,454	154,386	213,483	185,594
June	154,720	117,928	110,435	54,140
July	74,594	71,890	53,165	35,832
August	181,478	119,231	69,193	57,207
September	113,019	69,046	50,856	40,802
October	73,460	30,322	61,525	32,659
November	69,067	24,703	72,698	63,853
December	82,452	41,700	97,396	72,201
Totals	2,166,884	$1,371,319	1,861,421	$1,049,670

INTEREST ON DEPOSITS.

The several banks in San Francisco which pay interest on deposits announced during 1903, the following rates per annum, payable semi-annually on the dates named.

Bank.	July 1, 1903. Ordinary.	July 1, 1903. Term.	January 1. 1904. Ordinary.	January 1. 1904. Term.
California Safe Deposit	3.00	3.60	3.00	3.60
Columbus Savings	3.25	....	3.25	....
French Savings	3.12½	....	3.12½	....
German Savings	3.12½	....	3.25	....
Hibernia Savings	3.12½	....	3.25	....
Humboldt Savings	3.12½	....	3.25	....
Mutual Savings	3.00	....	3.20	....
S. F. Savings Union	3.00	3.42	3.00	3.50
Savings and Loan	3.25	....	3.25	....
Security Savings	3.20	....	3.25	....
Union Trust Co.	3.00	3.30	3.00	3.25
Central Trust Co.	3.00	3.60	3.00	3.60
Market Street Bank	....	....	3.50	....
City and County Bank	3.00	....	3.00	....
Italian American Bank	3.60	....	3.60	....

INSURANCE.

Statistics of the Fire and Marine Insurance business transacted in the State during the last two years, as reported to the Insurance Commissioner, are as follows:

	1903.	1902.
FIRE INSURANCE.		
Amount written	$522,928,503 00	$486,501,972 00
Premiums on same	8,288,354 90	7,339,984 39
Losses paid	4,342,785 60	2,655,301 58
Ratio of losses to premiums	52.4	36.2
MARINE INSURANCE.		
Amount written	$210,567,904 00	$212,601,297 00
Premiums on same	1,511,365 30	1,692,599 26
Losses paid	1,034,522 92	1,074,070 22
Ratio of losses to premiums	68.4	63.5
This business was apportioned as follows:		
TO COMPANIES OF THIS STATE.		
Fire Insurance—		
Amount written	$38,016,887 00	$37,014,531 00
Premiums on same	669,681 04	607,772 12
Losses paid	315,569 93	212,029 06
Ratio of losses to premiums	47.1	34.9
Marine Insurance—		
Amount written	$31,541,270 00	$32,751,873 00
Premiums on same	271,580 87	296,133 35
Losses paid	142,228 54	193,322 25
Ratio of losses to premiums	52.4	65.2
TO COMPANIES OF OTHER STATES.		
Fire Insurance—		
Amount written	$254,571,365 00	$221,774,946 00
Premiums on same	4,036,864 07	3,380,841 86
Losses paid	2,123,241 19	1,265,583 10
Ratio of losses to premiums	52.2	37.4
Marine Insurance—		
Amount written	$11,527,261 00	$9,929,981 00
Premiums on same	135,715 77	123,057 52
Losses paid	82,349 04	73,069 09
Ratio of losses to premiums	60.7	59.4
TO COMPANIES OF FOREIGN COUNTRIES.		
Fire Insurance—		
Amount written	$230,350,251 00	$227,712,493 00
Premiums on same	3,581,809 79	3,351,370 41
Losses paid	1,903,947 48	1,171,689 42
Ratio of losses to premiums	53.2	35.1
Marine Insurance—		
Amount written	$167,499,373 00	$169,219,443 00
Premiums on same	1,104,068 66	1,273,408 39
Losses paid	809,845 34	807,678 88
Ratio of losses to premiums	73.3	63.4

REAL ESTATE.

The monthly totals of sales in the city and county of San Francisco during 1903 and the preceding year, are as follows:

Month	1903 Number	1903 Amount	1902 Number	1902 Amount
January............	572	$5,484,118	469	$3,993,583
February..........	562	4,330,643	440	2,593,489
March	631	4,283,687	500	3,668,013
April.............	624	4,101,124	570	5,329,010
May..............	586	4,261,938	468	3,977,432
June..............	566	3,276,675	469	3,808,816
July..............	493	3,800,500	415	2,646,285
August............	463	2,794,108	420	3,232,723
September.........	429	3,829,105	523	5,227,830
October..	469	3,259,314	590	4,262,367
November.........	499	3,912,355	444	3,832,045
December.........	471	4,376,590	505	4,818,919
Totals	6,365	$47,710,157	5,813	$47,396,512

The totals of sales for thirty-seven years past are as follows:

Year	Amount	Year	Amount
1867...............	$17,640,367	1886	$15,119,760
1868...............	27,217,026	1887...............	20,745,059
1869...............	29,937,717	1888...............	24,744,479
1870...............	15,630,192	1889...............	33,768,969
1871...............	12,717,792	1890...............	36,545,887
1872...............	13,127,458	1891...............	27,431,135
1873...............	12,383,752	1892...............	20,518,955
1874...............	23,893,903	1893...............	13,621,492
1875...............	35,889,374	1894...............	14,227,050
1876...............	24,058,666	1895...............	15,947,361
1877...............	18,549,991	1896...............	11,545,331
1878...............	14,583,967	1897...............	12,903,025
1879...............	10,318,744	1898...............	10,747,102
1880...............	13,994,989	1899...............	14,555,137
1881...............	12,233,933	1900...............	18,527,814
1882...............	15,127,750	1901...............	29,147,969
1883...............	15,876,408	1902...............	47,396,512
1884...............	13,374,207	1903...............	47,710,157
1885...............	13,134,354		

The records of mortgages and releases during 1903 and for a series of years, are as follows:

By Whom Taken or Released.	Mortgages. No.	Amount.	Releases. No.	Amount.
Private Individuals............	1,903	$ 5,567,572	1,591	$6,114,969
Hibernia Savings and Loan Society	1,293	10,308,205	1,108	7,019,350
Savings and Loan Society.. ..	211	1,417,031	144	508,385
French Savings and Loan Society..	215	1,198,550	74	472,381
German Savings and Loan Society..	571	5,025,715	438	2,790,064
Humboldt Bank......	262	1,086,850	122	664,100
San Francisco Savings Union.....	230	3,014,840	206	1,725,515
Security Savings Bank...........	98	776,600	69	679,600
Mutual Savings Bank......	311	1,924,225	175	879,105
Columbus Savings and Loan ociet	86	487,300	57	232,400
Union Trust Company....S.. .y	2	3,750	12	246,000
Central Trust Company.........	12	79,350	7	14,850
Totals..................	5,194	$30,889,988	4,003	$21,346,699

MORTGAGES.

Years.	Number.	Amount.
1902	4,783	$25,254,542
1901............................	4,111	20,148,304
1900............................	4,010	17,034,453
1899............................	4,909	13,817,496
1898............................	4,395	12,356,870
1897............................	4,322	13,817,716
1896............................	4,215	14,272,584
1895............................	4,747	17,652,007
1894............................	4,343	17,562,719
1893............................	3,791	13,743,444
1892............................	4,305	16,060,918

RELEASES.

Years.	Number.	Amount.
1902............................	3,953	$20,249,190
1901......	3,311	15,472,143
1900............................	3,230	14,711,964
1899............................	2,926	13,880,306
1898............................	2,602	10,154,754
1897............................	2,774	10,245,709
1896............................	2,680	10,768,545
1895............................	2,778	13,174,353
1894............................	2,639	12,666,359
1893............................	2,414	9,388,664
1892............................	2,674	10,315,614

CALIFORNIA PROPERTY.

Showing the State rate of taxation on each $100 of valuation from the organization of the State Government to the year 1903, inclusive:

YEARS.	Total Assessed Value of all Property in California.	Value of Personal Property.	Percentage of Personal Property.	State Rate of Taxation.
1850	$ 57,670,689	$ 13,968,797	24.22	$0.50
1851	49,231,052	20,935,116	42.52	.65
1852	64,579,375	24,213,395	37.49	.65
1853	95,335,646	33,674,000	35.32	.60
1854	111,191,630	39,040,428	35.11	.60
1855	103,887,193	34,858,319	33.56	.60
1856	115,007,440	40,942,699	35.60	.70
1857	126,059,461	59,149,630	46.92	.70
1858	125,955,877	54,185,728	43.01	.60
1859	131,060,279	56,580,344	43.17	.60
1860	148,193,540	68,369,383	46.06	.60
1861	147,811,617	73,350,591	49.62	.60
1862	160,369,071	74,014,666	46.15	.77
1863	174,104,955	80,496,645	46.23	.92
1864	179,164,730	78,117,375	43.60	1.25
1865	183,534,312	79,782,436	43.47	1.15
1866	200,368,826	92,490,635	46.15	1.13
1867	212,205,339	100,105,600	47.17	1.13
1868	237,483,175	105,112,083	44.26	1.00
1869	260,563,879	104,723,592	40.19	.97
1870	277,538,134	108,001,588	38.90	.865
1871	267,868,126	86,174,230	32.17	.865
1872	637,232,823	219,942,323	30.40	.50
1873	528,747,043	118,425,520	22.20	.50
1874	611,495,197	210,779,127	34.46	.649
1875	618,083,315	199,243,292	32.07	.605
1876	595,073,177	140,431,866	25.27	.735
1877	586,953,022	128,780,824	21.77	.63
1878	584,578,036	118,304,451	20.23	.55
1879	549,220,968	112,325,850	20.45	.625
1880	666,399,985	174,514,906	26.18	.64
1881	659,835,762	160,058,309	24.24	.655
1882	608,642,036	134,048,419	22.02	.596
1883	765,729,430	167,338,644	21.85	.497
1884	821,078,767	166,394,997	20.26	.452
1885	859,512,384	172,760,681	27.90	.544
1886	816,446,700	151,937,132	18.60	.56
1887	956,740,805	165,663,387	17.31	.608
1888	1,107,952,700	173,273,458	15.63	.504
1889	1,111,550,979	170,661,836	15.35	.722
1890	1,101,137,290	169,489,475	15.39	.58
1891	1,239,647,063	189,599,783	15.29	.446
1892	1,275,816,228	187,008,874	14.66	.434
1893	1,216,700,283	173,853,273	14.59	.576
1894	1,205,918,403	163,581,104	13.56	.493
1895	1,138,282,013	157,726,988	13.85	.685
1896	1,266,593,065	142,353,345	11.24	.429
1897	1,089,814,836	120,592,875	11.07	.51
1898	1,130,885,697	128,855,959	11.39	.488
1899	1,193,764,673	164,070,620	13.74	.601
1900	1,218,292,457	184,380,015	15.13	.498
1901	1,241,705,803	189,506,344	15.26	.48
1902	1,290,750,465	200,164,271	15.50	.382
1903	1,598,603,226	269,488,904	16.85	.561

The area and population of the counties of the State, together with the assessed valuation of all descriptions of property in each county during the last two years, makes the following showing:

County.	Area in Square Miles.	Population 1900.	Assessed Valuation 1903.
Alameda	840	130,197	$128,681,766
Alpine	575	509	422,063
Amador	568	11,116	4,918,908
Butte	1,764	17,117	16,057,766
Calaveras	990	11,200	6,177,275
Colusa	1,080	7,364	12,188,096
Contra Costa	750	18,046	21,753,956
Del Norte	1,546	2,408	2,882,445
El Dorado	1,891	8,986	4,668,840
Fresno	5,940	37,862	34,302,205
Glenn	1,400	5,150	10,645,524
Humboldt	3,507	27,104	24,911,492
Inyo	10,224	4,377	2,316,319
Kern	8,159	16,480	24,050,871
Kings	1,257	9,871	7,883,009
Lake	1,332	6,017	3,258,020
Lassen	4,750	4,511	4,590,748
Los Angeles	3,957	170,298	169,268,166
Madera	2,140	6,364	6,732,495
Marin	516	15,702	14,489,582
Mariposa	1,580	4,720	2,270,146
Mendocino	3,460	20,465	13,131,995
Merced	1,750	9,215	14,877,086
Modoc	4,097	5,076	4,076,680
Mono	2,796	2,167	1,151,109
Monterey	3,450	19,380	18,962,554
Napa	800	16,451	13,840,291
Nevada	958	17,789	7,203,349
Orange	780	19,696	13,812,566
Placer	1,484	15,786	9,677,724
Plumas	2,361	4,657	2,792,091
Riverside	7,008	17,897	16,373,296
Sacramento	1,007	45,915	41,333,337
San Benito	1,476	6,633	6,499,068
San Bernardino	20,055	27,929	21,392,228
San Diego	8,400	35,090	20,807,594
San Francisco	42	342,782	564,070,301
San Joaquin	1,370	35,452	34,740,535
San Luis Obispo	3,500	16,637	13,680,235
San Mateo	470	12,094	18,999,564
Santa Barbara	2,450	18,934	18,849,976
Santa Clara	1,355	60,216	61,390,817
Santa Cruz	425	21,512	12,560,071
Shasta	4,050	17,318	10,902,036
Sierra	910	4,017	1,844,560
Siskiyou	6,078	16,962	10,560,650
Solano	911	24,143	20,195,481
Sonoma	1,540	38,480	30,380,419
Stanislaus	1,486	9,550	12,834,208
Sutter	611	5,886	6,621,047
Tehama	3,200	10,996	11,674,562
Trinity	3,276	4,383	1,651,362
Tulare	4,935	18,375	17,447,042
Tuolumne	2,282	11,166	7,089,725
Ventura	1,850	14,367	11,171,219
Yolo	1,017	13,618	17,640,406
Yuba	625	8,620	5,898,350
Totals	156,931	1,485,053	$1,598,603,226

CALIFORNIA PRODUCTS.

The annual yield of some of the leading products of the State, with approximate values, for a series of years, and trade estimates for 1903 are as follows:

DRIED FRUITS.

\multicolumn{3}{c	}{PRUNES.}	\multicolumn{3}{c}{APPLES.}
Year.	Pounds.	Value.	Year.	Pounds.	Value.
1888....	8,050,000	$ 193,000	1888...	550,000	$ 40,000
1889....	17,150,000	860,000	1889....	500,000	36,000
1890....	16,200,000	810,000	1890....	1,000,000	75,000
1891....	27,500,000	1,360,000	1891....	1,800,000	110,000
1892....	22,500,000	1,140,000	1892....	2,750,000	170,000
1893....	52,180,000	2,000,000	1893....	3,800,000	230,000
1894....	44,750,000	1,700,000	1894....	5,850,000	350,000
1895....	64,500,000	2,800,000	1895..	4,560,000	275,000
1896....	55,200,000	2,400,000	1896....	2,350,000	140,000
1897....	97,780,000	3,750,000	1897....	5,250,000	320,000
1898....	90,420,000	3,600,000	1898....	3,520,000	215,000
1899....	112,827,000	3,950,000	1899....	5,900,000	356,000
1900....	159,460,000	4,650,000	1900....	6,360,000	390,500
1901....	81,600,000	2,400,000	1901...	6,450,000	392,000
1902....	197,000,000	5,670,000	1902....	9,750,000	5,862,000
1903....	115,000,000	3,467,000	1903....	9,000.000	5,475,000

\multicolumn{3}{c	}{PEACHES.}	\multicolumn{3}{c}{APRICOTS.}
Year.	Pounds.	Value.	Year.	Pounds.	Value.
1888....	8,650,000	$ 600,000	1888....	3,250,000	$ 300,000
1889....	5,250,000	370,000	1889....	2,500,000	225,000
1890....	12,250,000	850,000	1990....	8,500,000	765,000
1891....	13,250,000	925,000	1891....	13,500,000	1,080,000
1892....	13,500,000	940,000	1892....	12,500,000	1,040,000
1893....	16,800,000	1,160,000	1893....	9,500,000	800,000
1894....	30,540,000	2,120,000	1894....	28,750,000	2,250,000
1895....	24,500,000	1,705,000	1895....	10,650,000	900,000
1896....	16,460,000	1,050,000	1896....	6,740,000	610,000
1897....	27,150,000	1,890,000	1897....	30,125,000	2,450,000
1898....	10,960,000	765,000	1898....	8,240,000	750,000
1899....	34,800,000	2,430,000	1899....	11,600,000	925,000
1900....	34,340,000	2,260,000	1900....	28,080,000	2,250,000
1901....	29,510,000	1,982,000	1901....	15,750,000	1,260,000
1902....	50,420,000	3,587,000	1902....	37,525,000	3,108,000
1903....	30.000,000	1,987,000	1903....	19,000.000	1,720,000

Pears.

Year.	Pounds.	Value.
1888....	150,000	$ 10,000
1899....	140,000	9,700
1890....	600,000	42,000
1891....	1,000,000	68,000
1892....	2,250,000	157,500
1893....	2,640,000	180,750
1894....	6,530,000	457,200
1895....	5,400,000	375,000
1896....	9,650,000	675,500
1897....	6,350,000	434,000
1898....	6,620,000	460,000
1899....	5,760,000	403,000
1900....	14,550,000	1,018,500
1901....	6,510 000	460,000
1902....	5,250,000	465,000
1903....	4,500,000	430,000

Plums.

Year.	Pounds.	Value.
1888....	365,000	$ 15,000
1889....	330,000	13,500
1890....	1,000,000	42,000
1891....	1,250,000	51,000
1892....	2,000,000	84,000
1893....	1,500,000	62,000
1894....	2,760,000	112,500
1895....	4,500,000	190 000
1896....	2,100,000	87,000
1897....	3,250,000	135,000
1898....	2,460,000	100,000
1899....	3,360,000	136,000
1900....	3.900,000	160,000
1901....	3,450,000	120,000
1902....	2,560,000	103,500
1903 ..	2,200,000	96,000

Nectarines.

Year.	Pounds.	Value.
1888....	345,000	$20,750
1889....	275,000	16,500
1890....	525,000	32,000
1891....	625,000	38,000
1892....	720,000	45,000
1893....	780,000	47,500
1894....	1,250,000	75,000
1895....	1,325,000	80,000
1896....	625,000	37,500
1897....	285,000	17,250
1898....	190,000	12,000
1899....	840,000	50,500
1900....	875,000	52,500
1901....	650,000	42,000
1902....	910,000	56,250
1903....	600,000	43,500

Figs.

Year.	Pounds.	Value.
1888....	175,000	$ 8,750
1889....	225,000	11,250
1890....	360,000	18,000
1891....	365,000	18,250
1892...	500,000	25,000
1893....	890,000	45,000
1894....	1,550,000	77,500
1895....	2,750,000	140,000
1896...	2,165,000	108,000
1897....	3,250,000	160,000
1898....	4,780,000	240,000
1899....	5,800,000	290,000
1900....	6,000,000	300,000
1901....	6,500,000	325,000
1902....	7,250,000	357,500
1903	7,500,000	372,000

Dried Grapes.

Year.	Pounds.	Value.
1888....	2,340,000	$ 70,200
1889...	2,500,000	75,000
1890....	10,500,000	275,000
1891....	5,500,000	150,000
1892...	4,000,000	120,000
1893....	4,880,000	145,000
1894....	4,510,000	135,000
1895....	4,250,000	125,000
1896....	2,700,000	80,000
1897....	3,450,000	103,000
1898....	640,000	19,000
1899....	450,000	13,000
1900....	480,000	14,500
1901....	350,000	12,000
1902....	375,000	13,750
1903....	400,000	15,000

Hops.

Year.	Bales.	Pounds.
1888....	35,000	6,860,000
1889....	35,400	6,938,400
1890....	28,400	5,566,400
1891....	36,150	7,035,400
1892....	39,800	7,800,800
1893....	51,400	10,074,400
1894....	67,500	13,230,000
1895....	52,000	10,192,000
1896....	35,000	6,860,000
1897....	45,000	8,820,000
1898....	44,500	8,722,000
1899....	59,000	11,564,000
1900....	36,000	7,056,000
1901....	48,000	9,360,000
1902....	53,000	10,176,000
1903...	47.500	9,120,000

Walnuts.

Year.	Pounds.	Value.
1888....	1,000,000	$ 72,000
1889....	1,500,000	105,000
1890...	2,000,000	142,000
1891....	2,124,000	148,000
1892....	2,950,000	205,000
1893....	2,866,000	200,000
1894....	5,805,000	420,000
1895....	4,620,000	325,000
1896....	8,230,000	580,000
1897....	7,970,000	490,000
1898....	11,300,000	795,000
1899....	11,160,000	786,000
1900....	10,860,000	775,000
1901....	13,800,000	990,000
1902...	17,140,000	1,230,000
1903....	11,500,000	925,000

Almonds.

Year.	Pounds.	Value.
1888....	220,000	$ 25,000
1889....	450,000	50,000
1890....	250,000	28,000
1891....	500,000	60,000
1892....	1,066,000	120,000
1893....	720,000	80,000
1894....	2,125,000	235,000
1895....	1,850,000	205,000
1896....	3,210,000	356,000
1897....	4,750,000	525,000
1898....	900,000	100,000
1899....	4,640,000	515,000
1900....	5,480,000	600,000
1901....	3,000,000	288,000
1902....	6,540,000	524,250
1903....	6,000.000	476,500

ORANGES.			LEMONS.		
Season.	Cars.	Boxes.	Season.	Cars.	Boxes.
1888-89.	2,782	1,007,084	1888-89.	26	8,684
1889-90.	3,476	1,278 312	1889-90.	34	11,356
1890-91.	3,980	1,440,760	1890-91.	40	13,360
1891-92.	4,538	1,642,750	1891-92.	52	17,368
1892-93.	5,960	2,156,520	1892-93.	65	21,710
1893-94.	5,270	1,407,740	1893-94.	145	48,430
1894-95	7,985	2,890,570	1894-95.	335	111,890
1895-96.	7,268	2,631,016	1895-96.	565	186,610
1896-97.	7,682	2,670,884	1896-97.	1,378	460,252
1897-98.	16,120	5,835,440	1897-98.	2,410	804,940
1898-99.	11,280	4,083,360	1898-99.	1,230	410,820
1899-00.	18,978	6,870,036	1899-00.	2,520	781,200
1900-01.	25,340	8,200,080	1900-01.	3,260	1,010,600
1901-02.	19,910	7,207,420	1901-02.	1,830	585,600
1902-03.	24,560	8,890,720	1902-03.	3,150	982,800
1903-04.	32,000	11,584,000	1903-04.	3,850	1,201,200

HONEY.		BEET SUGAR.	
Year.	Pounds.	Year.	Pounds.
1888.	3,500,000	1888.	4,280,500
1889.	2,200,000	1889.	5,170,350
1890.	5,000,000	1890.	9,250,200
1891.	4,000,000	1891.	8,175,450
1892.	1,240,000	1892.	8,624,890
1893.	2,680,000	1893.	21,801,330
1894.	4,275,000	1894.	40,204,100
1895.	4,000,000	1895.	49,232,700
1896.	5,350,000	1896.	64,510,000
1897.	7,878,000	1897.	70,740,000
1898.	1,820,000	1898.	36,180,000
1899.	2,822,000	1899.	54,890,000
1900.	2,208,000	1900.	60,638,000
1901.	8,112,000	1901.	137,400,000
1902.	5,125,000	1902.	147,535,000
1903.	3,650,000	1903.	151,000,000

RAISINS.

The annual production of Raisins in California and the approximate value of the yearly crops for a series of years past is as follows:

Year	20. Lb. Bxs.	Pounds.	Value.
1870	1,200	24,000	$ 1,350
1871	2,000	40,000	2,100
1872	3,500	70,000	3,400
1873	5,950	119,000	6,000
1874	9,000	180,000	9,100
1875	11,000	220,000	12,000
1876	19,000	380,000	20,000
1877	32,000	640,000	34,000
1878	48,000	960,000	50,000
1879	65,000	1,300,000	68,000
1880	75,000	1,500,000	80,000
1881	90,000	1,800,000	91,000
1882	115,000	2,300,000	120,000
1883	125,000	2,500,000	132,000
1884	175,000	3,500,000	181,000
1885	475,000	9,500,000	490,000
1886	703,000	14,060,000	720,000
1887	800,000	16,000,000	825,000
1888	1,250,000	25,000,000	1,260,000
1889	1,633,900	32,678,000	1,640,000
1890	1,900,000	38,000,000	1,920,000
1891	2,600,000	52,000,000	2,650,000
1892	2,850,000	57,000,000	2,900,000
1893	4,250,000	85,000,000	4,300,000
1894	5,150,000	103,000,000	5,180,000
1895	4,658,000	93,160,000	4,672,000
1896	3,412,530	68,230,600	3,430,000
1897	4,685,200	93,704,000	4,725,000
1898	4,031,550	80,631,000	4,050,000
1899	3,578,400	71,568,000	3,590,000
1900	4,716,750	94,335,000	4,740,000
1901	3,712,500	74,250,000	3,765,000
1902	5,400,000	108,750,000	5,432,500
1903	5,600,000	112,000,000	5,586,500

CALIFORNIA'S GOLD.

Gold was discovered by John W. Marshall on January 24, 1848, at Sutter's Mill, near Coloma, El Dorado County. Since that time the annual production has been as follows:

Year.	Production.	Year.	Production.
1848	$ 500,000	1876	$16,099,559
1849	14,500,000	1877	15,237,729
1850	45,270,000	1878	18,839,508
1851	75,938,000	1879	19,626,166
1852	85,250,000	1880	20,030,745
1853	74,250,000	1881	19,223,000
1854	69,433,000	1882	17,146,500
1855	65,850,000	1883	24,316,873
1856	65,300,000	1884	13,615,000
1857	57,680,000	1885	12,779,725
1858	50,500,000	1886	14,716,506
1859	51,200,000	1887	13,588,614
1860	45,000,000	1888	12,750,000
1861	41,884,000	1889	11,212,913
1862	38,854,000	1890	12,309,793
1863	30,150,000	1891	12,728,869
1864	26,600,000	1892	12,571,900
1865	28,515,000	1893	12,422,811
1866	25,500,000	1894	13,923,281
1867	25,135,000	1895	15,334,317
1868	22,500,000	1896	17,181,562
1869	21,780,000	1897	15,871,401
1870	25,600,000	1898	15,906,478
1871	19,447,354	1899	15,336,031
1872	18,143,314	1900	15,863,355
1873	17,280,951	1901	15,730,700
1874	17,617,124	1902	16,910,320
1875	16,876,211	1903	17,500,000

Total product in 56 years.................................$1,517,327,610

SILVER.

The production of Silver in California for a series of years past is as follows:

Year	Production.	Year.	Production.
1887	$1,632,003	1896	$ 422,464
1888	1,700,000	1897	452,789
1889	754,793	1898	414,055
1890	1,060,613	1899	504,012
1891	953,157	1900	1,510,344
1892	463,602	1901	1,229,356
1893	537,157	1902	616,412
1894	297,332	1903	740,000
1895	599,789		

COUNTIES.	1902. VALUE.	1901. VALUE.	1900. VALUE.	1899. VALUE.
Alameda	$666,838	$786,366	$639,771	$508,709
Alpine	14,129	27,747		
Amador	1,679,113	1,888,191	1,479,009	1,593,720
Butte	926,251	879,767	500,786	504,795
Calaveras	2,371,013	2,355,372	1,905,856	1,303,188
Colusa	194,500	115,107	13,930	1,420
Contra Costa	55,141	101,900	146,900	135,113
Del Norte	5,450	10,612	3,483	4,450
El Dorado	381,578	347,263	426,420	425,346
Fresno	670,058	480,696	609,847	497,234
Humboldt	79,555	108,425	118,827	235,274
Inyo	184,414	668,618	420,586	473,851
Kern	3,481,926	2,423,918	1,867,856	1,027,366
Kings	19,000	5,000	5,000	11,550
Lake	288,231	331,684	172,745	204,103
Lassen	23,654	6,100	20,483	28,898
Los Angeles	1,697,932	1,642,591	2,155,198	1,729,964
Madera	121,151	400,825	268,467	115,620
Marin	206,600	128,227	202,500	81,150
Mariposa	647,298	542,975	171,516	565,636
Mendocino	9,898	10,720	8,448	8,788
Merced	1,656	12,453		
Mono	549,298	522,911	752,121	749,556
Monerey	39,253	50,169	19,175	17,378
Napa	410,968	516,388	493,100	701,416
Nevada	2,155,839	2,145,840	1,916,899	2,231,898
Orange	824,742	187,341	259,174	112,077
Placer	1,018,487	1,025,184	1,128,882	1,117,812
Plumas	381,203	403,832	369,379	381,166
Riverside	334,622	316,608	285,112	272,848
Sacramento	555,138	302,882	259,439	233,755
San Benito	328,231	255,219	205,650	290,495
San Bernardino	3,308,002	1,844,239	1,965,143	1,859,351
San Diego	562,730	514,522	402,061	381,215
San Francisco	395,100	156,947	58,400	275,694
San Joaquin	70,598	80,456	39,862	111,880
San Luis Obispo	200,391	116,083	85,626	68,548
San Mateo	330,745	15,725	16,500	58,225
Santa Barbara	315,550	300,148	528,438	318,528
Santa Clara	471,122	421,150	497,386	391,940
Santa Cruz	205,296	195,779	191,091	251,392
Shasta	3,730,049	6,737,571	5,574,026	4,661,981
Sierra	332,466	576,182	663,159	450,474
Siskiyou	1,094,745	1,067,451	1,010,383	991,871
Solano	170,140	12,600	24,700	16,937
Sonoma	198,803	173,147	157,135	142,330
Stanislaus	19,026	29,169	21,405	11,769
Tehama	3,500	6,000	2,200	19,800
Trinity	731,261	752,280	698,689	715,595
Tulare	62,398	69,526	21,566	20,810
Tuolumne	1,830,329	1,710,171	1,659,258	1,650,880
Ventura	483,986	350,570	476,161	613,450
Yolo	450	2,300	1,760	384
Yuba	155,632	189,754	284,631	189,939
Unapportioned	73,619	33,280	1,406,803	485,802
Totals	$35,069,105	$34,355,981	$32,622,945	$29,313,460

COPPER.			BORAX.		
Year.	Pounds.	Value.	Year.	Pounds.	Value.
1887....	1,600,000	$ 192,000	1887....	2,029,380	$116,689
1888....	1,570,021	235,303	1888....	2,809,088	196,636
1889....	151,505	18,180	1889....	1,939,650	145,473
1890....	23,347	3,502	1890....	6.402,034	480,152
1891....	3,397.455	424,675	1891....	8,533,337	640,000
1892....	2,960,944	342,808	1892....	11,050,495	838,787
1893....	239,682	21,571	1893....	7,910,563	593,292
1894....	738,594	72,486	1894....	11,540,099	807,807
1895....	225,650	21,901	1895....	11,918,000	595,900
1896....	1,992,844	199,519	1896....	13,508,000	675,400
1897....	13,638,626	1,540,666	1897....	16,000,000	1,080,000
1898....	21,543,229	2,475.168	1898....	16,600,000	1,153,000
1899....	23,915,486	3,990,534	1899....	40,714,000	1,139,882
1900....	29,515,512	4,748,242	1900....	51,674,000	1,013,251
1901....	34,931,788	5,501,782	1901....	14,442,000	982,380
1902....	27,860,162	3,239,975	1902....	34,404,000	2.234,994

ASPHALT.			BITUMINOUS ROCK.		
Year.	Tons.	Value.	Year.	Tons.	Value.
1887....	4,000	$ 16,000	1887....	36,000	$160,000
1888....	3,100	39,500	1888....	50,000	257,000
1889....	3,000	30,000	1889....	40,000	170,000
1890....	3,000	30,000	1890....	40,000	160,000
1891....	4,000	40,000	1891....	39,962	154,164
1892....	7,550	75,500	1892....	24,000	72,000
1893....	9,150	161,250	1893....	32,000	192,036
1894....	11,698	233,800	1894....	31,214	115,193
1895....	25,525	170,500	1895....	38,921	121,586
1896....	20,914	362,590	1896....	49,456	122,500
1897....	22,697	404,350	1897....	45,470	128,173
1898....	25,690	482,175	1898....	46,836	137,575
1899....	15,060	308,130	1899....	40,321	116,097
1900....	12,575	253,950	1900....	25,306	71,495
1901....	21,634	313,219	1901....	24,052	66,354
1902...	34,511	349,344	1902....	33,490	43,411

\<Salt\>			\<Coal\>		
Year.	Tons.	Value.	Year	Tons.	Value.
1887....	28,000	$112,000	1887....	50,000	$150,000
1888....	30,800	92,400	1888....	95,000	380,000
1889....	21,000	63,000	1889....	121,280	288,232
1890....	8,729	57,085	1890....	110,711	283,019
1891....	26,094	90,303	1891....	93,301	204,902
1892...	23,570	104,788	1892...	85,178	209,711
1893...	50,500	213,000	1893....	72,603	167,555
1894....	49,131	140,087	1894....	59,887	139,862
1895...	53,031	150,576	1895....	79,858	193,790
1896....	64,743	153,244	1896....	70,649	161,335
1897....	67,851	157,520	1897...	87,449	196,255
1898....	93,421	170,855	1898....	143,045	337,475
1899....	82,654	149,588	1899....	160,941	420,109
1900....	89,338	204,754	1900....	176,956	535,531
1901....	126,218	366,376	1901....	150,724	401,772
1902....	115,208	205,876	1902....	88,460	248,622

Clay (Pottery.)			Gypsum.		
Year.	Tons.	Value.	Year.	Tons.	Value.
1887....	75,000	$37,500	1887...	2,700	$27,000
1888..	75,000	37,500	1888....	2,500	25,000
1889...	75,000	37,500	1889....	3,000	30,000
1890....	100,000	50,000	1890....	3,000	30,000
1891....	100,000	50,000	1891....	2,000	20,000
1892....	100,000	50,000	1892....	2,000	20,000
1893....	24,856	67,284	1893....	1,620	14,280
1894....	28,475	35,073	1894....	2,446	24,584
1895....	37,660	39,685	1895...	5,158	51,014
1896....	41,907	62,900	1896....	1,310	12,580
1897....	24,592	30,290	1897....	2,200	19,250
1898....	28,947	33,747	1898....	3,100	23,600
1899....	40,600	42,700	1899....	3,663	14,950
1900....	59,636	60,956	1900....	2,522	10,088
1901	55,679	39,144	1901....	3,875	38,750
1902..	67,933	74,163	1902...	10,200	53,500

California Mineral Products.

LEAD.			LIME.	
Year.	Tons.	Value.	Year.	Value.
1887	580	$52,200	1887	$368,750
1888	450	38,250	1888	381,750
1889	470	35,720	1889	416.780
1890	400	36,000	1890	350,000
1891	570	49,020	1891	300,000
1892	680	54,400	1892	300,000
1893	333	24,975	1893	301,276
1894	475	28,500	1894	337,975
1895	796	49,364	1895	457,784
1896	646	38,805	1896	332,617
1897	298	20,264	1897	291,456
1898	328	23,907	1898	278,558
1899	360	30,642	1899	343,760
1900	520	41,600	1900	315,231
1901	360	28,820	1901	434,133
1902	175	12,230	1902	460,140

GRANITE.		ALL MINERALS.	
Year.	Value.	Year.	Total Value
1887	$150,000	1887	$19,785,868
1888	57,000	1888	19,469,320
1889	1,329,018	1889	16,681,731
1890	1.200,000	1890	18,039,666
1891	1,300,000	1891	18,872,413
1892	1,000,000	1892	18,300,168
1893	531,322	1893	18,811,261
1894	228,816	1894	20,203,294
1895	224,329	1895	22,844,663
1896	201,004	1896	24,291,398
1897	188,024	1897	25,142,441
1898	147,732	1898	27,289,079
1899	141,070	1899	29,313,460
1900	295,772	1900	32,622,945
1901	519,285	1901	34,355,981
1902	255,239	1902	35,069,105

RECEIPTS OF LEADING PRODUCTS.

The following shows the monthly receipts at San Francisco from California, Oregon and Washington during 1903:

MONTHS.	FLOUR, barrels. California.	FLOUR, barrels. Oregon, etc.	WHEAT, centals. California.	WHEAT, centals. Oregon, etc.	BARLEY, centals. California.	BARLEY, centals. Oregon, etc.	OATS, centals. California.	OATS, centals. Oregon, etc.	HOPS, bales. California.	HOPS, bales. Oregon, etc.
January	54,409	29,814	776,235	87,480	137,950	730	7,705	3,681	500	10
February	77,144	28,681	573,813	74,165	152,507	60	21,723	1,902	1,033	....
March	96,562	29,825	489,046	482,280	148,291	....	20,914	11,947	316	....
April	50,963	18,553	203,355	28,850	117,697	8,445	8,165	22,264	1,352	....
May	66,774	26,434	163,831	33,785	106,326	22,445	8,068	6,450	526	....
June	94,991	35,484	49,816	39,677	184,067	1,955	10,180	3,666	262	24
July	80,429	32,996	56,079	35,820	220,901	400	50,644	6,434	817	....
August	128,279	33,777	220,352	65,291	762,197	....	65,035	44,451	772	50
September	111,469	26,944	110,163	60,838	807,094	1,640	53,822	13,792	7,975	....
October	101,267	29,425	179,547	64,353	859,604	22,642	7,220	26,322	7,660	145
November	79,136	40,371	90,976	35,086	366,539	65,360	3,355	29,617	3,769	....
December	59,355	33,895	219,087	105,131	654,383		14,967	48,332	4,448	
Totals	1,000,778	366,199	3,132,300	1,082,933	4,517,456	123,677	217,798	218,858	29,430	229
1902	1,379,259	364,293	8,902,646	217,897	5,928,805	15,104	555,977	259,498	14,631	346
1901	1,325,093	349,914	9,864,255	9,360	5,943,032	....	570,600	233,402	8,913	22
1900	1,389,959	272,584	7,625,002	170,157	3,810,121	529	502,620	210,742	8,493	1,895
1899	1,178,094	363,903	3,457,173	291,803	4,230,114	87,079	449,521	241,435	8,015	782
1898	936,265	383,288	3,602,514	1,405,447	1,407,976	680,951	216,290	572,616	12,511	236
1897	970,805	330,532	8,921,191	696,515	4,457,720	4,127	240,945	284,655	7,862	253
1896	1,277,158	318,704	11,936,571	587,638	4,902,803	31,674	237,475	449,989	9,069	1,041

PRODUCE RECEIPTS.

The receipts of the leading commodities of produce at San Francisco, from all sources, during 1903, and the totals for a series of years makes the following showing:

1903	Flour, qr. sks.	Wheat, ctls.	Barley, ctls.	Oats, ctls.	Beans, sks.	Corn, ctls.	Rye, ctls.	Potatoes sks.	Onions, sks.	Bran, sks.	Middlings. sks.	Hay, Tons.	Hops, Bales.	Musd, sks.	Flax-seed sks.	Wool, Bales.
Jnry	345,629	870,715	140,337	16,284	34,407	12,798	2,662	133,146	14,582	55,194	14,599	12,364	537	408	26,979	1,136
February	423,080	656,951	152,567	26,748	13,826	15,136	7,665	121,595	10,253	97,879	11,210	12,333	1,033	87	37,392	598
Mch	465,919	596,236	148,539	37,442	20,360	29,685	6,760	108,388	8,408	56,525	13,594	11,585	316	505	3,697	3,685
April	285,434	232,205	126,412	38,065	21,712	11,445	5,671	88,589	7,774	14,168	11,764	13,518	1,362	....	5	11,082
May	339,487	194,098	135,511	16,422	21,821	9,789	3,610	68,529	14,177	12,773	7,900	12,773	526	977	8	13,271
June	517,796	93,098	203,400	13,816	16,521	10,902	5,143	81,115	24,075	58,617	12,492	13,813	276	2	1,369	4,068
July	453,720	91,619	264,973	71,839	9,322	6,380	6,040	90,536	15,409	49,009	15,836	21,077	837	468	....	4,821
August	630,193	283,135	915,230	160,457	11,432	14,355	5,636	123,909	14,466	51,557	14,659	26,604	772	....	....	5,924
September	532,651	173,485	1,012,690	176,799	79,987	16,824	7,687	93,815	23,794	49,956	12,814	22,202	7,975	328	2,627	5,829
October	513,126	217,665	957,313	127,652	254,368	7,328	5,905	123,121	22,659	58,315	14,947	16,067	7,805	747	5,570	10,320
Nvbr	478,576	126,552	429,950	49,942	101,554	16,550	3,425	142,139	12,037	79,023	13,749	8,705	3,769	839	....	3,796
December	462,298	324,218	733,075	71,218	62,961	12,546	4,660	139,172	9,280	48,157	16,174	10,450	4,448	....	8,974	2,078
Ttls, 1903	5,467,909	3,889,977	5,251,997	806,714	648,271	163,738	46,784	1,314,054	176,923	584,759	159,768	181,491	29,656	4,366	86,616	66,608
Totals, 1902	6,974,214	9,120,543	5,943,909	819,115	756,320	148,604	361,585	1,301,706	224,222	619,584	217,316	155,024	14,023	4,210	97,179	71,760
Ttls, 1	6,700,029	9,874,615	5,943,035	837,221	623,114	107,852	200,608	1,480,440	212,034	578,766	150,561	149,874	8,935	9,440	65,730	78,985
Ttls, 1	7,056,351	8,565,190	3,702,625	726,386	543,691	176,548	111,305	1,466,877	182,331	701,220	151,363	161,163	10,077	9,773	65,826	46,607
Ttls, 1	6,024,642	3,778,654	4,233,694	698,887	404,151	190,404	103,740	1,148,919	194,184	580,434	140,591	148,961	8,540	20,424	37,849	89,421
Totals, 1	5,253,977	4,961,680	2,076,821	780,559	450,082	298,467	43,306	1,203,601	177,991	672,253	128,445	128,993	13,033	4,718	23,017	58,675
Ttls, 1	5,200,910	9,647,248	4,527,187	536,353	586,800	541,530	110,935	1,114,463	130,566	555,898	124,127	147,410	7,394	16,887	17,879	100,097
Totals, 1	6,197,625	12,641,706	5,102,014	68,222	566,565	257,871	214,807	1,115,788	152,033	607,459	124,127	141,663	9,887	38,342	41,183	76,083
Totals, 1	5,203,094	12,255,849	2,798,638	630,805	562,086	212,166	44,180	1,079,000	140,305	520,853	138,331	142,788	11,932	58,782	96,672	95,814
Totals, 1	4,511,217	8,766,242	2,076,920	687,152	509,720	324,032	42,601	1,168,479	....	....	....	142,927	11,057	54,211	37,186	102,144
Ttls, 1	4,481,950	12,667,224	4,237,493	606,584	515,226	330,149	73,600	1,313,270	259,151	....	....	127,653	10,229	49,648	11,497	89,672
Totals, 1	5,332,405	10,435,610	2,746,878	593,398	648,909	262,042	72,999	1,259,157	....	....	....	123,810	7,650	28,307	51,891	96,380
Ttls, 1	5,862,388	18,183,133	2,710,538	595,782	402,076	369,904	139,336	1,274,607	....	....	....	126,540	9,418	24,851	69,011	86,352
Ttls, 1	5,917,700	14,209,226	1,851,346	532,332	420,595	367,680	146,967	1,355,418	....	....	....	132,042	10,154	29,412	56,155	101,490
Ttls, 1	5,597,109	13,246,621	2,255,560	586,484	368,135	213,712	51,273	1,351,897	....	....	....	124,264	14,149	27,941	72,203	109,746
Totals, 1	4,354,420	12,917,228	2,792,631	609,529	269,057	221,098	28,543	1,239,430	....	....	....	127,701	17,952	26,108	95,905	105,388
Totals, 1	3,600,315	9,602,631	2,055,366	414,812	423,530	281,600	32,277	961,200	....	....	....	117,360	....	37,734	58,195	110,769
Ttls, 1	4,885,772	16,527,503	2,184,560	508,717	361,320	218,100	26,275	1,079,593	....	....	....	99,442	....	43,828	88,704	114,098

NAVAL CONSTRUCTION.

The following is a complete list of warships built for the United States Navy by the Union Iron Works at San Francisco:

Name	Displacement Tons	Type	Horse power	Speed Knots	Launched
Charleston	4,040	Protected Cruiser	6,660	18.20	July 19, 1888
San Francisco	4,088	Protected Cruiser	10,604	20.17	Oct. 26, 1889
Monterey	4,350	Armored Monitor	5,810	16	April 28, 1891
Olympia	5,870	Protected Cruiser	17,313	21.68	Nov. 5, 1892
Oregon	10,500	Armored Battleship	12,000	16	Oct. 26, 1893
Marietta	1,000	Gunboat	1,040	12	March 18, 1897
Wheeling	1,000	Gunboat	1,003	12	March 18, 1897
Farragut	240	Torpedo Boat	5,600	30.60	July 16, 1898
Wisconsin	11,500	Armored Battleship	12,766	18 54	Nov. 26, 1898
Wyoming	2,700	Harbor Defense Monitor	2,900	12.70	Sept. 8, 1900
Perry	420	Torpedo Boat Destroyer	8,000	29	Oct 27, 1900
Preble	420	Torpedo Boat Destroyer	8,000	29	March 2, 1901
Ohio	12,440	Armored Battleship	14,600	18	May 18, 1901
Paul Jones	420	Torpedo Boat Destroyer	7,840	28.90	June 14, 1902
Grampus	120	Submarine Boat	70	8.50	July 31, 1902
Pike	120	Submarine Boat	70	8.50	Jan. 14, 1903
Tacoma	3,500	Protected Cruiser	4,500	16.50	June 2, 1903
California	13,800	Armored Cruiser	23,000	22	Building
South Dakota	13,400	Armored Cruiser	23,000	22	Building
Milwaukee	9,700	Protected Cruiser	21,000	22	Building

*Lost, November 7, 1899, on the north coast of Luzon, Philippine Islands.

SHIP BUILDING SUMMARY.

The following is a classified list of new vessels built on the Pacific Coast and documented at San Francisco for a series of years past:

Year	Vessels Steam	Vessels Sail	Total Vessels	Tonnage Gross	Tonnage Net
1887	23	31	54	17,629	13,908
1888	31	27	58	21,921	17,360
1889	28	18	46	8,544	7,091
1890	16	29	45	12,063	10,175
1891	9	35	44	8,939	8,585
1892	23	54	79	9,885	8,915
1893	6	15	21	2,897	2,394
1894	3	14	17	2,577	2,095
1895	6	16	22	1,584	1,350
1896	7	8	15	3,393	2,384
1897	4	6	10	961	705
1898	39	8	47	17,337	10,532
1899	13	7	20	6,675	5,701
1900	33	18	51	29,221	22,779
1901	25	16	41	11,519	9,669
1902	21	21	42	26,226	20,095
1903	21	4	25	21,025	14,210

SHIPBUILDING IN 1903.

List of the new vessels built on the Pacific Coast during the year 1903 that were documented at San Francisco.

Rig	Name.	Builder.	Where Built.	Gross T'nn'ge.	Net T'nn'ge
Steamer...	Hercules	H. Anderson	San Francisco	20.89	20
Steamer...	Pedro Costa	W. F. Stone & Co...	San Francisco	51.57	32
Steamer...	Lagunitas	W. A. Boole & Son..	Oakland	767.98	767
Schooner	Annie E. Smale		Marshfield, Or..	845.41	809
Steamer...	Rita Newman	W. A. Boole & Son..	Oakland	182.36	120
Steamer...	Whittier	Union Iron Works..	San Francisco	1,295.57	798
Steamer...	Ada Warren	R. W. Schultz	San Francisco	45.81	26
Steamer...	Cazadero	John W. Dickie	Alameda	1,682.69	991
Steamer...	Ramona	Risdon Iron Works	Alameda	575.85	362
Steamer...	Francis H. Leggett.	Newport News Co...	Newport News, Va.	1,606.65	975
Steamer...	Gretta A	M. J. Nunes	Freeport	53 33	38
Steamer...	San Gabriel	United Eng. Works	Alameda	484.99	312
Steamer..	San Jose	John W. Dickie	Alameda	1,115.46	758
Steamer...	Yerba Buena	John W. Dickie	Alameda	1,115.46	758
Steamer...	Pilot	W. J. Campbell	San Francisco	88.10	43
Schooner.	Sausalito	W. F. Stone & Co...	San Francisco	367.26	326
Steamer...	Brunswick	Rebuilt	Alameda	512.01	349
Steamer...	Topo	Hay & Wright	Alameda	229.67	173
Steamer...	Dauntless	Risdon Iron Works	San Francisco	269.90	144
Schooner	Ellen	E. Munder	San Francisco	84.15	72
Steamer...	Pomo		Fairhaven, Cal	368.41	235
Steamer...	Elizabeth	W. F. Stone & Co...	San Francisco	363.44	284
Steamer...	Arizonian	Union Iron Works..	San Francisco	8,671.60	5,621
Schooner	Siafiafi	M. Turner	Benicia	38.77	30
Steamer...	Chinega	United Eng. Works	San Francisco	188 01	167
	Totals			21,025.34	14,210

SHIP BUILDING IN 1902.

List of the new vessels built on the Pacific Coast during the year 1902 that were documented at San Francisco.

Rig.	Name.	Builder.	Where Built.	Gross Tonnage	Net Tonnage
Schooner	Soquel	W. F. Stone & Co.	San Francisco	767	698
Steamer	Phœnix	Hay & Wright	Alameda	256	160
Steamer	Santa Monica	W. F. Stone & Co.	San Francisco	497	318
Steamer	Spokane	Union Iron Works	San Francisco	2,036	1,289
Steamer	Redwood City	J. W. Dickie	Alameda	258	158
Barkentine	Amazon	Matthew Turner	Benicia	1,167	1,105
Steamer	St. Helena	Gratto & Reimers	San Francisco	344	263
Steamer	Prentiss	W. A. Boole & Son	Oakland	406	267
Schooner	C. A. Close	J. W. Dickie	Alameda	401	370
Schooner	Jas. F. McKenna	H. Anderson	San Francisco	95	81
Schooner	Charles W	E. Munder	San Francisco	80	71
Barkentine	Makaweli	W. A. Boole & Son	Oakland	899	821
Schooner	Mariposa	H. Anderson	San Francisco	95	81
Schooner	Covina	Schultze Bros	San Francisco	83	74
Schooner	Oakland	W. F. Stone & Co.	San Francisco	418	383
Steamer	Surprise	E. Munder	San Francisco	110	65
Schooner	Undine	H. Anderson	San Francisco	95	81
Schooner	M. Turner	Matthew Turner	Benicia	816	763
Barkentine	Fullerton	Hay & Wright	Alameda	1,554	1,494
Steamer	Isleton	Charles Ruling	Wood Island, Cal	615	534
Schooner	Ruby	J. W. Dickie	Alameda	345	306
Steamer	Ramona	J. W. Dickie	Alameda	1,061	671
Steamer	Sea Rover	Fulton Ship Bldg Co	San Francisco	199	116
Steamer	A. H. Payson	W. A. Boole & Son	Oakland	158	93
Steamer	Priscilla	Hay & Wright	Alameda	51	31
Steamer	Suisun City	A. M. Nelson	San Francisco	152	129
Schooner	Salem	W. F. Stone & Co.	San Francisco	767	698
Schooner	Redwood City	E. Munder	San Francisco	37	32
Schooner	Virginia	Hay & Wright	Alameda	585	541
Steamer	Sea Fox	J. W. Dickie	Alameda	69	35
Steamer	Centralia	J. W. Dickie	Alameda	487	324
Barkentine	Koko Head	W. A. Boole & Sons	Oakland	1,084	1,011
Steamer	Alaskan	Union Iron Works	San Francisco	8,671	5,621
Steamer	Nahualate	Geo. W. Kneass	San Francisco	20	14
Steamer	Kingfisher	Risdon Iron Works	San Francisco	263	141
Schooner	Taraug	Matthew Turner	Benicia	83	72
Barkentine	Puako	W. A. Boole & Son	Oakland	1,084	1,011
Steamer	Lady Nau	Peter Swanson	Belvedere	40	30
Steamer	Chignik	Andrew Wilson	San Francisco	16	6
Steamer	Ryba	H. P. Gray	Alameda	32	14
Schooner	Bedouin	J. F. Crosby	Alameda	20	15
Schooner	Mary Carathima	Geo. Carathima	Vallejo	10	8
Totals				26,226	20,095

SHIP BUILDING IN 1901.

New vessels built on the Pacific Coast during 1901 and documented at San Francisco.

Rig.	Name.	Builder.	Where Built.	Gross Tonnage	Net Tonnage
Steamer	Jersey	Jarvis & Son	Stockton	41	39
Steamer	Hanalei	Alexander Hay	Alameda	666	502
Steamer	Acme	John W. Dickie	Alameda	416	269
Sloop	Geo. F. Haller	Risdon Iron Works	Alameda	139	81
Steamer	Sea Prince	Fulton Iron Works	San Francisco	58	27
Steamer	Tyonie	R. W. Schultz	San Francisco	59	36
Steamer	Mohawk	J. R. Cresty	San Francisco	18	6
Steamer	Ugashik	G. W. Kneass	San Francisco	21	8
Steamer	Toglak	G. W. Kneass	San Francisco	21	8
Schooner	Katata	John Twigg & Sons	San Francisco	12	9
Steamer	Uyak	J. C. Beetle	Alameda	22	12
Steamer	Oneida	James Madison	San Francisco	21	7
Schooner	Crockett	E. Munder	San Francisco	62	56
Steamer	Newtown	Matthew Turner	Benicia	77	64
Schooner	Solano	Matthew Turner	Benicia	728	692
Steamer	Chilcat	Fulton Iron Works	San Francisco	172	98
Steamer	Hilda	United Eng. Works	San Francisco	18	6
Steamer	Ouinnat	United Eng. Works	San Francisco	31	14
Steamer	Alitak	United Eng. Works	Alameda	115	73
Steamer	Tamalpais	Union Iron Works	San Francisco	1,554	957
Schooner	Mindoro	Hay & Wright	Alameda	679	642
Steamer	Kayak	United Eng. Works	Alameda	679	642
Schooner	Helen	John A. Lockhart	Sausalito	15	9
Schooner	Kona	Alexander Hay	Alameda	679	642
Barkentine	Lahaina	W. A. Boole & Son	Oakland	1,067	994
Schooner	W. H. Marston	W. F. Stone	San Francisco	1,169	1,110
Schooner	Geo. W. McNear	H. Anderson	San Francisco	99	88
Steamer	Alma	F. C. Laurentzen	Rio Vista	11	10
Schooner	H. Eppinger	E. Munder	San Francisco	96	89
Steamer	Warrior	William Muller	Wilmington	122	83
Steamer	Gualala	John W. Dickie	Alameda	225	158
Steamer	Gov. M. B. M	E. J. Stone	San Francisco	14	10
Steamer	Valletta	W. J. Delonoy	Benicia	419	368
Steamer	Fox	R. W. Schultz	San Francisco	20	18
Schooner	Samar	Alexander Hay	Alameda	710	678
Barkentine	Amaranth	Matthew Turner	Benicia	1,109	1,062
Steamer	Elaine	W. F. Stone	San Francisco	14	9
Steamer	Martha Jane	J. E. Hicks	Sacramento	50	45
Sloop	Union	P. Swanson	Belvedere	13	9
Schooner	Theo. Roosevelt	Henry Schroeder	San Francisco	62	51
Schooner	Shell	Oliver Ortley	Alviso	16	13

SHIP BUILDING IN 1900.

List of the new vessels built on the Pacific Coast during the year 1900 that were documented at San Francisco.

Rig.	Name.	Builders.	Where Built.	Gross Tonnage.	Net Tonn'ge
Schooner	Expansion	Alex. Hay	Alameda	545	512
Steamer	Potrero	Risdon Iron Works.	Alameda	531	452
Steamer	Commodore	E. J. Stone	San Francisco	44	33
Schooner	Stanley		Fairhaven	355	253
Steamer	Reporter	John F. Twigg	San Francisco	38	26
Steamer	Robt. Dollar		Hoquiam, Wash	1,389	845
Schooner	Annie L.	E. Munder	San Francisco	60	53
Barkentine	Jas. L. Eviston		Marshfield, Or.	755	662
Steamer	Richmond	Fulton Iron Works.	San Francisco	135	77
Schooner	Churchill		North Bend, Or.	655	600
Steamer	Rainier		Hoquiam, Wash.	800	519
Steamer	Meteor	A. M. Wilson	San Francisco	68	40
Steamer	Santa Ana		Marshfield, Or.	1,250	814
Steamer	Nome City	H. D. Bendixsen	Fairhaven	1,660	1,294
Steamer	Kvichak		Portland, Or.	1,063	610
Steamer	Onisbo	Chas. Ruling	Woodland, Cal	632	605
Schooner	Luzon	Alex. Hay	Alameda	545	512
Steamer	Shelikof	Risdon Iron Works.	Alameda	173	101
Schoouer	Rosamond	Matthew Turner	Benicia	*1,080	985
Steamer	Eureka	C. P. Doe	Wilmington	484	312
Schooner	Wm. Olsen	E. B. Wright	Alameda	523	491
Steamer	Alexander Volta	Fulton Iron Works.	San Francisco	38	23
Steamer	Cordelia Heald	John L. Heald	Oakland	69	39
Steamer	John L. Kimball	C. G. White	Everett, Wash	1,588	1,208
Schooner	A. B. Johnson		Aberdeen, Wash	529	460
Steamer	Alton	James Gillis	Stockton	106	93
Schooner	Commerce	Alex. Hay	Alameda	658	621
Schooner	Forest Home		Marshfield, Or	763	682
Schooner	Ariel	Matthew Turner	Benicia	726	684
Schooner	Bainbridge	W. F. Stone	Port Blakely, Wash	566	496
Steamer	Santa Barbara	W. F. Stone	San Francisco	695	527
Steamer	San Pablo	Union Iron Works.	San Francisco	1,584	966
Steamer	Mandalay		North Bend, Or.	438	266
Steamer	Coronado		Aberdeen, Wash.	578	381
Schooner	Forester	Alex. Hay	Alameda	658	621
Steamer	Nonpareil	A. M. Wilson	San Francisco	62	31
Steamer	Eclipse	Matthew Turner	Benicia	211	163
Schooner	Nome	Matthew Turner	Benicia	231	193
Schooner	York	Matthew Turner	Benicia	231	198
Steamer	California**	Union Iron Works.	San Francisco	5,879	4,597
Schooner	R. C. Slade		Aberdeen, Wash.	673	601
Steamer	Rio Vista	E. Jarvis	Stockton	13	10
Steamer	King Fisher	R. W. Schultz	San Francisco	11	3
Steamer	Dawn	J. C. Beetle	Alameda	12	9
Steamer	Queen	Geo. W. Kneass	San Francisco	24	16
Steamer	Uganuk	John F. Twigg	San Francisco	13	8
Steamer	Islam	J. C. Beetle	Alameda	11	7
Steamer	Dorothy	W. F. Stone	San Francisco	8	5
Steamer	Letha R. Thomas	W. F. Stone	San Francisco	11	7
Steamer	Kid	Denis Sullivan	San Francisco	14	12
Schooner	Pathfinder	Matthew Turner	Benicia	86	71
	Total Tonnage			29,221	22,779

*Tonnage changed.

**Built for American-Hawaiian Steamship Company of New York.

As above stated the list comprises only the new vessels that were documented here. There were others built on the Coast, or in course of construction at the close of the year.

PACIFIC COAST TRADE.

The foreign trade of the Pacific Coast ports as shown by Custom House statistics during 1903 and for the five preceding years is as follows:

EXPORTS.

District.	1898.	1899.	1900.	1901.	1902.	1903.
Alaska	$ 64,419	$ 30,370	$2,532,198	$2,830,296	$ 1,573,537	$ 1,614,378
Hawaii			63,212	92,410	41,968	38,897
Humboldt, Cal.	151,594	192,367	248,020	233,154	409,803	673,877
Los Angeles, Cal.	8,614	691		110	237	733
Oregon	257,365	130,786	87,125	167,034	155,517	43,843
Puget Sound, Wash	15,649,512	15,498,991	19,612,077	26,810,563	34,856,859	27,450,507
San Diego, Cal.	144,928	2,629,366	1,573,238	1,058,394	159,832	314,616
San Francisco, Cal.	31,998,805	34,270,833	37,940,334	37,690,908	37,897,793	32,650,248
Southern Oregon				7,784	20,364	9,277
Willamette, Or.	12,801,913	7,273,233	9,007,043	11,927,476	11,524,391	9,965,904
Total	$61,077,150	$60,026.637	$71,063,247	$80,813,130	$86,640,301	$72,762,280

IMPORTS.

District	1898.	1899.	1900.	1901.	1902.	1903.
Alaska	$ 231,106	$ 272,847	$ 544,500	$ 532,786	$ 495,287	$ 526,834
Hawaii			1,285,567	3,081,949	2,981,473	3,643,699
Humboldt, Cal	1,241	2.643	831	1,908	2,264	8,201
Los Angeles, Cal.	620,585	857,323	858,273	862,555	653,146	1,379,302
Oregon	23,837	22,593	9,442	5,394	3,715	20,598
Puget Sound, Wash	4,969,566	8,774.811	5,686,256	9,212,206	12,722,765	12,133,230
San Diego, Cal.	249,440	465,114	605,738	564,841	355,825	433,835
San Francisco, Cal.	36,057,958	45,767,110	39,402,935	37,267,279	36,078,270	36,552,187
Southern Oregon						
Willamette, Or.	1,538,887	1,617,162	1,510,075	1,664,409	2,912,565	2,708,677
Total	$43,692,620	$57,779,603	$49,903,617	$53,193,327	$56,208,250	$57,406,563

AMERICAN COMMERCE.

The foreign trade of the United States during 1903 and for a series of years preceding was as follows:

EXPORTS.

Years.	Atlantic ports.	Gulf ports.	Mexican border ports.	Pacific ports.	Northern border and Lake ports.	Interior ports.	Total.
1893	$ 642,798,894	$131,272,337	$10,257,106	$38,935,502	$ 52,844,942	....	$ 876,108,871
1894	616,964,745	120,071,849	7,842,214	31,901,916	48,321,524	....	825,102,248
1895	596,244,559	120,300,517	9,456,585	41,323,860	57,534,615	....	824,860,136
1896	701,114,790	170,452,067	13,079,106	58,109,021	63,081,720	$ 537	1,005,837,241
1897	772,210,869	181,028,211	12,503,778	63,757,679	70,208,508	....	1,099,700,045
1898	892,299,004	202,213,778	13,755,997	61,077,150	85,916,958	283,379	1,255,546,266
1899	896,532,699	203,368,668	18,295,824	60,026,637	97,039,277	204,866	1,275,467,971
1900	1,007,331,868	269,602,629	23,952,224	71,063,247	105,399,653	596,492	1,477,946,113
1901	967,306,139	286,423,623	21,091,035	80,813,130	109,473,533	268,400	1,465,375,860
1902	876,668,535	257,117,589	26,312,984	86,640,301	113,966,370	156	1,360,705,935
1903	919,901,648	331,596,006	26,557,923	72,761,077	133,864,212	1,129	1,484,681,995

IMPORTS.

Years.	Atlantic ports.	Gulf ports.	Mexican border ports.	Pacific ports.	Northern border and Lake ports.	Interior ports.	Total.
1893	$642,017,157	$23,828,271	$11,690,959	$42,438,310	$48,742,000	$7,532,227	$776,248,924
1894	561,917,691	18,261,817	4,839,937	41,891,106	43,116,293	6,286,097	676,312,941
1895	666,525,645	18,240,986	3,508,967	46,280,572	58,640,532	8,472,645	801,669,317
1896	564,591,938	16,907,176	3,265,497	42,630,130	46,965,529	7,219,286	681,579,556
1897	616,303,353	17,756,220	4,357,113	50,965,808	46,733,790	6,478,947	742,595,229
1898	522,454,966	13,581,717	5,595,559	43,692,620	42,674,712	6,964,874	634,964,448
1899	654,472,890	20,073,280	4,866,232	57,779,603	53,695,939	8,079,556	798,967,410
1900	680,896,076	26,221,750	5,974,725	49,903,617	56,631,969	9,521,577	829,149,714
1901	707,303,987	29,824,241	13,610,845	53,193,327	64,798,449	11,689,061	880,419,910
1902	775,545,306	35,365,542	14,230,246	56,208,250	75,119,815	12,851,794	969,320,953
1903	788,609,803	39,027,740	12,112,383	57,406,563	83,356,557	14,934,129	995,447,175

The destinations of shipments from the United States to foreign countries during 1903 and for a series of years preceding were as follows:

EXPORTS.

Years.	Europe.	North America.	South America.	Asia and Oceania.	Africa and other countries.	Total.
1893......	$ 679,616,358	$125,283,901	$34,322,834	$31,038,953	$ 5,846,740	$ 876,108,781
1894......	642,025,857	111,009,647	34,626,296	30,729,262	6,711,186	825,102,248
1895......	634,386,087	114,225,264	34,171,572	33,073,633	9,003,580	824,860,136
1896......	778,105,762	120,640,196	34,235,923	55,822,854	17,032,506	1,005,837,241
1897......	858,049,510	129,468,932	33,506,140	62,005,036	16,679,427	1,099,709,045
1898......	981,230,370	149,164,257	35,102,408	71,937,761	18,111,470	1,255,546,266
1899......	959,202,820	168,854,567	37,421,700	91,386,490	18,602,394	1,275,467,971
1900......	1,116,399,524	198,788,019	41,248,051	98,531,349	22,979,170	1,477,946,113
1901......	1,099,574,016	199,239,040	42,553,758	94,356,953	29,652,093	1,465,375,860
1902......	984,752,850	204,432,970	38,944,090	96,204,562	36,351,461	1,360,685,933
1903......	1,087,049,843	227,322,260	46,357,644	92,736,777	31,215,471	1,484,681,995

IMPORTS.

Years.	Europe.	North America.	South America.	Asia and Oceania.	Africa and other countries.	Total.
1893......	$392,161,248	$170,874,163	$103,540,680	$102,706,126	$ 6,966,707	$776,248,924
1894......	317,511,443	160,081,965	103,856,505	88,696,826	6,166,202	676,812,941
1895......	431,539,496	138,923,253	117,406,577	105,252,034	8,547,987	801,669,347
1896......	360,213,449	106,400,055	99,785,611	105,529,008	9,651,438	681,579,556
1897......	407,970,382	101,762,584	103,412,125	119,884,603	9,535,585	742,595,229
1898......	324,726,482	97,830,811	83,075,415	121,194,394	8,137,346	684,964,448
1899......	402,512,977	123,464,933	91,728,862	169,520,002	11,740,636	798,967,410
1900......	441,610,461	130,361,458	102,706,638	143,445,861	11,025,306	829,149,714
1901......	454,496,214	158,731,376	120,384,181	135,907,052	10,901,087	880,419,910
1902......	513,731,154	172,990,251	109,401,111	160,711,952	12,482,402	969,316,870
1903......	527,878,256	182,014,342	113,260,952	161,434,499	10,859,126	995,447,175

Classified, the annual foreign trade of the United States for a series of years past, as shown by Custom House reports, is as follows:

YEARS.	IMPORTS.			EXPORTS.		
	Free of duty.	Dutiable.	Total.	Domestic.	Foreign.	Total.
1867	$ 16,923,552	$354,552,623	$371,476,175	$ 294,983,527	$15,155,340	$ 310,138,867
1868	18,404,354	349,602,218	368,006,572	269,844,993	11,476,475	281,321,468
1869	21,775,643	416,680,251	438,455,894	324,421,333	12,954,655	337,375,988
1870	21,189,105	439,942,953	461,132,058	387,780,302	15,805,708	403,586,010
1871	47,316,643	525,794,456	578,111,099	445,563,259	14,788,829	460,352,088
1872	94,094,635	561,870,064	655,964,699	452,143,553	16,694,895	468,887,948
1873	141,473,322	453,774,726	595,248,048	550,098,492	17,659,875	567,757,867
1874	159,076,057	403,039,850	562,115,907	553,929,842	25,948,211	569,872,553
1875	145,185,903	357,967,033	503,152,936	497,263,737	13,683,685	510,947,422
1876	128,031,139	299,316,026	427,347,165	575,735,804	14,980,825	590,666,629
1877	154,456,844	325,789,456	480,246,300	607,566,495	12,735,917	620,302,412
1878	139,443,607	292,368,876	431,812,483	723,286,821	13,805,252	737,092,078
1879	174,643,157	338,959,689	513,602,796	754,656,755	10,503,070	765,159,825
1880	206,583,345	490,223,881	696,807,176	875,564,075	14,119 347	889,683,422
1881	206,910,261	463,299,187	670,209,448	814,162,951	19,386,176	833,549,127
1882	214,036,390	538,807,117	752,848,507	749,911,309	18,070,687	767,981,946
1883	205,111,054	481,955,162	687,066,216	777,528,718	17,685,598	795,209,316
1884	203,321,386	425,940,474	629,261,860	733,768,764	15,597,466	749,366,428
1885	195,782,174	392,086,499	587,868,673	673,598,507	14,656,292	688,249,798
1886	219,887,787	443,541,402	663,429,189	699,519,430	18,884,591	718,404,021
1887	239,781,913	469,036,565	708,818,478	703,319,692	11,981,352	715,301,044
1888	248,590,235	476,821,186	725,411,871	679,597,477	12,163,573	691,761,050
1889	261,164,484	509,357,481	770,521,965	814,154,864	12,951,488	827,106,347
1890	288,528,328	534,869,398	823,397,726	845,999,603	11,502,945	857,502,548
1891	429,835,677	398,985,266	828,820,943	957,835,551	13,176,095	970,509,646
1892	446,978,931	593,952,024	840,980,955	923,237,315	15,183,345	938,420,660
1893	417,344,174	258,904,750	776,248,924	854,729,454	21,879,327	876,108,781
1894	383,371,933	292,941,008	676,312,941	807,312,116	17,790,132	825,102,248
1895	384,816,131	416,853,216	801,669,347	807,742,415	17,117,721	824,860,136
1896	322,952,457	358,627,099	681,579,556	986,830,080	19,007,161	1,005,837,241
1897	377,288,396	365,306,833	742,595,229	1,079,834,296	19,874,749	1,099,709,045
1898	268,384,173	366,580,275	634,964,448	1,233,558,140	21,988,126	1,255,546,266
1899	350,897,220	448,070,190	798,967,410	1,252,982,344	22,585,627	1,275,467,971
1900	342,288,761	486,860,958	829,149,714	1,453,010,112	24,936,001	1,477,946,113
1901	381,512,618	498,907,292	880,419,910	1,438,078,651	27,297,209	1,465,375,860
1902	408,640,299	560,676,571	969,316,870	1,333,268,491	27,417,442	1,360,685,933
1903	437,394,968	558,052,207	995,447,175	1,457,575,865	27,106,130	1,484,681,995

RAINFALL IN SAN FRANCISCO.

Compiled by U. S. Weather Bureau.

SEASON.	July.	Aug.	Sept.	Oct.	Nov.	Dec.	Total 6 Mos.	Jan.	Feb.	Mar.	Apr.	May.	June.	Total 6 Mos.	Total Season
1849-50	....	....	....	3.14	8.66	6.20	18.00	8.34	1.77	4.53	.46	....	....	15.10	33.10
1850-51	....	....	.33	....	.92	1.05	2.30	.72	.54	1.94	1.23	.67	....	5.10	7.40
1851-52	....	....	1.03	.21	2.12	7.10	10.46	.58	.14	6.68	.26	.82	....	7.98	18.44
1852-53	....	....	....	.80	5.31	13.20	19.31	3.92	1.42	4.86	5.37	.38	....	15.95	35.26
1853-54	....	.04	.46	.12	2.28	2.32	5.22	3.88	8.04	3.51	3.12	.02	.08	18.65	23.87
1854-55	....	.01	.15	2.41	.34	.81	3.72	3.67	4.77	4.64	5.00	1.88	....	19.96	23.68
1855-56	....	....	....	....	.67	5.76	6.43	9.40	.50	1.60	2.94	.76	.03	15.23	21.66
1856-57	.02	....	.07	.45	2.79	3.75	7.08	2.45	8.59	1.62	....	.02	.12	12.80	19.88
1857-58	....	.05	....	.93	3.01	4.14	8.13	4.36	1.83	5.55	1.55	.34	.05	13.	21.81
1858-59	.05	.16	....	2.74	.69	6.14	9.78	1.28	6.32	3.02	.27	1.05	....	12.	
1859-60	....	.02	.03	.05	7.28	1.57	8.95	1.64	1.60	3.99	3.14	2.86	.09	13.	
1860-61	.21	....	....	.91	.58	6.16	7.86	2.47	3.72	4.08	.51	1.00	.08	11.	
1861-62	....	....	....	.02	4.10	9.51	13.66	24.36	7.53	2.20	.73	.74	.05	35.	22.22
1862-63	....	....	....	.40	.15	2.35	2.90	3.63	3.19	2.06	1.61	.23	....	10.	18.11
1863-64	....	....	.03	....	2.55	1.80	4.38	1.83	....	1.52	1.57	.78	....	5.	10.08
1864-65	....	.21	.01	.13	6.68	8.91	15.94	5.14	1.34	.74	.94	.63	....	8.	24.
1865-66	....	....	.24	.26	4.19	.58	5.27	10.88	2.12	3.04	.12	1.46	.04	17.	22.79
1866-67	....	....	.11	....	3.35	15.16	18.62	5.16	7.20	1.58	2.36	....	....	16.	34.93
1867-68	....	.04	....	.20	3.41	10.69	14.34	9.50	6.13	6.30	2.31	.03	.23	24.	38.84
1868-69	....	....	....	.15	1.18	4.34	5.67	6.35	3.90	3.14	2.19	.08	.02	15.	
1869-70	....	....	.12	1.29	1.19	4.31	6.91	3.89	4.78	2.00	1.53	.20	....	12.	
1870-71	....	....	.03	....	.43	3.38	3.84	3.07	3.76	1.29	1.98	.21	....	10.	
1871-72	....	....	.03	.11	3.72	16.74	20.60	4.22	6.97	1.64	1.10	.16	.02	14.68	
1872-73	....	....	.14	.21	2.62	7.25	10.22	2.17	4.24	.78	.52	.01	.08	7.80	35
1873-74	.03	.15	....	.68	1.31	10.12	12.29	4.85	1.83	3.55	1.04	.34	.08	11.69	21.98
1874-75	....	....	.08	2.73	5.92	.28	9.01	6.97	.20	1.08	.02	.11	1.01	9.39	18.40
1875-76	....	....	....	.22	6.73	3.08	10.03	6.41	3.96	4.37	1.04	.18	.02	15.98	26.01
1876-77	.01	.01	.38	3.36	.25	....	4.01	4.32	1.18	1.05	.26	.18	.01	7.03	11.04
1877-78	.02	....	....	.65	1.57	2.66	4.90	11.97	12.52	4.56	1.06	.16	.01	30.28	35.18
1878-79	.01	T	.55	1.27	.57	.58	2.98	3.52	4.90	8.75	1.89	2.35	.05	21.46	24.44
1879-80	.01	.02	T	.78	4.03	4.46	9.30	2.23	1.87	2.08	10.06	1.12	....	17.36	26.66
1880-81	....	....	....	.05	.33	12.33	12.71	8.69	4.65	.90	2.00	.22	.69	17.15	29.86
1881-82	....	....	.25	.54	1.94	3.85	6.58	1.68	2.96	3.45	1.22	.21	.04	9.56	16.14
1882-83	....	....	.26	2.66	4.18	2.01	9.11	1.92	1.04	3.01	1.51	3.52	.01	11.01	20.12
1883-84	....	....	.42	1.48	1.60	.92	4.42	3.94	6.65	8.24	6.33	.23	2.57	27.96	32.38
1884-85	....	.04	.33	2.55	.26	7.68	10.86	2.53	.30	1.01	3.17	.04	.19	7.24	18.10
1885-86	.06	....	.11	.72	11.78	4.99	17.66	7.42	.24	2.07	5.28	.37	.01	15.39	33.05
1886-87	.23	....	.01	1.48	.84	2.07	4.63	1.90	9.24	.84	2.30	.06	.07	14.41	19.04
1887-88	....	.01	.29	....	.99	3.34	4.63	6.81	.94	3.60	.11	.38	.27	12.11	16.74
1888-89	.01	.01	.98	.13	3.99	5.80	10.92	1.28	.72	7.78	.96	2.17	.08	12.94	23.86
1889-90	.01	....	....	7.28	2.90	13.81	24.00	9.61	5.16	4.73	1.18	1.07	.10	21.85	45.85
1890-91	.02	....	.31	....	....	3.25	3.58	.98	7.26	1.96	2.44	1.25	.11	14.00	17.58
1891-92	.10	.02	.77	.04	.56	5.62	7.11	2.42	2.90	2.85	1.39	1.86	T	11.42	18.58
1892-93	....	....	.02	1.65	3.91	5.08	10.66	3.05	2.75	4.08	1.03	.15	.33	11.39	22.05
1893-94	.02	....	.21	.16	4.18	2.25	6.82	5.99	2.69	.60	.50	1.31	56	11.65	18.47
1894-95	....	T	....	2.64	1.73	.88	9.01	14.26	8.14	.28	2.85	5.16	.72	....	17.15	21.25
1895-96	.01	....	.77	.11	1.78	1.43	4.10	8.14	.28	2.85	5.16	.72	....	17.15	21.25
1896-97	.04	.09	.52	1.55	4.56	4.34	11.10	2.26	4.41	4.56	.27	.61	.22	12.33	23.48
1897-98	T	T	.10	1.70	1.05	1.22	4.07	1.12	2.13	.24	.19	1.44	.19	5.31	9.88
1898-99	....	....	T	1.06	.86	.46	1.62	4.00	3.67	.10	7.61	.62	.86	.01	12.87	16.87
1899-1900	....	....	T	....	3.92	3.79	2.65	10.36	4.11	.64	1.91	1.08	.32	05	8.11	18.47
1900-01	....	....	T	.46	1.48	3.91	1.37	7.22	5.79	5.03	80	1.64	.69	T	13.95	21.17
1901-02	T	T	T	.78	.64	3.48	.90	5.80	1.23	7.27	2.65	.98	1.05	T	13.18	18.98
1902-03	T	T	T	1.70	1.98	2.32	6.00	3.73	1.76	6.23	.56	T	T	12.28	18.28

T indicates a trace of precipitation.

MONTHLY AND ANNUAL MEAN TEMPERATURE AT STATIONS IN CALIFORNIA DURING SEASON OF 1901-02.

Compiled by U. S. Weather Bureau.

STATIONS.	1902. July	Aug.	Sept.	Oct.	Nov.	Dec.	1903. Jan.	Feb.	Mar.	Apr.	May.	June.	Annual Mean.
Anaheim	67.4	71.2	67.9	64.9	59.0	61.0	62.2	55.7	57.2	62.4	68.1	69.7	63.9
Angiola	77.5	76.4	74.8	62.2	49.0	44.6	42.1	43.2	53.4	56.6	66.6	75.7	60.2
Antioch	75.0	73.2	72.1	65.0	54.8	50.8	50.6	45.8	55.1	60.0	72.1	79.7	62.8
Aptos	61.8	63.1	62.1	57.1	49.3	47.0	51.2	47.4	51.4	52.8	62.2	63.8	55.8
Auburn	79.7	.....	.....	61.8	52.9	46.0	44.8	41.8	48.4	55.0	73.6	79.0	.....
Azusa	72.7	73.2	72.8	65.0	57.6	54.8	56.2	52.2	58.0	61.4	63.8	70.0	63.1
Bakersfield	78.4	77.6	75.4	.....	.....	47.2	44.9	45.1	54.8	58.4	69.2	77.3	.....
Berkeley	63.0	63.3	63.6	59.0	52.1	48.2	46.4	46.1	50.8	53.4	57.6	62.9	55.5
Biggs	77.7	74.2	72.5	61.3	49.9	45.2	48.4	41.4	49.1	57.5	68.5	75.0	59.6
Bishop	72.2	69.5	67.4	55.0	42.4	38.4	42.4	36.4	44.5	50.4	59.6	69.0	53.9
Blue Canon	71.8	67.8	64.3	52.4	40.2	38.5	39.8	32.7	38.6	44.8	57.1	64.8	51.1
Boca	62.1	57.6	56.6	.....	.....	27.0	28.7	14.2	31.6	37.1	45.9	52.2	.....
Bodie	54.4	51.3	48.4	35.2	24.7	22.2	23.0	11.3	21.0	30.2	40.0	49.9	34.3
Bowman's Dam	66.7	66.4	64.6	49.8	38.6	36.0	36.0	29.1	34.6	41.8	54.8	63.2	48.5
Branscomb	.....	.....	.....	.....	.....	.....	.....	.....	44.3	46.6	56.2	61.2	.....
Byron	77.2	73.8	69.9	60.4	52.1	45.5	44.0	43.6	50.7	58.4	65.6	73.0	59.5
Cabazon	79.6	75.2	77.3	64.6	58.0	60.2	55.7	49.3	57.8	59.8	61.8	74.8	64.5
Caliente	84.8	80.3	83.6	64.0	58.0	48.6	45.7	44.2	49.4	56.7	78.0	86.0	63.6
Calistoga	68.3	71.1	72.0	62.0	55.5	51.4	44.7	48.8	50.6	55.8	64.0	70.8	59.6
Campbell	65.4	66.4	65.2	58.6	50.8	47.0	44.8	51.4	52.4	58.6	63.0	55.9
Cedarville	65.4	66.5	61.4	49.2	37.2	32.6	32.1	23.2	37.8	41.0	52.8	63.8	46.9
Chico	76.2	75.9	72.4	.....	.....	46.2	41.8	41.3	51.0	56.4	68.4	75.0	.....
Chino	78.1	78.4	71.2	63.0	57.3	50.0	52.1	46.9	54.3	57.2	67.7	70.6	61.4
Cisco	57.1	56.0	55.8	42.4	32.2	29.6	31.2	22.2	30.8	36.2	50.3	64.8	42.3
Claremont	69.1	68.2	68.4	61.4	53.4	49.4	52.2	47.0	52.9	59.4	60.6	66.0	59.0
Cloverdale	72.7	70.4	68.8	60.4	51.6	47.2	42.7	46.8	50.0	55.8	63.8	73.0	59.0
Colfax	78.0	76.6	75.8	58.3	44.7	44.8	41.5	37.4	41.4	52.0	66.3	75.8	57.7
Colton	72.9	71.9	71.1	61.2	52.7	49.1	53.4	48.2	54.6	58.2	62.7	70.1	60.5
Colusa	76.6	74.5	71.9	61.4	50.6	45.2	42.7	41.0	51.0	55.8	67.6	74.4	59.6
Corning	80.3	77.0	75.4	65.4	53.3	47.6	47.1	44.1	50.6	55.4	66.9	77.3	61.7
Craftonville	73.7	74.2	69.5	63.0	48.4	48.4	49.9	43.0	51.5	55.5	59.9	69.1	58.8
Crescent City	56.6	57.2	55.4	54.6	50.2	47.0	46.6	44.8	47.9	48.8	52.2	57.7	51.5
Cuyamaca	60.8	62.2	59.2	48.4	39.1	36.5	37.7	28.2	39.2	41.2	49.8	59.7	46.8
Davisville	77.2	76.7	73.6	64.0	52.5	47.6	46.0	43.6	53.4	56.7	68.2	75.6	61.3
Delano	87.0	83.8	81.6	70.1	54.5	46.8	46.4	47.0	56.9	.....	.....	82.8	.....
Delta	76.6	75.4	71.4	55.7	51.8	44.4	46.0	41.1	45.0	51.4	71.4	77.5	59.0
Drytown	75.0	72.2	70.5	60.1	49.3	45.1	42.6	43.0	51.1	53.6	68.6	71.5	58.1
Dunnigan	82.8	78.6	75.1	63.0	51.6	47.2	44.2	47.7	53.2	59.0	76.3	82.6	63.4
Dunsmuir	71.1	71.3	63.0	50.4	41.8	41.3	43.2	36.4	43.4	47.4	62.4	70.6	53.8
Durham	77.2	74.2	72.6	61.7	51.1	46.2	43.0	44.0	51.3	55.6	66.6	74.7	59.8
El Cajon	69.4	71.3	70.6	63.6	56.1	53.4	53.3	49.8	5..6	58.2	64.4	68.4	61.2
El Dorado	73.6	72.1	70.1	56.8	48.0	44.9	43.9	42.2	48.4	54.2	66.1	74.0	57.9
Elmdale	76.0	74.8	72.5	62.4	50.4	45.8	48.4	44.1	53.1	55.4	64.6	73.4	59.7
Elmira	84.0	80.0	78.4	65.4	58.8	50.1	46.8	46.8	54.9	62.0	76.8	72.4	64.7
Elsinore	78.5	74.4	75.7	65.8	56.2	53.2	58.6	49.0	54.2	58.4	63.5	73.6	62.6
Escondido	71.2	71.2	68.8	61.0	52.4	48.5	49.6	46.8	54.0	56.2	63.6	72.0	59.6
Eureka	56.2	57.0	55.0	55.7	51.8	49.8	48.6	45.1	49.2	48.7	51.5	56.2	52.1
Fallbrook	70.0	70.2	69.4	61.0	58.8	51.9	53.2	47.4	55.0	57.3	61.8	69.0	60.0
Farmington	75.8	72.8	69.8	61.9	50.1	45.5	45.7	41.2	50.0	54.2	66.2	73.4	58.9
Fernando	78.5	72.8	73.6	67.0	61.5	52.7	53.4	46.8	55.0	58.1	58.7	68.3	61.8
Folsom	75.6	75.1	72.2	61.8	52.0	47.5	45.0	44.8	53.6	57.4	69.8	76.5	61.0
Fort Ross	57.8	59.4	61.2	62.6	52.1	49.3	48.4	45.6	50.0	50.8	53.1	58.0	54.0

Monthly and Annual Mean Temperature.

(CONTINUED.)

STATIONS.	1902. July.	Aug.	Sept.	Oct.	Nov.	Dec.	1903. Jan.	Feb.	Mar.	Apr.	May.	June.	Annual Mean.
Fresno	80.4	78.4	76.0	64.4	51.2	47.0	43.8	45.8	54.9	57.5	67.8	77.2	62.0
Fruto	80.5	72.8	75.8	63.5	49.6	45.7	43.5	42.4	49.9	55.1	71.0	74.9	60.4
Galt	75.0	74.0	71.7	64.2	54.2	48.8	50.8	45.8	51.6	57.5	65.4	71.0	60.4
Georgetown	72.6	72.6	72.7	58.6	46.1	44.5	45.0	40.4	44.6	49.4	60.2	69.2	56.3
Gilroy	66.5	67.0	63.8	59.2	50.3	47.0	44.2	41.6	51.5	54.8	59.5	66.9	56.0
Gonzales	63.8	65.6	64.2	58.6	50.6	47.8	49.0	44.6	51.4	53.4	58.0	64.6	56.0
Greenville	62.8	64.2	61.0	50.8	40.1	35.2	34.5	26.6	40.9	44.7	54.8	66.2	46.8
Guinda	80.3	76.7	72.8	59.9	47.3	42.7	40.7	42.2	48.6	56.6	68.7	77.9	59.5
Hanford	79.6	75.9	74.2	62.6	49.5	43.6	40.8	41.3	54.2	62.3	75.4	79.0	61.5
Healdsburg	69.0	67.0	66.6	59.4	51.6	47.7	45.4	45.7	50.1	54.4	64.0	77.0	58.2
Hollister	66.2	65.6	66.0	60.0	51.1	47.8	47.6	45.2	52.5	54.2	59.2	65.2	56.7
Hornbrook	69.7	69.2	63.4	52.8	43.0	45.4	41.4	33.0	43.4	48.6	54.8	67.9	52.7
Huron	85.8	83.6	76.4	61.4	52.0	47.5	44.8	45.3	55.4	61.0	......	82.4	......
Idyllwild	62.8	64.1	62.2	54.0	43.6	42.0	......	......	38.7	......	52.4	61.6	......
Imperial	88.2	90.2	85.7	74.2	58.4	52.8	56.4	55.8	69.2	74.4	82.5	98.6	73.4
Independence	77.0	74.9	72.8	60.2	45.4	40.4	44.5	37.6	48.1	54.0	64.2	75.0	57.8
Indio	88.8	93.3	89.5	75.8	61.4	51.5	58.2	55.0	64.9	72.6	81.0	91.1	73.6
Ione	77.8	80.4	73.6	59.9	45.4	44.2	44.8	43.4	49.4	54.8	67.2	73.8	59.6
Iowa Hill	71.4	70.8	70.8	57.4	47.8	45.6	46.4	41.0	45.3	51.0	61.9	68.8	56.5
Jackson	73.6	72.2	72.4	60.6	49.4	46.5	45.8	43.9	48.1	52.2	62.5	70.4	58.1
Keeler	82.3	80.2	76.0	63.6	50.0	43.8	43.9	40.8	52.0	60.5	69.8	86.4	62.4
Kings City	68.1	68.6	67.9	58.1	48.4	48.4	49.3	45.4	52.3	54.1	61.1	66.6	57.4
Knights Ldg	78.2	72.4	72.6	64.7	50.7	52.0	46.9	43.5	49.4	57.8	68.8	75.0	60.5
Lakeport (near)	73.6	73.8	73.0	59.6	49.7	44.6	44.8	42.4	47.8	53.7	62.8	70.1	58.0
La Porte	59.0	59.0	57.3	45.2	35.8	32.7	35.1	28.2	34.0	39.0	51.4	58.8	44.6
Le Grand	79.6	76.7	74.2	62.5	49.4	46.2	44.6	44.0	53.5	57.6	67.5	......	......
Lemon Cove	79.8	78.4	77.8	67.7	55.7	48.1	45.1	47.0	56.2	60.0	70.2	78.7	63.7
Lick Observat'ry	66.7	66.9	68.2	58.0	41.6	41.8	43.7	34.9	39.8	43.7	54.0	61.6	51.8
Livermore	71.6	70.6	69.8	61.8	52.9	48.3	47.4	46.6	52.9	55.4	62.8	68.2	59.0
Lodi	73.0	70.6	69.0	60.0	50.2	45.8	44.6	43.0	52.4	54.6	64.5	71.4	58.3
Los Angeles	68.4	68.8	69.2	63.2	58.2	56.0	56.6	52.0	56.2	58.0	60.8	66.3	61.1
Los Banos	78.1	77.8	72.9	65.7	52.5	46.2	45.6	43.4	53.4	55.3	74.6	79.8	62.1
Los Gatos	68.3	68.2	66.9	59.5	50.8	48.7	47.0	45.9	51.0	53.6	60.6	66.2	57.2
Mammoth Tank	89.2	92.6	88.0	77.0	64.2	54.2	60.1	56.4	......	72.9	77.3	87.8	......
Manzana	81.5	74.8	79.7	62.8	49.2	42.6	46.2	40.4	50.4	54.8	66.6	......	......
Marysville	74.8	75.6	75.1	67.0	56.6	48.8	46.6	44.5	50.8	59.8	68.9	74.5	61.9
Meadow Valley	63.4	63.6	61.8	48.6	39.0	34.4	34.9	26.6	37.0	40.0	51.7	59.9	46.7
Mendota	79.8	80.4	71.8	64.1	......	51.9	47.4	44.2	56.8	62.7	71.8	82.6	......
Menlo Park	68.8	69.2	66.4	60.2	59.6	49.6	50.7	42.8	58.1	55.1	61.8	67.4	58.7
Merced	77.4	76.4	74.5	63.0	50.1	44.4	41.4	42.8	52.0	55.8	66.7	80.1	60.4
Mercury	75.8	68.6	68.8	61.6	55.0	51.4	51.2	49.6	53.7	58.2	65.2	70.3	60.8
Milton (near)	76.3	74.2	73.8	63.7	51.8	47.6	43.4	44.6	52.7	54.4	64.4	72.7	60.0
Modesto	81.5	78.9	76.4	66.3	58.2	48.4	47.2	51.2	57.2	62.8	68.4	75.6	64.3
Mojave	80.4	76.8	77.8	62.2	53.8	42.0	46.5	42.0	49.0	51.4	68.7	76.2	60.5
Montague	......	......	......	......	......	......	38.1	33.2	42.6	47.0	57.0	65.8	......
Monterey	60.2	61.4	64.7	62.4	54.2	51.4	49.2	48.1	55.0	56.4	58.2	61.3	56.9
Monterio	70.2	72.6	71.8	61.0	48.2	47.2	48.4	41.2	48.5	......	......	66.8	......
Mt. Tamalpais	76.3	65.8	69.6	56.2	47.4	44.4	45.9	41.8	43.8	49.2	58.1	64.2	55.2
Napa	69.3	69.6	68.7	61.8	51.8	47.8	45.0	46.8	51.1	54.6	62.0	66.6	58.0
Needles	93.0	93.2	87.2	73.4	......	48.8	......	49.8	64.7	72.4	81.8	91.5	......
Nevada City	66.2	66.1	65.5	55.2	44.8	43.1	43.7	37.7	43.2	47.6	58.3	65.0	53.0
Newcastle	......	80.8	74.6	62.6	50.1	45.4	42.4	44.9	51.6	56.4	66.4	73.2	......
Newhall	73.4	73.8	73.0	62.5	52.3	46.1	54.8	53.4	57.4	63.2	69.0	74.5	62.8
Newman	77.8	76.6	78.4	63.8	51.2	45.4	42.4	45.1	52.4	57.2	66.8	75.8	60.6
Niles	67.2	67.1	66.4	60.6	52.6	49.0	47.8	47.0	52.8	55.3	60.5	64.3	57.6
North Bloomfield	70.6	70.5	69.5	55.4	43.6	41.6	43.2	36.8	42.2	47.6	59.0	67.2	53.9
North San Juan	69.0	72.7	73.8	61.0	51.0	46.7	42.5	40.6	49.0	53.7	63.6	69.7	57.4
Oakdale	76.3	74.4	70.0	70.0	48.2	43.4	41.8	41.0	50.1	58.2	63.5	71.9	58.6
Oakland	65.2	65.0	64.0	60.2	52.9	49.0	47.5	46.8	53.2	55.6	59.8	64.1	56.9
Ogilby	95.4	93.8	92.0	82.2	64.9	57.2	65.6	52.9	......	77.5	88.4	95.6	......

Monthly and Annual Mean Temperature.

(CONTINUED)

STATIONS	1902. July	Aug.	Sept.	Oct.	Nov.	Dec.	1903. Jan.	Feb.	Mar.	Apr.	May.	June.	Annual Mean.
Ontario	74.0	73.8	72.8	62.6	58.8	50.4	58.3	49.2	55.3	59.8	63.6	71.0	61.6
Orland	88.2	84.7	76.2	68.4	59.8	48.5	45.2	45.2	49.7	56.4	65.9	71.9	63.3
Oroville	74.5	75.3	71.4	59.0	46.4	42.4	39.3	42.1	43.8	54.4	68.0	75.4	58.1
Palermo	76.0	74.8	72.1	60.1	49.8	45.8	41.7	43.8	50·8	55.0	65.2	73.6	59.0
Palm Springs	85.5	83.9	83.7	73.8	61.0	51.3	58.1	58.8	59.0	65.7	72.0	79.6	69.0
Paso Robles	69.1	65.7	66.4	56.6	46.2	42.4	44.8	41.7	48.6	52.3	59.7	68.1	55.1
Peachland	68.2	65.9	65.0	59.9	52.6	48.2	46.6	46.3	51.0	55.3	62.3	68.2	57.5
Pine Crest	66.0	66.0	67.6	62.0	57.6	55.0	58.6	52.2	53.4	56.7	57.2	64.0	59.7
Placerville	68.8	67.3	66.0	54.5	44.4	42.7	42.1	88.8	46.2	45.6	58.4	66.3	58.7
Point Lobos	56.9	59.4	60.0	57.6	54.2	50.0	47.4	47.6	51.8	53.0	53.5	56.8	54.0
Point Reyes	54.0	57.6	59.0	56.4	53.6	51.2	50.7	48.6	51.2	50.4	50.0	54.2	51.1
Pollasky	92.4	85.6	81.7	68.8	54.8	47.6	44.9	44.1	55.6	64.6	82.1	......	......
Porterville	77.8	77.5	75.8	64.8	53.4	47.7	45.2	46 1	54.7	58.7	67.0	76.0	62.1
Poway	70.8	71.3	70.8	68.3	55.8	52.8	58.6	49.6	57.0	58.7	64.0	69.0	61.4
Quincy	68.8	63.8	58.4	49.2	40.0	35.0	34.4	25.8	40.8	45.1	55.8	63.6	48.0
Red Bluff	80.0	78.6	76.3	68.3	51.3	45.4	43.6	44.5	50.1	56.2	68.8	76.6	61.2
Redding	79.6	79.0	76.4	62.8	50.4	·45.4	44.4	44.7	49.6	55.8	68.0	76.1	61.0
Redlands	75.2	74 5	74.6	64.4	54.6	51.5	58.0	48.6	54.5	57.4	63.4	70.9	61.9
Reedley	79.2	76.0	73.0	61.1	49.4	47.2	44.8	45.6	55.8	58.2	71.4	80.6	61.9
Rio Vista	76.0	71.9	70.2	62.2	51.6	46.5	44.4	45.0	51.8	56.0	65.2	71.4	59.4
Riverside	72.0	71.2	71.0	62.0	53.2	50.8	52.0	48.4	54.0	57.9	62.8	68 8	60.3
Rocklin	78.3	76.9	74.2	63.8	53.0	48.6	47.4	46.7	55.4	59.2	69.6	76.4	62.5
Rosewood	78.4	76.7	72.5	59.2	48.2	42.6	43.2	40.6	47.8	53.1	65.8	75.2	58.6
Sacramento	73.2	71.4	70.7	61.8	51.4	46.9	48.4	45.5	52.2	56.1	65.2	71.0	59.1
Salinas	61.8	64.2	65.2	58.8	51.0	48.8	50.2	46.4	53.8	54.0	58 0	61.3	56.1
Salton	97.6	97.8	93.5	78.4	62.6	55.1	58.3	56.4	66.0	72.6	79.1	89.4	75.6
San Bernardino	73.6	78.0	72.8	63.1	54.3	51.4	52.6	49.1	54.6	58.0	63.8	70.6	61.4
San Diego	65.4	66.8	66.2	62.6	58.3	55.8	56.8	52.2	57.6	58.4	60.5	63.2	60.3
San Francisco	59.5	60.6	61.9	59.3	54.8	50.6	47.8	48.9	52.2	54.0	55.2	58.5	55.3
Sanger	81.4	85.7	78.9	69.4	55.6	48.6	46.4	43.6	57.2	60.5	73.4	82.0	65 2
San Jacinto	75.2	73.6	74.4	63.4	52.9	50.0	50.7	46.2	53.1	57.0	63.3	71.8	61.0
San Jose	66.8	67.4	67.6	62.2	53.2	50.3	48.8	47.8	54.0	56.2	61.0	65.6	58.4
San Leandro	64.5	64.8	64.2	59.4	51.6	47.2	46.5	45.2	52.6	54.3	59.5	63.8	56.1
San Luis Obispo	63.9	63.7	65.3	61.8	55.8	52.6	55.0	49.0	53.5	55.7	56.4	63.4	58.0
San Mateo	69.1	66.9	66.9	62.4	53.5	48.6	49.1	48.0	53.2	55.8	60.4	69.5	58.6
San Miguel	72.3	69.5	69.9	61.2	51.9	45.8	47.4	44.8	51.7	56.8	62.7	74.0	59.0
Santa Barbara	65 3	65.4	66.0	61.8	57.6	54.2	56.4	51.1	54.6	57.0	58.4	63.4	59.3
Santa Clara	65.0	64.4	63.8	58.5	51.0	49.8	47.8	46.2	52.7	53.6	59.5	63.8	56.3
Santa Cruz	61.6	62.8	62.2	58.0	52.0	49.6	49.4	46.0	51.2	53.6	56.6	61.9	55.4
Santa Margarita	72.2	70.2	67.4	59.7	51.6	47.9	47.7	43.7	55.3	51.1	62.1	68.2	58.1
Santa Maria	63.7	64.5	65.3	62 2	55.6	52.3	54.8	49.6	55.3	57.2	59.3	63.7	58.6
Santa Monica	62.8	63.0	63.7	58.2	55.7	58.6	54.9	49.3	52.6	54.6	57.2	61.9	57.5
Santa Paula	72.1	71.0	70.6	62.7	59.5	59.3	61.6	54.2	55.5	64.8	68.1	70.0	64.1
Santa Rosa	66.8	66.0	65.8	58.6	51.4	46.6	45.6	44.8	49.1	52.8	59.0	65.8	56.0
Selma	81.6	75.2	75.3	61.2	51.8	44.4	46.8	48.2	50.9	59.1	72.0	78.0	61.6
Shasta	81.4	80.4	77.7	63.4	50.1	44.6	47.6	44.6	49.7	57.2	69.8	77.4	62.0
Sierra Madre	70.1	69.8	70.2	62.8	56.2	53.8	55.2	50.0	54.2	57.1	60.4	67.2	60 6
Sisson	67.8	67.8	61.0	52.9	40.5	35.3	34.7	31.0	39.2	45.7	55.0	65.8	49.7
Soledad	67.8	62.6	61.3	56.8	55.3	56.3	56.6	45.2	52.8	58.5	63.3	69.5	58.8
Sonoma	70.1	68.7	67.9	......	......	50.3	46.6	50.6	51.8	57.2	63.4	67.2	......
Stockton	72.6	71.0	68.7	60.6	50.0	45.1	42.8	43.5	51·4	54.8	64.3	70.7	58.0
Storey	77.8	76.7	78.4	61.0	48.2	45.0	45.6	43.7	51·4	55.9	66.1	74.0	59.9
Suisun	72.1	69.2	69.1	63.2	53.6	48.0	46.4	46.6	52·9	56.2	62.5	69.0	59.1
Summerdale	65.0	64.8	65.6	52.6	40.5	39.9	41.4	34.0	37·6	41.8	52.5	61.2	49.7
Summit	64.0	62.2	56.6	44.2	30.9	28.1	30.9	23.0	29·2	33.7	44.4	56.7	42.0
Susanville	67.0	65.8	61.6	49.8	37.5	32.5	31.8	17.0	37·1	44.5	55.1	62.7	46.9
Tehachapi	74.0	70.5	68.0	59.1	46.2	38.9	37.3	32.4	40·4	44.2	58.2	70.0	53.8
Tehama	85.5	82.1	78.7	65.2	54.9	50.4	47.0	46.4	58·0	60.6	73.2	81.6	64.9
Tejon Rancho	79.8	77.8	76.8	63.4	51.2	49 2	47.2	46.4	53·8	55.6	66.6	75.2	61.9
Tequisquita Rancho	66.2	67.2	66.4	60.9	51.1	48.0	48.0	45.8	52.0	54.6	59.9	66.0	57.2

Monthly and Annual Mean Temperature.

(CONTINUED)

STATIONS.	1902. July.	Aug.	Sept.	Oct.	Nov.	Dec.	1903. Jan.	Feb.	Mar.	Apr.	May.	June.	Annual Mean.
Tracy	79.9	74.1	72.1	62.9	53.0	48.1	49.5	47.8	56.5	60.2	72.6	76.7	62.8
Truckee	52.4	57.2	49.9	39.0	35.1	29.2	27.7	15.8	31.8	37.9	49.3	55 3	40.0
Tulare	78.0	76.4	74.2	63.8	53.1	48.3	45.5	46.2	53.4	57.8	67.5	76.6	61.9
Tustin	72.8	74.2	72.8	67.8	60.2	56.2	59.2	55.4	60.9	63.2	67.7	73.0	65.1
Ukiah	68.8	68.6	67.1	54.0	49.1	45.0	45.9	43.6	48.7	52.4	61.8	68.2	56.4
Upland	70.6	70.8	71.8	62.8	55.2	51.8	52.5	47.8	52.2	55.0	59.4	67.8	59.8
Upper Lake	71.0	72.0	70.0	57.6	48.4	42.7	48.3	42.9	46.5	51.6	61.0	67.5	56.2
Upper Mattole	59.5	61.4	59.2	52.5	49.9	45.9	46.2	44.2	49.2	50.2	52.8	56.8	52.3
Vacaville	75.2	78.0	72.7	62.1	52.6	47.5	44.2	45.4	51.6	56.0	66.1	74.4	60.1
Valley Springs	81.7	78.8	77.1	64.5	......	47 2	46.0	45.4	51.0	58.9	70.0	76.1	......
Ventura	64.9	......	65.7	62.2	58.6	......	58.7	53.6	56.4	56.6	56 6	64.2	......
Vina	83.7	78 8	76.1	63.4	57.8	46.4	45.4	45.4	48.7	59.4	66.7	83.4	62.9
Visalia	80.2	76.9	73.8	61.8	50.4	46.0	43.5	......	52.6	57.2	67.4	75.6	......
Volcano	99.6	99.4	92 0	75.2	63.0	59.4	61.5	58.1	73.1	69.4	78.5	88.5	76.b
Wasco	83.2	80.6	76.8	63.7	50.2	45.3	42.4	43.5	53.8	58.7	69.2	77.6	62.1
Watsonville	62.9	64.5	61.0	57.3	57.0	50.7	56.5	48.8	55.9	59.2	62.6	62.8	58.2
Westley	83.1	77.6	75.2	64.2	53.4	50.4	46.6	46.8	52.1	58.8	69.0	76.5	63.1
Wheatland	73.5	71.8	70.4	60.9	49.6	45.4	42.5	43.4	50.4	54.4	65.4	72.7	58.4
Williams	83.1	80.4	77.0	65.5	54.7	50.3	49.1	47.1	55.4	60.4	74 0	83.0	65.0
Willits	68.8	69.0	68.6	56.4	49.0	44.2	45.3	43.4	46.8	49.8	59.0	67 8	55.7
Willows	77.6	75.4	73.8	60.8	51.0	45.7	43.1	43.9	50.1	55.3	66.8	75.8	59.9
Winters	86.5	80.6	82.8	71.6	54.7	47.1	40.9	40.6	53.2	59.4	73.6	85.0	64.7
Woodland	80.5	76.6	71.7	60.0	57.4	47.8	45 4	40.1	50.2	53.8	68.6	78.0	60.8
Zenia	......	......	......	......	......	41.8	44.3	40.0	43.8	46.6	56.4	60 6	......

MONTHLY AND SEASONAL PRECIPITATION AT STATIONS IN CALIFORNIA, SEASON OF 1902–1903.

Compiled by U. S. Weather Bureau

STATIONS	July.	Aug.	Sept.	Oct.	Nov.	Dec.	Jan.	Feb.	March.	April.	May.	June.	Total Season.
Anaheim	T	.00	.00	.40	1.86	3.83	1.22	2.61	5.58	4.47	.00	.00	19.47
Angiola	T	.00	.00	.00	.63	.54	.75	.11	.90	.22	.00	.00	3.15
Antioch	.00	.10	.00	.20	1.21	1.26	2.92	1.48	3.45	.75	.00	.00	11.27
Aptos	.00	.00	.00	2.95	2.86	2.10	5.42	2.62	7.32	1.62	.00	.00	24.89
Auburn	.00			2.40	3.55	6.15	11.80	1.00	9.60	1.80	T	.00	
Azusa	T	.10	.07	.41	2.19	8.14	2.26	1.57	9.00	4.30	.14	.00	23.08
Bakersfield	.00	T	.00	.35	.88	.36	1.27	.59	.82	.49	T	.22	4.98
Berkeley	.00	T	.00	2.35	3.21	3.69	5.17	2.05	7.81	1.11	.02	T	25.41
Biggs	.00	.00	.00	1.63	2.85	3.27	3.58	1.51	6.19	.13	.00	.00	19.16
Bishop	T	.12	.05	.28	.97	.03	.46	.20	.35	.14	T	.20	2.80
Blue Canon	.00	.00	.00	5.18	8.14	10.19	14.67	5.90	14.10	2.40	.40	T	58.98
Boca	.10	.00	.00			1.60	6.40	1.50	.90	.70	.20	T	
Bodie	.08	.40	.00	.58	1.47	.15	2.88	1.04	.78	.88	.60	.31	9.12
Bowman's Dam	.09	T	.02	5.86	10.04	12.99	19.97	5.99	17.32	2.54	.94	.40	76.16
Branscomb	.01	.07	T	5.88	27.29	15.66	22.30	6.82	9.53	1.08	.19	.24	89.07
Byron	.00	.00	.00	1.25	1.20	.65	2.10	1.40	4.10	1.50	.00	.00	12.20
Cabazon	T	.00	.00	.00	.75	1.00	.15	1.76	3.20	4.76	.00	.00	11.62
Caliente	.00	.00	.00	.00	1.98	1.30	2.15	2.60	1.92	2.42	.00	.02	12.39
Calistoga	.00	.00	.00	8.01	7.24	4.90	7.83	1.15	7.55	.41	.00	.00	37.09
Campbell	.00	.00	.00	1.35	2.17	.86	2.69	1.64	6.22	.81	.00	.00	15.74
Cedarville	1.15	.23	.46	.81	1.76	2.09	2.65	.50	1.05	.11	.39	1.78	12.48
Chico	.00	.00	.00	2.11	6.31	2.92	3.90	2.15	6.23	.40	.25	T	24.27
Chino	.00	.00	.00	.35	1.26	2.62	.81	1.97	6.80	2.21	.00	.00	16.02
Cisco	T	T	T	6.70	3.40	6.50	5.85	2.80	10.60	4.20	.40	.00	40.45
Claremont	.05	.00	T	.37	1.51	2.61	2.38	.45	8.59	2.85	.00	.00	18.81
Cloverdale	.00	.01	.00	6.22	10.58	4.45	6.49	2.89	7.05	.84	.00	.22	38.20
Colfax	.00	.00	.00	3.95	6.06	7.88	10.80	4.00	12.95	3.50	.10	T	49.22
Colton	.00	.00	.00	.15	.97	1.66	1.42	1.60	5.51	4.37	.00	.00	15.68
Colusa	.00	T	.00	1.57	2.64	1.62	2.74	1.27	4.91	.08	T	T	14.83
Corning	.00	.00	.00	2.45	5.55	1.97	1.95	1.20	5.23	.15	.15	T	18.65
Craftonville	.10	.00	T	.00	1.47	1.58	.90	1.60	5.85	4.75	.70	.00	16.95
Crescent City	.47	.06	.76	4.29	18.59	17.29	24.38	6.06	10.06	3.40	1.32	.19	86.87
Cuyamaca	1.54	.00	T	1.01	5.09	3.66	3.96	7.31	6.13	8.21	.69	.00	37.60
Davisville	.00	.00	.00	2.03	1.95	2.05	2.93	2.18	4.43	.62	.00	.00	16.19
Delano	.00	.00	.00	.89	1.01	.22	1.05	1.15	1.38			T	
Delta	T	.28	.00	4.57	14.33	9.68	11.86	3.67	14.74	.88	.51	.02	60.04
Drytown				1.20	2.90	2.15	6.30	1.70	9.03	2.20	.00	.00	
Dunnigan	.00	T	.00	2.79	3.73	1.09	3.93	1.26	5.00	.12	T	T	17.92
Dunsmuir	T	.05	.00	6.09	14.76	9.13	10.33	1.50	6.47	.02	.00	.20	48.53
Durham	.00	.00	.00	1.85	4.89	8.73	3.73	1.77	6.19	.38	.24	.00	22.78
El Cajon	.75	.00	.00	.20	1.73	2.21	.84	2.97	1.83	1.29	.14	T	11.46
El Dorado	.00	.00	.00	2.41	4.63	4.56	8.96	2.22	11.31	2.16	.20	.00	36.45
Elmdale	.00	.00	.00	.39	1.54	.59	2.84	.72	4.91	.15	T	.00	11.11
Elmira	.00	.00	.00	3.28	3.09	1.96	3.79	2.16	4.75	.90	.00	.00	19.88
Elsinore	.08	.00	.00	.13	1.26	3.04	.81	2.50	6.55	1.71	T	.00	16.08
Escondido	.15	.00	.00	.28	2.35	3.04	1.58	3.67	2.78	3.84	T	.00	17.69
Eureka	.25	T	.14	2.34	10.88	8.33	16.07	3.80	7.42	1.23	.70	.57	51.73
Fallbrook	.23	.00	.00	.29	2.86	4.00	3.11	3.33	5.19	4.35	.08	.05	23.49
Farmington	.00	T	.00	.55	2.11	1.29	2.93	1.35	6.68	1.50	.00	.00	16.41
Fernando	.00	.00	.00	.35	4.39	3.08	.77	1.19	4.83	4.20	.00	.00	18.75
Folsom	.00	.01	T	1.85	2.15	4.15	5.23	1.57	9.27	.89	T	.01	25.16
Fort Ross	.00	.00	.00	8.95	14.16	7.87	9.85	5.21	12.87	.36	.01	.09	59.87

233

Monthly and Seasonal Precipitation.

(CONTINUED.)

STATIONS	1902. July.	Aug.	Sept.	Oct.	Nov.	Dec.	1903. Jan.	Feb.	March.	April.	May.	June.	Total Season.
Fresno	.00	T	.00	.42	2.25	.54	1.86	.65	2.25	.50	T	T	8.50
Fruto	.00	.00	.00	2.75	3.70	1.10	2.55	2.05	4.45	.80	.00	.00	17.40
Galt	.00	T	.00	.86	1.52	1.85	4.17	1.72	7.88	.05	.00	.00	18.05
Georgetown	.00	.05	.00	8.77	6.66	7.76	14.77	2.72	16.60	2.06	.70	.08	55.12
Gilroy	.00	.00	.00	1.43	1.85	1.27	8.31	1.97	6.44	1.21	.00	.00	17.48
Gonzales	.00	.00	.00	.17	2.11	.67	2.77	.98	2.46	.16	.00	.00	9.32
Greenville	.48	.16	.04	8.79	5.26	7.49	7.44	2.86	7.36	1.05	.54	.64	36.56
Guinda	.00	T	.00	2.20	2.95	2.05	4.29	2.16	4.28	.33	T	T	18.21
Hanford	.00	.00	.00	.36	1.67	.56	1.31	.38	1.71	.50	.00	.00	6.49
Healdsburg	T	T	.00	6.10	9.46	4.71	7.55	8.86	7.60	.89	T	T	39.17
Hollister	.00	.00	T	.31	2.03	1.02	2.78	1.86	4.30	.84	.00	.00	12.64
Hornbrook	T	.60	.00	.42	8.42	3.08	6.15	.60	2.22	.00	.09	1.10	17.68
Huron	.00	.00	.00	.11	.62	.40	.88	.37	1.82	.58	......	.00	......
Idyllwild	.33	.00	T	.10	3.80	2.00	3.82	3.00	6.76	6.10	.49	.09	26.49
Imperial	.55	.00	.00	.00	.13	1.75	T	.06	.03	T	T	T	2.52
Independence	.17	.18	T	.08	.41	.04	.71	.27	.34	.19	T	.02	2.36
Indio	.10	.00	.00	.00	.50	.80	.00	.00	.00	.75	.00	.00	......
Ione	.00	.00	.00	1.03	2.55	2.28	5.23	1.07	8.56	1.67	.00	.00	22.89
Iowa Hill	.00	.15	.00	3.09	5.70	8.27	12.54	3.39	12.00	2.66	.88	.06	48.74
Jackson	.00	T	.00	2.46	4.51	8.73	9.12	1.62	11.84	1.31	.04	T	34.63
Keeler	T	T	T	.00	.50	.10	.00	.10	T	T	T	T	0.70
Kings City	.00	.00	.00	.80	2.28	.59	1.19	1.40	1.76	.67	T	.00	8.19
Knights Landing	.00	.00	.00	2.23	2.85	......	4.27	2.37	5.25	.65	.00	.00	......
Lakeport (near)	.00	T	.00	3.92	4.35	2.47	5.87	2.02	4.20	.20	T	T	22.53
La Porte	.02	T	.18	6.94	10.87	12.84	16.42	8.14	16.71	2.18	.33	.25	69.88
Le Grand	.00	.00	.00	.50	2.14	1.14	2.39	.98	4.51	.25	.00	.00	11.91
Lemon Cove	T	.00	.00	.51	2.05	1.23	2.22	.94	4.04	1.68	.12	.10	12.89
Lick Observatory	.00	.00	.00	2.05	3.01	3.11	8.86	2.20	9.89	1.12	.05	T	30.29
Livermore	T	.18	.00	.47	2.07	.87	8.19	.94	5.65	.81	.12	.00	14.25
Lodi	.00	T	.00	.66	1.54	1.52	3.21	1.79	10.31	.23	.00	.00	19.26
Los Angeles	T	T	T	.40	2.08	2.50	2.10	1.52	6.98	3.77	T	.02	19.32
Los Banos	.00	.00	.00	.07	1.00	.25	1.55	.80	2.67	.00	.00	.00	6.34
Los Gatos	.00	.00	T	2.80	4.90	1.89	5.98	2.51	10.17	.73	.00	T	28.98
Mammoth Tank	.28	.00	.00	.00	T	.61	.00	.00	.00	.00	.00	.00	......
Manzana	.00	.00	.00	.08	1.99	1.78	.60	.96	3.02	3.46	.00	......	......
Marysville	.00	T	.00	1.86	4.43	2.55	5.00	1.70	5.09	.63	T	T	21.26
Meadow Valley	.13	.02	.14	4.31	9.83	10.66	9.48	3.48	20.85	1.83	.48	.47	61.68
Mendota	.00	.00	.00	.12	......	1.18	1.11	.55	1.93	T	.00	.00	......
Menlo Park	.00	.00	.00	1.36	1.85	.77	4.14	1.68	6.20	1.10	.00	.00	17.10
Merced	.00	T	.00	T	2.25	.36	2.24	.63	6.41	T	.00	.00	11.89
Mercury	T	.03	.00	7.51	11.12	5.51	9.28	3.05	8.79	.25	.00	.00	45.54
Milton	.00	T	.00	1.11	2.55	1.61	4.52	.96	8.08	.79	.00	T	19.62
Modesto	.00	.00	.00	.40	1.55	.65	2.34	.68	5.16	1.45	.00	.00	12.28
Mojave	.00	.00	.00	T	.84	.21	.02	.50	.35	1.00	.00	.00	2.92
Montague	......	......	......	......	......	......	2.18	.10	1.81	.08	.07	.32	......
Monterey	.00	.00	.00	.50	1.66	1.17	3.43	1.88	5.98	.80	.00	.00	15.42
Monterio	.00	.00	.00	.10	3.94	3.00	1.94	1.90	3.08	......	......	.96	......
Mt. Tamalpais	.03	T	.00	2.61	3.82	3.27	6.37	1.79	6.77	.79	T	T	25.45
Napa	.00	.02	.00	4.84	4.13	2.94	3.22	2.11	4.99	1.13	T	.00	23.38
Needles	.12	.18	.60	.00	2.20	.55	......	.00	.65	T	.00	.00	......
Nevada City	.00	.00	.00	8.95	5.91	7.65	10.62	2.36	13.80	1.46	.52	.16	46.43
Newcastle	......	.00	.00	2.09	3.05	4.75	8.88	1.95	10.00	1.24	.00	.00	......
Newhall	.00	.00	.00	.82	8.70	2.45	1.13	1.77	4.29	5.48	.00	.00	19.64
Newman	T	.00	.00	.61	1.58	.49	1.47	.78	4.31	.07	T	.00	9.26
Niles	.00	.00	.00	1.06	2.49	1.46	4.26	1.36	5.82	.75	.00	.00	17.20
North Bloomfield	.09	.04	T	4.43	6.09	8.05	12.72	2.80	15.04	1.91	.59	.21	51.97
North San Juan	.00	.02	.03	3.77	6.08	9.66	12.88	2.60	13.70	1.14	.08	.15	50.11
Oakdale	.00	.00	.00	1.30	2.37	.68	3.27	.92	5.58	1.42	.00	.00	15.49
Oakland	.00	T	.00	T	1.98	2.37	3.14	4.02	1.68	7.42	.55	T	21.16
Ogilby	.04	.00	.00	.00	.55	.05	.00	T	.00	.00	.00	.00	0.64

Monthly and Seasonal Precipitation.

(CONTINUED)

STATIONS.	1902. July.	Aug.	Sept.	Oct.	Nov.	Dec.	1903. Jan.	Feb.	March.	April	May.	June.	Total Season.
Ontario	.00	.00	.00	.26	1.22	2.39	1.34	2.11	7.24	3.43	T	.00	17.99
Orland	.00	.00	.00	2.66	4.60	1.62	2.27	1.70	4.20	.28	T	T	17.83
Oroville	.00	.00	.00	2.85	8.60	4.46	5.30	1.88	6.90	.12	.15	.04	24.25
Palermo	.00	T	.00	2.43	3.49	4.62	6.62	1.12	6.55	.14	.16	.04	25.17
Palm Springs	.00	.00	.00	.00	.70	.70	.00	.00	.70	.00	.00	.00	2.10
Paso Robles	.00	.00	.00	1.08	.71	.96	2.19	1.85	4.16	.79	.00	.00	11.24
Peachland	.08	.09	.08	6.29	7.46	5.31	9.86	3.60	9.98	8.37	.02	.02	42.61
Pine Crest	.00	.00	.00	2.48	5.27	3.03	3.13	1.48	6.83	8.12	.14	T	25.43
Placerville	.00	.14	.04	2.27	4.59	4.42	9.88	2.35	11.85	2.11	.11	.00	37.21
Point Lobos	T	.00	.00	1.91	2.20	2.10	8.84	1.72	5.72	.67	.00	T	18.16
Point Reyes	.00	T	.00	3.68	2.88	2.48	2.64	1.39	3.88	.51	.00	.00	17.46
Pollasky	.00	.00	.00	.45	2.21	.84	2.82	.81	2.66	.46	.00		
Porterville	.01	.00	.00	.56	1.42	.79	1.80	.78	1.85	1.02	.01	.01	8.25
Poway	.80	.00	.00	.38	3.03	2.27	2.22	2.88	2.96	1.95	.11	.00	16.55
Quincy	.40	T	.02	5.03	7.90	7.68	9.31	2.17	7.45	.52	.55	.92	41.95
Red Bluff	.00	T	.00	3.44	6.64	3.89	2.78	1.53	4.99	.88	1.06	.01	24.22
Redding	.01	.08	.00	5.51	7.72	6.24	10.14	2.68	9.60	1.09	2.29	.02	45.33
Redlands	.07	.00	.00	.06	1.40	1.50	1.16	1.41	5.86	4.88	.48	.00	15.82
Reedley	.00	.00	.00	.50	1.58	.88	2.16	.97	2.58	1.26	.04	.00	9.97
Rio Vista	T	T	.00	1.38	1.69	1.89	2.86	1.47	4.35	.65	.05	T	14.34
Riverside	T	.00	T	.09	1.09	1.64	.94	1.24	5.22	2.49	.03	.00	12.74
Rocklin	.00	.02	.00	2.03	2.30	4.63	7.34	2.19	9.61	1.49	.00	T	29.61
Rosewood	.00	.15	.00	2.58	5.45	3.50	4.79	2.05	4.83	.51	.49	.08	24.38
Sacramento	.00	T	.00	1.67	2.02	2.91	3.05	1.70	4.81	.46	T	T	16.62
Salinas	.00	.00	.00	.52	1.43	1.39	3.14	1.88	3.02	.17	.00	.00	11.05
Salton	.30	.00	.00	.00	.22	.98	.00	.15	.27	1.83	.00	.00	3.25
San Bernardino	.01	.00	.00	.09	1.94	1.94	1.96	1.67	6.47	3.10	.24	.00	17.42
San Diego	.92	T	T	.06	1.58	3.58	.69	2.27	1.17	1.40	.14	T	11.76
San Francisco	T	T	T	1.70	1.98	2.82	3.73	1.76	6.28	.56	T	T	18.28
Sanger	.00	.00	.00	.30	1.51	.47	1.73	.52	1.93	.73	.00	.00	7.19
San Jacinto	.10	.00	.00	.06	1.25	2.12	1.32	1.37	4.54	4.99	.00	.00	15.75
San Jose	.00	.00	.00	.95	2.18	.92	2.74	1.27	4.99	.84	.00	.00	13.89
San Leandro	.00	.00	.00	2.24	3.00	3.25	4.89	1.94	6.61	.74	.00	.00	22.67
San Luis Obispo	T	T	.00	2.00	1.52	1.48	3.67	3.18	4.98	1.66	.00	T	18.49
San Mateo	.00	.00	.00	1.85	3.37	1.90	6.30	2.45	6.83	1.15	.00	.00	23.85
San Miguel	.00	.00	.00	.55	.61	.34	1.27	1.06	2.96	.53	.00	.00	7.45
Santa Barbara	.00	.00	.00	1.48	4.01	2.24	2.06	1.63	6.12	2.91	.27	.00	20.72
Santa Clara	.00	.02	.00	1.12	2.22	1.15	3.09	1.50	5.74	.82	.00	.00	15.66
Santa Cruz	.00	.00	.00	2.10	2.74	2.23	6.25	2.07	11.06	.25	.00	.00	26.70
Santa Margarita	.00	.00	.00	2.73	1.20	1.05	8.50	1.85	6.38	2.19	.00	.00	23.85
Santa Maria	.00	.00	.00	1.02	2.59	.79	1.80	1.91	3.97	.71	T	.00	12.79
Santa Monica	.00	.00	.00	.60	3.12	2.72	1.14	2.11	6.55	2.84	.02	.00	19.10
Santa Paula	.00	T	.00	T	3.25	1.16	1.66	1.30	6.14	2.65	.10	.00	16.26
Santa Rosa	T	T	.00	3.70	5.00	4.43	6.38	2.58	6.49	.60	T	.03	29.21
Selma	.00	.00	.00	.16	1.53	.66	1.87	.84	2.23	.53	.00	.00	7.82
Shasta	.00	.01	.00	6.55	12.14	7.37	17.24	1.84	14.03	1.30	.57	T	61.05
Sierra Madre	T	.00	.00	.56	3.91	3.26	4.84	1.78	9.24	4.06	.33	.19	28.17
Sissou	.88	4.16	.11	5.28	11.12	4.39	8.18	1.76	8.57	.13	.21	.83	44.62
Soledad	.00	.00	.00	.14	1.75	.61	.97	1.07	1.42	.49	.00	.00	6.45
Sonoma	.00	.04	.00	5.07	4.87	2.91	5.46	2.01	5.49	.50	.00	.00	25.85
Stockton	.00	.00	.00	.66	1.30	1.26	2.50	1.12	7.29	.33	.08	T	14.54
Storey	.00	.00	.00	.35	1.14	1.67	1.53	.78	2.49	.38	.00	.00	8.36
Suisun	.00	.01	.00	2.40	2.59	1.63	3.64	1.71	4.46	.05	.00	.00	16.49
Summerdale	T	.00	.00	4.85	6.92	3.95	14.13	3.70	11.83	3.37	.79	.29	49.83
Summit	.00	1.00	.00	2.30	7.50	4.60	10.50	3.20	11.10	1.70	.80	T	42.70
Susanville	.54	.09	.12	.78	2.48	3.04	8.71	1.13	2.45	.41	.58	.82	15.65
Tehachapi	.00	.00	.82	.20	1.90	1.02	1.10	2.50	.90	1.30	.00	.05	9.29
Tehama	.00	.00	.00	1.84	5.10	2.79	2.40	1.30	6.84	.41	.69	T	20.87
Tejon Rancho	.00	.00	T	.20	2.68	2.06	2.19	1.27	1.86	1.42	T	T	11.68
Tequisquita Rancho	.00	.00	.00	.81	1.44	1.25	2.87	1.30	5.56	.02	.00	.00	13.25

(CONTINUED)

STATIONS.	1902. July.	Aug.	Sept.	Oct.	Nov.	Dec.	1903. Jan.	Feb.	March.	April.	May.	June.	Total Season.
Tracy	.00	.05	.00	.29	.96	.52	1.96	.65	5.59	.26	.00	.00	10.28
Truckee	.45	1.10	.00	.50	2.20	3.60	8.00	1.00	4.15	3.40	.53	.98	25.91
Tulare	.00	00	.00	.24	1.32	.50	1 60	.68	1.88	.41	T	.00	6.63
Tustin	T	T	T	.24	1.19	2.82	1.49	1.18	5.73	3.00	.00	.0(	15 65
Ukiah	.00	.00	.00	4.66	9.21	5.71	7.26	2.50	5.20	.01	T	T	34.55
Upland	.00	.00	.00	.41	2.05	2.54	3 97	2.10	9.45	4.00	.68	.00	25.15
Upper Lake	.00	.07	.00	3.60	5 15	3.70	6.23	1.91	4.90	.20	.08	T	25.84
Upper Mattole	.07	.00	.08	7.94	23.02	15.98	23.05	6.62	15.65	1.88	.74	.88	95.86
Vacaville	.00	T	.00	3.53	3.21	2.00	4.95	1.83	6.26	.01	T	T	21.79
Valley Springs	.00	.00	.00	1.53	3.12	3.11	6.57	1.28	7.92	2.50	.00	.00	26.03
Ventura	.00	......	.00	.45	3.60	....	.88	1.08	5.25	2.04	.00	.00	....
Vina	.00	T	.00	1.63	5.66	2.00	1.70	.78	4.73	.00	.90	.00	17.40
Visalia	.00	.00	.00	.64	1.37	.71	1.77	.60	2.17	.25	T	.05	7.56
Volcano	.80	.00	T	.00	.95	.95	.00	.00	.00	.00	.00	.00	2.70
Wasco	.00	.00	.0c	.25	.85	.36	1.40	.65	.60	.20	.00	.00	4.81
Watsonville	.00	.00	.00	1.06	2.51	1.66	4.10	2.27	6.86	.08	.00	.00	18.54
Westley	.00	.00	.00	.00	.76	.70	1.51	.92	5.10	2.02	.07	.00	11.08
Wheatland	.00	.04	.00	2.00	2.11	3.81	6.31	1.66	6.51	.49	.07	.00	23.30
Williams	.00	T	.00	1.44	2.95	1.07	2.10	1.34	3.62	.80	.00	.00	13.32
Willits	.00	.02	.00	5.55	16.00	9 66	12.36	4.15	7.56	.18	T	.02	55.50
Willows	.00	T	.00	2.20	4.32	.96	2.48	1.35	5.76	T	.03	T	17.10
Winters	.00	.00	.00	1.26	3.40	1.25	4.23	2.22	6.24	.00	.00	.00	18.60
Woodland	.00	.00	.00	2.13	2.60	2.13	1.89	.47	4.12	1.00	T	.00	14.34
Zenia	.19	.08	.12	4.66	17.99	11.95	17.29	5.37	9.6.	.76	.43	.79	69.25

T indicates a trace of precipitation.

NORMAL CLIMATOLOGICAL DATA FOR SAN FRANCISCO, CALIFORNIA, FOR THIRTY-TWO YEARS.

Compiled by the United States Weather Bureau.

	Jan.	Feb.	March.	April.	May.	June.	July.	Aug.	Sept.	Oct.	Nov.	Dec.
Temperature												
Mean for Month	50°	52°	54°	55°	57°	59°	59°	59°	61°	60°	56°	52°
Highest mean Year	55° 1873	57° 1886	58° 1885	59° 1889	60° 1890	62° 1888	62° 1885	63° 1894	65° 1889	64° 1887	59° 1894	54° 1885
Lowest mean Year	46° 1890	48° 1887	49° 1897	52° 1896	53° 1898	56° 1894	56° 1901	56° 1891	58° 1899	57° 1881	53° 1897	49° 1895
Highest Date and Year	78° 26th 1899	80° 18th 1899	80° 7th 1892	88° 14th 1888	97° 28th 1857	100° 29th 1891	98° 15th 1888	92° 22d 1891	94° 22d 1894	94° 6th 1899	83° 16th 1895	72° 8th 1893
Lowest Date and Year	29° 15th 1888	32° 5th 1887	33° 3d 1896	40° 7th 1891	44° 16th 1894	47° 19th 1893	47° 31st 1893	47° 8th 1893	49° 30th 1894	45° 14th 1881	38° 27th 1896	34° 24th 1879
Precipitation.												
Mean for Month	4.53	3.50	3.05	1.85	0.76	0.21	0.02	0.01	0.31	1.31	2.72	4.44
Greatest fall Year	24.36 1862	12.52 1878	8.75 1879	10.06 1880	3.52 1888	2.57 1884	0.23 1886	0.21 1864	1.06 1898	7.28 1889	11.78 1885	15.16 1866
Lowest fall Year	0.58 1852	0.00 1864	0.24 1898	0.00 1857	0.00 *	0.00 *	0.00 *	0.00 *	0.00 *	0.00 *	0.00 1890	0.00 1876
Greatest rainfall in 24 hours, date and year	4.67 29th 1881	3.60 4th & 5th 1887	3.31 4th & 5th 1879	2.43 23d & 24th 1896	1.29 4th & 5th 1889	1.23 11th & 12th 1884	0.23 16th 1886	0.06 29th & 30th 1896	1.04 29th & 30th 1894	2.03 17th & 18th 1889	8.98 28d 1874	3.14 18th & 19th 1871
Average No. days with .01 of an in. or more	11	10	10	7	4	2	1	0	2	4	7	11
Clouds & Weather.												
Average No. Clear days	11	10	11	12	13	14	12	10	14	16	15	12
Average No. partly Cloudy days	10	10	11	12	12	11	14	15	12	11	9	10
Average No. Cloudy days	10	8	9	6	6	5	6	6	4	4	6	9
Wind.												
Prevailing direct'n	N	SW	W	W	W	W	SW	SW	W	W	W	SE
Highest velocity Direction Date Year	57 SE 3d 1901	49 S 25th 1902	60 S 1st 1902	47 NW 23d 1871	45 W 11th 1897	48 SW 30th 1878	41 W 15th 1898	42 SW 2d 1893	40 W 27th 1899	41 W 10th 1899	56 SE 30th 1892	60 SE 23d 1892

* Many years.

FROSTS.

Average date of first "Killing" in autumn, December 10th.
Average date of last "Killing" in spring, January 25th.

NORMAL CLIMATOLOGICAL DATA FOR FRESNO, CALIFORNIA, FOR FIFTEEN YEARS.

Compiled by the United States Weather Bureau.

	Jan.	Feb.	March	April	May	June	July	Aug.	Sept.	Oct.	Nov.	Dec.
Temperature.												
Mean for Month	45°	51°	54°	61°	67°	75°	82°	81°	74°	63°	55°	46°
Highest mean / Year	51° 1896	54° 1898	59° 1900	67° 1888	72° 1897	80° 1859	85° 1859	86° 1858	83° 1858	69° 1888	59° 1894	49° 1896
Lowest mean / Year	42° 1898	47° 1890	49° 1897	55° 1896	63° 1899	69° 1894	79° 1895	75° 1899	68° 1893	60° 1899	52° 1897	44° 1895
Highest / Date and Year	69° 15th 1893	8° 20th 1896	86° 6th 1899	101° 25th 189-	104° 21st 1892	112° 30th 1891	114° 1st 1891	113° 11th 1898	111° 24th 1888	95° 4th 1889	82° 7th 1894	72° 5th 1895
Lowest / Date and Year	20° 1st 1888	24° 6th 1899	28° 1st 1888	34° 5th 1895	38° 1st 1899	45° 2d 1899	51° 8th 1891	50° 31st 1887	44° 22d 1895	36° 17th 1892	27° 25th 18-8	23° 21st 1897
Precipitation.												
Mean for Month	1.54	1.34	1.75	1.11	0.50	0.18	T	0.01	0.26	0.67	1.15	1.79
Greatest fall / Year	4.14 1895	4.35 1884	4.22 1-93	3.42 1884	1.69 1884	1.16 1893	0.07 1896	0.15 1896	1.26 1890	3.17 1889	9.54 1885	4.09 1894
Lowest fall / Year	0.34 1889	0.00 1885	0.17 1887	0.00 1898	0.00 1897	0.00 *	0.00 *	0.00 *	0.00 *	0.00 1890	0.08 1884	0.33 1900
Greatest rainfall in 24 hours, date and year	1.46 4th & 5th 1895	1.48 9th 1893	1.22 20th 1893	1.68 21th 1896	0.94 14th & 15th 1894	0.74 5th 1894	0.06 25th 1896	0.15 30th 1896	1.12 29th 1890	1.73 22d & 23d 1889	1.33 16th 1888	2.10 29th & 30th 1891
Average No. days with .01 of an in. or more	8	6	8	8	3	1	0	0	1	3	4	9
Clouds & Weather.												
Average No. Clear days	9	15	13	19	21	26	29	25	25	20	17	9
Average No. partly Cloudy days	8	7	10	8	7	3	2	6	3	7	7	9
Average No. Cloudy days	14	6	8	3	3	1	0	0	2	4	6	13
Wind.												
Prevailing direct'n	NW	NW	NW	NW	NW	NW	NW	W	NW	NW	NW	NW
Highest velocity / Direction / Date / Year	32 NW 16th 1898	30 NW 10th 1894	38 SE 2d 1896	30 NW 15th 1894	34 NW 30th 1894	30 NW 17th 1891	24 E 4th 1896	24 N 4th 1891	26 W 20th 1895	25 W 16th 1892	30 W 30th 1892	25 NW 29th 1887

* Many years.

FROSTS.

Average date of first "Killing" in autumn, December 1st.
Average date of last "Killing" in spring, March 19th.

NORMAL CLIMATOLOGICAL DATA FOR SACRAMENTO, CALIFORNIA, FOR FIFTY YEARS.

Compiled by the United States Weather Bureau.

	Jan.	Feb.	March.	April.	May.	June.	July.	Aug.	Sept.	Oct.	Nov.	Dec.
Temperature.												
Mean for Month. ...	46°	50°	55°	59°	64°	70°	74°	73°	70°	63°	54°	47°
Highest mean...... Year..................	53° 1873	55° 1877	60° 1885	68° 1857	70° 1865	77° 1858	81° 1854	77° 1888	76° 1853	78° 1853	58° 1894	51° 1861
Lowest mean...... Year..................	42° 1888	46° 1880	49° 1880	53° 1896	58° 1860	65° 1894	69° 1859	66° 1873	65° 1854	58° 1881	49° 1880	43° 1890
Highest............ Date and Year...	72° 30th 1899	80° 18th 1899	80° 30th 1882	89° 28th 1888	98° 26th 1888	106° 30th 1891	107° 21st 1891	110° 11th 1898	106° 11th 1888	98° 3d 1885	78° 1st 1890	69° 8th & 9th 1893
Lowest............ Date and Year....	19° 14th & 15th 1888	21° 13th 1884	29° 15th 1880	36° 17th 1892	39° 12th 1880	44° 1st 1890	48° 17th 1887	48° 30th 1887	44° 18th 1882	36° 14th 1881	27° 28th 1880	24° 29th 1878
Precipitation.												
Mean for Month. ...	3.83	2.80	2.85	1.74	0.80	0.12	0.03	0.01	0.18	0.76	2.09	4.87
Greatest fall........ Year..................	15.04 1862	8.50 1854	10.00 1850	14.20 1880	3.25 1889	1.45 1884	0.68 1860	0.20 1896	1.26 1895	6.02 1889	11.34 1885	13.40 1852
Lowest fall......... Year..................	0.15 1889	0.04 1899	0.04 1898	T 1875 *	0.00 *	0.00 *	0.00 *	0.00 *	0.00 *	0.00 *	0.00 1890	0.00 1876
Greatest rainfall in 24 hours, date and year............	2.06 29th 1881	2.48 4th & 5th 1887	2.94 8th & 9th 1884	7.24 21st 1880	1.94 5th 1889	0.82 11th & 12th 1884	0.04 4th 1895	0.20 30th 1896	0.88 29th 1894	1.86 21st & 22d 1859	4.29 17th & 18th 1885	2.96 2d 1880
Average No. days with .01 of an in. or more.............	9	8	9	6	4	1	0	0	2	3	5	10
Clouds & Weather.												
Average No. Clear days...	12	12	14	15	20	24	29	29	25	22	19	11
Average No. partly Cloudy days...............	9	9	9	10	8	5	2	2	4	7	6	9
Average No. Cloudy days...	10	7	8	5	3	1	0	0	1	2	5	11
Wind.												
Prevailing direct'n	SE	SE	SE	S	SW	S	S	S	W	S	N	SE
Highest velocity Direction............ Date................ Year................	48 SE 4th 1895	48 NW 10th 1894	48 SE 29th 1892	39 NW 22d 1897	44 NW 9th 1895	42 NW 12th 1886	30 NW 1st 1892	28 SW 5th 1896	36 NW 23d 1889	48 S 20th 1894	48 S 30th 1892	60 SE 9th 1894

* Many years.

FROSTS.

Average date of first "Killing" in autumn, November 15th.
Average date of last "Killing" in spring, February 16th.

NORMAL CLIMATOLOGICAL DATA FOR LOS ANGELES, CALIFORNIA, FOR TWENTY-FIVE YEARS.

Compiled by the United States Weather Bureau.

	Jan.	Feb.	March	April	May	June	July	Aug.	Sept.	Oct.	Nov.	Dec.
Temperature.												
Mean for Month	54°	55°	57°	60°	63°	67°	71°	71°	70°	64°	60°	56°
Highest mean Year	58° 1896	60° 1896	62° 1885	63° 1885	66° 1885	71° 1883	74° 1891	75° 1885	74° 1888	68° 1890	66° 1890	61° 1890
Lowest mean Year	49° 1890	51° 1880	52° 1880	56° 1896	60° 1894	63° 1894	65° 1880	68° 1900	60° 1880	60° 1886	56° 1880	53° 1891
Highest Date and Year	87° 9th 1896	88° 16th 1896	99° 29th 1879	99° 13th 1888	103° 25th 1896	105° 7th 1890	109° 25th 1891	106° 19th 1885	108° 21st 1885	105° 3d 1855	96° 3d 1890	88° 3d 1878
Lowest Date and Year	30° 29th 1880	28° 6th 1883	31° 9th 1893	38° 21st 1896	40° 16th 1888	46° 13th 1894	49° 12th 1888	50° 6th 1883	44° 23d 1880	40° 22d 1892	34° 19th 1886	30° 14th 1878
Precipitation.												
Mean for Month	2.90	3.09	2.85	1.17	0.47	0.08	0.02	0.04	0.05	0.80	1.26	3.58
Greatest fall Year	7.83 1890	13.37 1884	12.36 1884	5.06 1880	2.06 1892	1.39 1884	0.24 1886	0.61 1889	0.73 1894	6.95 1889	6.53 1900	15.80 1889
Lowest fall Year	0.20 1887	T 2 yrs	0.01 1885	0.02 1897	0.00 1886	0.00 4 yrs	0.00 9 yrs	0.00 8 yrs	0.00 9 yrs	0.00 1891	0.00 2 yrs	T 1900
Greatest rainfall in 24 hours, date and year	4.17 25th& 26th 1890	3.94 14th& 15th 1887	3.18 3d & 4th 1884	2.20 9th& 10th 1884	1.76 2d & 3d 1892	0.87 13th 1884	0.24 14th 1886	0.61 31st 1889	0.71 30th 1894	3.62 21st 1889	3.75 28th 1892	4.30 11th& 12th 1889
Average No. days with .01 of an in. or more	6	6	7	6	3	1	0	0	0	3	3	7
Clouds & Weather.												
Average No. Clear days	17	14	12	11	11	10	12	14	17	18	19	17
Average No. partly Cloudy days	8	9	12	12	14	17	18	16	12	10	8	9
Average No. Cloudy days	6	5	7	7	6	3	1	1	1	3	3	5
Wind.												
Prevailing direct'n	NE	NE	W	W	W	W	W	W	W	W	W	NE
Highest velocity Direction Date Year	48 NE 8th 1882	40 W 17th 1884	46 SW 12th 1881	42 W 12th 1888	30 NW 1st 1887	24 W 9th 1892	22 W 14th 1886	22 W 18th 1885	28 W 16th 1882	34 NE 7th 1887	43 NE 9th 1881	37 E 14th 1887

FROSTS.

Average date of first "Killing" in autumn—none reported.(?)
Average date of last "Killing" in spring, March 19th.

NORMAL CLIMATOLOGICAL DATA FOR RED BLUFF, CALIFORNIA, FOR TWENTY-FIVE YEARS.

Compiled by the United States Weather Bureau.

	Jan.	Feb.	March	April	May.	June.	July.	Aug.	Sept.	Oct.	Nov.	Dec.
Temperature.												
Mean for Month..	45°	49°	55°	59°	67°	75°	82°	81°	73°	64°	54°	47°
Highest mean...... Year..................	50° 1881	54° 1886	61° 1885	67° 1888	73° 1897	81° 1878	86° 1887	84° 1885	81° 1888	71° 1887	59° 1894	50° 1886
Lowest mean...... Year..................	39° 1890	43° 1887	48° 1897	52° 1896	60° 1899	69° 1894	78° 1884	74° 1889	60° 1882	56° 1881	50° 1897	42° 1891
Highest............ Date and Year....	77° 27th 1899	82° 25th 1888	86° 9th 1892	96° 24th 1898	110° 29th 1887	110° 30th 1891	115° 8th 1887	114° 22d 1891	108° 1st 1891	97° 5th 1892	88° 3d 1890	79° 5th 1885
Lowest............ Date and Year....	18° 14th 1888	22° 14th 1884	28° 16th 1880	34° 15th 1896	37° 7th 1879	44° 1st 1898	58° 1st 1881	52° 27th 1881	46° 12th 1893	32° 14th 1881	26° 30th 1880	25° 13th 1884
Precipitation.												
Mean for Month. ...	4.74	3.57	3.19	2.06	1.34	0.50	0.02	0.04	0.63	1.30	2.95	5.40
Greatest fall........ Year..................	20.71 1878	16.66 1878	7.81 1884	7.05 1880	3.02 1892	2.61 1888	0.17 1891	0.54 1896	2.91 1885	8.41 1889	17.05 1885	12.85 1880
Lowest fall... ...... Year..................	0.51 1887	0.01 1899	T 1885	0.58 1888	0.18 1884	0.00 3 yrs	0.00 8 yrs	0.00 14 yrs	0.00 4 yrs	0.00 1887	0.00 1890	0.52 1883
Greatest rainfall in 24 hours, date and year............	5.11 16th 1878	3.80 17th 1879	2.17 9th 1884	2.08 20th 1880	1.67 9th & 10th 1890	0.84 3d & 4th 1888	0.10 9th 1891	0.54 29th & 30th 1896	2.91 24th 1885	1.70 20th 1889	4.78 9th & 10th 1885	5.04 19th 1879
Average No. days with .01 of an in. or more.............	11	9	11	9	6	3	1	2	2	6	2	11
Clouds & Weather.												
Average No. Clear days...	13	13	9	13	16	22	28	29	25	20	17	11
Average No. partly Cloudy days...	9	9	11	11	10	6	3	2	4	8	7	9
Average No. Cloudy days ..	9	7	11	6	5	2	0	0	1	3	6	11
Wind.												
Prevailing direct'n	N	N	N	S	S	S	S	S	NW	N	N	N
Highest velocity Direction............ Date.................. Year.................	60 N 9th 1880	52 N 18th 1880	42 S 9th 1884	48 NW 15th 1880	40 S 6th 1889	42 S 14th 1888	36 S 8th 1887	26 S 31st 1889	40 N 30th 1882	46 N 14th 1878	44 N 27th 1885	52 N 19th 1879

FROSTS.

Average date of first "Killing" in autumn, November 20th.
Average date of last "Killing" in spring, March 15th.

APPENDIX.

RATES OF COMMISSIONS AND BROKERAGE.

TO BE CHARGED WHERE NO EXPRESS AGREEMENT TO THE CONTRARY EXISTS.

Adopted by the Chamber of Commerce of San Francisco, May 9th, 1871, as Amended to Date.

Commission on purchase of stocks, bonds and all kinds of securities, including the drawing of bills, for payment of same........... 1 per ct.

On sale of stocks, bonds and all kinds of securities, with guarantee of sale, and remittance in bill.. 1 per ct.

(But in this and all other cases where no charge is made for guarantee of Bill of Exchange, the party shall remit in first-class paper, without guarantee, unless the Bill be endorsed by him.

On purchase or sale of specie, gold dust or bullion, on amounts not exceeding $20,000.. 1 per ct.

On purchase or sale of specie, gold dust or bullion, on any excess over $20,000... ½ per ct.

For drawing or endorsing bills of exchange ....1¼ per ct.

On sale of bills of exchange without endorsement .... 1 per ct.

On sale of merchandise from domestic Atlantic ports, with guarantee 5 per ct.

On sale of merchandise from foreign ports, with guarantee ....7½ per ct.

On goods received on consignment, and afterwards withdrawn, on invoice cost...2½ per ct.

(The receipt of the Bill of Lading to be considered equivalent to receipt of the goods.

On purchase and shipment of merchandise, with funds in hand, on cost and charges, when not exceeding $2,500............ ..... 5 per ct.

On purchase and shipment of merchandise, with funds in hand, on excess over $2,500..3½ per ct.

On purchase and shipment of merchandise without funds in hand, on cost and charges.. 5 per ct.

For collecting and remitting delayed or litigated accounts..........10 per ct.

For collecting general claims....................................2½ per ct.

For collecting and paying or remitting money from which no other commission is derived.. 1 per ct.

For collecting freight by vessels from domestic Atlantic ports, on amount of freight list or charter party. ....2½ per ct.

For collecting freight by vessels from foreign ports, on amount collected..2½ per ct.

For attending to general average matters and collecting contributions,
- on the first $10,000, or any smaller amount.................... 5 per ct
- on any excess over $10,000 to $30,000........................ 2½ per ct.
- on any excess over $30,000.................................... 1 per ct.

(A deposit to cover probable amount of contribution, or security to the satisfaction of the merchant attending to the matter, to be furnished by the claimant of goods.)

For landing and re-shipping goods at this port from vessels in distress, on market value.. 1¼ per ct.

(The merchant entitled to such commission being held in all cases to have assumed the responsibility of the safe keeping of the Cargo, except as to damage resulting from natural accidents.)

For accepting and paying a bottomry on respondencia bond........ 2½ per ct. (Interest to be also allowed for the time used.)

On purchase or sale of vessels................................. 2½ per ct.

For entering, clearing and transacting ship's business on vessels with
- cargo or passengers, on vessels under 500 tons register........ $100
- on vessels from 500 to 1,000 tons register.................... $150
- on vessels over 1,000 tons register........................... $200

(If the vessel be chartered and cleared by different consignees, the commission not to exceed one-half of the above rates to each.)

For disbursements of vessels by consignees, with funds in hand..... 2½ per ct.
For disbursements of vessels by consignees, without funds in hand.. 5 per ct.
For procuring freight or passengers........................... 5 per ct.
For chartering vessels, on amount of freight, actual or estimated, to be considered due when the charter is effected.................. 5 per ct.

(But no charter to be considered as effected or binding until a memorandum or one of the copies of the charter party has been signed. Where no special rate of exchange is stipulated on outward charters, payable in sterling, the pound sterling to be valued at $4 86 U. S. gold coin.)

On giving bonds for vessels under attachment in litigated cases, on amount of liability.. 2½ per ct.

For receiving and transhipping, or otherwise forwarding goods, on invoice amount, on the first $3,000, or any smaller amount.... 2½ per ct.

For receiving and transhipping, or otherwise forwarding goods, on invoice amount, on any excess over $3,000.................... 1 per ct.

For effecting marine insurance, when no commission for sale or purchase is charged, on amount of premium...................... 5 per ct.

The foregoing commissions to be exclusive of brokerage and every charge actually incurred.

Brokerage, on purchase or sale of merchandise.................... 1 per ct.

On bonded goods in warehouse, as per class, per month, 37½ to 62½ cents per ton of 40 cubic feet, or of 2,000 lbs. On bonded goods stored outside or in yard of warehouse, 37½ cents per ton. On free goods, as per class, 25 to 37½ cents per ton of 2,000 lbs., or of 40 cubic feet.

In all cases a fraction of a month to be charged as a month.

REGULATIONS.

CONCERNING DELIVERY OF MERCHANDISE, PAYMENT OF FREIGHT, ETC.

When no express stipulation exists per Bill of Lading, goods are to be considered as deliverable on shore.

Freight on all goods to be paid, or secured to the satisfaction of the captain or consignee of the vessel, prior to the delivery of goods.

After the delivery to the purchaser of merchandise sold, no claim for damages, deficiency or other cause, shall be admissible, unless made within three days, and no such claim shall be admissible after goods sold and delivered have once left the city.

When foreign Bills of Lading do not expressly stipulate the payment of freight in a specific coin, foreign currency shall be reckoned according to the United States value thereof, and payment be made in any legal tender of the United States;

When foreign Bills of Lading expressly stipulate that the freight shall be paid in a specific coin, then the same must be procured, if required, or its equivalent given—the rate to be determined by the current value at the time in San Francisco.

When no special agreement is contained in a charter party, lay days shall commence as follows: For vessels from foreign ports with general cargo, as soon as vessel is in her discharging berth, and a general order has been issued by the Custom House.

For vessels with Coal from Atlantic or Australian ports, five running days after arrival, provided that discharging berth can be procured.

In the case of coal-laden vessels, when no special quantity is fixed by the charter party, the minimum quantity to be discharged per working day shall be 150 tons.

In the case of grain-loading vessels, when the charterer does not furnish stiffening within forty-eight hours from the time notice is given him by the captain or consignee, the time lost should count as lay days on the charter.

For tare on Wool Bags, two pounds is to be allowed for each new sack, and three and one-half pounds for each second-hand sack.

For tare on China Sugar, four pounds is to be allowed for each mat containing four pockets of about 25 pounds each.

All other rates of tare are to be allowed as by custom in New York, except when otherwise provided.

For vessels loaded with general cargo, when no special quantity is fixed by the charter party, the minimum quantity to be discharged per weather working day shall be two hundred tons.

ARBITRATION CLAUSE BILLS OF LADING.

"Any disputed claim against the vessel not exceeding $100.00 to be settled by the Arbitration Committee of the Chamber of Commerce of the port in which dispute arises or by arbitrators selected by the parties in interest, and to be binding on said parties, arbitration fees to be paid by looser or loosers."

Stevedore Rates, Rates of Pilotage, Rates of Dockage and Tolls

STEVEDORE RATES.
DISCHARGING.
Per 2240 lbs.

Coal, Full Cargo	$ .35
Cement	.32½
Coal, Navy Yard	.36¼
Pig Iron & Ballast	.40
Chalk and Sulphur	.35
Sheet and Bar Iron—under 100 tons	1.00
" " " over 100 tons	.75
R. R. Iron	.60
Boiler Plates—Medium	.60
" " Large	.90
Scrap Iron	.90
Jute and Seeds—40 cub. ft.	.32½
Soda, Bleaching Powder and Paints	.35
Nitrate, Sulph. of Ammonia and Shale	.45
Coke, Glass, Fire Brick	.70
Structural Iron, Blooms and Shafting	1.25
Slab Block, Marble and Machinery up to Two Tons	1.50
" " over Two Tons	2.00
Other Mdse. not Specified (Weight or Measurement)	.35

LOADING.

Wheat—2240 lbs.	.30
Barley and Flour—2000 lbs.	.30
Bran—40 cub. ft.	.30
Canned & Barreled Salmon, 2240 lbs.	.45
Canned Fruit—2000 lbs.	.45
Orchilla and Pulu, Gen'l. Mdse. 40 cub. ft.	.35
Wine and Tallow in Barrells—2000 lbs.	.75
Lumber, per Thousand ft.	1.40

Oakland or Stream 10c extra

Ties, per Thousand ft.	.75
Structural and Scrap Iron per ton—2000 lbs.	1.00

BALLAST

Supplied and Put on Board—2000 lbs.	1.00
Lighterage when Required	.50
Hauling Ballast where Carts can be used from the City Wharf	.
Where Lighters must be used	.60

CHARGES FOR ENTERING.

Survey	$3.00
Entry	2.50
Official certificate and oath	.20

CHARGES FOR CLEARANCE.

Clearance...	$2.50
Official certificate and oath..........................	.20
Post entry, if any....................................	2 00

RATES OF PILOTAGE.

INTO OR OUT OF THE HARBOR OF SAN FRANCISCO.

All vessels under five hundred tons, five dollars per foot draught; all vessels over five hundred tons, five dollars per foot draught and four cents per ton for each and every ton registered measurement; when a vessel is spoken, inward or outward bound, and the services of a pilot are declined, one-half of the above rates shall be paid. In all cases where inward-bound vessels are not spoken until inside the bar, the rates of pilotage and one-half pilotage above provided shall be reduced fifty per cent. Vessels engaged in the whaling or fishing trade shall be exempt from all pilotage, except where a pilot is actually employed.

RATES OF DOCKAGE, TOLLS AND WHARFAGE.

Extracts from Rules and Regulations of Board of State Harbor Commissioners,.

DOCKAGE.

EACH RATE IS FOR A DAY OF TWENTY-FOUR (24) HOURS. OR ANY PART THEREOF.

50.—For all ocean vessels, steam or sail, and all sail vessels, steamboats, and barges navigating the bay of San Francisco and the rivers and other waters flowing into it, of two hundred net registered tons or under, 2 cents per ton; for all such vessels of over two hundred net registered tons, $4 for the first two hundred tons, and ¾ of a cent for each additional ton.

51.—All vessels docking at a wharf with freight on board shall be charged full rates, unless additional cargo is to be taken on board. All vessels discharging shall be charged full rates *until* ready for "stiffening," when they may be placed on half rates. After receiving "stiffening" they shall be charged full rates until through discharging.

52.—Vessels while taking in cargo, or receiving or discharging ballast, or lying idle, or occupying outside berths, or moored in docks, slips, basins or canals, are subject to only half rates of dockage; *provided*, that vessels not used for carrying freight or passengers, or that are engaged in towing, shall not be entitled to such half rates.

53.—When the per diem dockage of a vessel, as above prescribed, is not a multiple of five, it must be reduced or increased, as the case may be, to the nearest such multiple; *provided*, that if it be equally near to two such multiples, it must be increased to the first such multiple above.

54 —All bills for dockage must be paid when due, whether approved by the master or not. Failure to pay said bills on presentation will subject the vessels to be placed on the Delinquent List, and to the penalties provided by law. Errors, if any, will be rectified by the Board.

55.—When a vessel of any kind is charged or has paid dockage at a wharf for any day, she may use the same or any other wharf during that day without further charge, no matter how often she may leave and return; *provided*, a receipt for payment or transfer card from the Wharfinger at the first wharf be produced; and on application of the master the Wharfinger is required to issue such transfer card.

RATES OF DOCKAGE ON LIGHTERS.

56.—A dockage rate of 1 cent per ton per day will be charged on all lighters in the following cases:

When discharging or loading at a wharf.

When discharging into or loading from a vessel lying at a wharf, or when lying at a wharf or in a slip with cargo on board.

When transporting from a wharf to a vessel, or from a vessel to a wharf, but one dockage will be made per day.

TOLLS.

57.—A ton is by weight 2,000 pounds, unless otherwise specified; by measurement, 40 cubic feet.

58.—Merchandise, for the purpose of tolls or wharfage, must be computed by weight or measurement, as the one mode or the other will give the greater number of tons.

59.—Of the following articles 2,240 pounds constitute a ton: Coal, railroad iron, pig iron, gypsum, asphaltum, ores, crude or boiled sulphur, paving stones, sand, and ballast.

TOLLS PER TON.

60—On Merchandise (except where otherwise specified), per ton	5 cents
On 400 pounds or less	1 "
On 800 pounds or less and more than 400 pounds	2 "
On 1,200 pounds or less and more than 800 pounds	3 "
On 1,600 pounds or less and more than 1,200 pounds	4 "
On 2,000 pounds or less and more than 1,600 pounds	5 "

[Tolls on merchandise, when measured or charged a higher rate, to be collected according to the foregoing subdivisions.]

TOLLS CHARGED OTHERWISE THAN BY THE TON.

61.—On the following articles toll must be paid as follows:

On Hay, per ton	5 cents
On Fir, Redwood, Spruce, and all soft-wood lumber, per 1,000 feet, board measure	5
On Oak, Hickory, Ash, and all hard-wood lumber, per 1,000 feet, board measure	10
On Lumber or Timber discharged in the water in any slip, dock, basin, or canal, the same as if discharged on a wharf.	
On Piles discharged in any slip, dock, basin, or canal, per pile	3
On Fence Posts, per 100	5
On Railroad Ties, per 1,000 feet of lumber, board measure, contained therein (32 or 24 feet to a tie, according to size)	5

Tolls.

On Redwood Shingles, per 40 bundles	5 cents
On Cord Wood, per cord	5 "
On Tan Bark and Stave Bolts, per cord	5 "
On Fire Bricks, per 1,000	15 "
On Bricks (other than Fire Bricks) discharged on, or loaded from, any wharf, per 1,000	10 "
On Bricks (other than Fire Bricks) discharged from any vessel lying at any wharf, or in any slip, dock, or basin, into another vessel, or received into any such vessel from any lighter or other vessel, per 1,000	5 "
On Wool or Cotton in sacks, per sack	1 "
On Wool or Cotton in bales, strapped, per bale	1½ "
On Hops in bales, per bale	1 "
On Hides of Cattle (green or dry) per hide	¼ "
On Skins, per skin	1/16 "
On Cattle, Horses, and Mules, per head	5 "
On Colts and Calves under a year old, per head	2½ "
On Crushed Rock (long ton)	5 "
On Sheep and Hogs, per head	1 "
On Reapers, Mowers, Horse Rakes, Hay Presses, Gang Plows, Cultivators, and Wheeled Vehicles, set up, each	10 "
On Headers and Separators, set up, each	20 "
On Empty Barrel (merchandise) stays	¼ "
On Laths, per 60 bundles	5 "
On Shakes, per 100 bundles	5 "
On Charcoal, per 35 sacks (of 55 pounds each)	5 "
On Cement, 5 barrels to the ton	5 "
On Lime, 8 barrels to the ton	5 "
On Beef, Pork, or Fish, 6 barrels to the ton	5 "
On Sugar or Syrup, 6 barrels to the ton	5 "
On Empty Sugar Barrels	¼ "
On Wine or Liquor, per barrel	1¼ "
On Wine or Liquor, per pipe	5 "
On Cocoanuts, per 1,000	15 "
On Bananas, per bunch	¼ "
On Salmon, per ton of 2,000 pounds	5 "
Crude Oil, (whether in barrels or bulk), per ton of 2,000 pounds	5 "

Crude Oil, naptha, gasoline, etc. conveyed either inward or outward, over or through any wharf, bulkhead or other State structure, or loaded or discharged in any slip, basin or channel, per ton of 2,000 pounds .... 5 cents

62. (The weight of crude oil contained in tanks or vessels or conveyed to or from shipping to be computed on the basis of 7¾ pounds per gallon, *if actual weight is not obtainable.*)

63 On Empty Packages being returned to the owner, who uses them to send commodities to market, no tolls will be charged.

64. No tolls will be charged on grain, flour, or mill stuffs for passing over the wharves under the Board's jurisdiction; but such articles will be subject to the same rules and rates of wharfage as are imposed on other merchandise, except on Sections 1 and 2 of the seawall.

65. The term "grain" is intended to and does include wheat, barley, oats, corn, and rye; the term "flour" includes only the flour of wheat, and "millstuffs" includes only bran, middlings, shorts, and ground food.

66. No tolls will be charged on donkey engines or stevedores' tools when taken on the wharf for the purpose of loading or discharging a vessel; nor on milk, butcher, baker, ice, or laundry wagons on their daily trips to supply customers.

67. Merchandise landed on a wharf, and not removed therefrom, may be reshipped from the same wharf, on the payment of one toll and the wharfage, if any, due thereon.

68. Merchandise, except hay and bricks (other than fire bricks), discharged from a vessel lying at any wharf or within any slip, into lighters or other vessels, or received into any such vessel from lighters or other vessels, is subject to the same rates of toll as if discharged on or loaded from a wharf.

69. When the tolls have been paid on merchandise, on its discharge into lighters, it may be landed thence on a wharf, or discharged into a vessel, without the payment of further tolls; except bricks (other than fire bricks), which shall be charged as follows: on bricks, 5 cents per one thousand.

WHARFAGE.

70. Merchandise, except wheat, barley, oats, corn, rye, flour, bran, middlings, shorts, beans, and seeds, on Sections 1 and 2 of the seawall, must be removed from the wharf before 6 o'clock P. M. on the day following the one on which it was placed thereon; but Wharfingers are hereby authorized, when the owners or consignees of merchandise desire it, and it can be done without interfering with the business of the wharf, to allow merchandise to remain on the wharf after the prescribed time, at a wharfage charge equal to an additional toll for every forty-eight hours or part thereof. If merchandise be not removed within twenty-four hours after notice by the Wharfinger, it shall be liable to the penalties of Section 2524 of the Political Code, as amended November 29, 1889.

71. *Provided,* That parties engaged in the lumber business at the northern extremity of East street may be permitted to utilize Pier No. 51 (Powell street Wharf) for the storage of lumber at the rate of 10 cents per M. feet per month or a less time exceeding four days. All lumber to be removed on the order of the Chief Wharfinger.

75. All vessels carrying oil for fuel must store the same in steel or iron tanks.

76. No vessel carrying oil for fuel in wooden tanks or wooden compartments shall be allowed to lie alongside or make fast to any other vessel while the same is lying at any Dock, Pier or Wharf, or to lie alongside or make fast to any structure under the jurisdiction of the Board of State Harbor Commissioners.

RULES AND REGULATIONS FOR THE HANDLING OF FUEL OIL AT DOCKS, PIERS AND WHARVES ON THE WATERFRONT OF THE CITY AND COUNTY OF SAN FRANCISCO, CALIFORNIA.

77. All oil for fuel purposes must be delivered through a steam pump so as to pump the oil into the vessel to be supplied as quickly as possible, and all vessels carrying oil for fuel must be kept clear of rubbish, etc., which is liable to catch fire from sparks.

78. No vessel loaded with Coalinga oil or any other oil which will flash below 110 degrees Fahrenheit shall be permitted to haul alongside of any vessel or structure.

79. No vessel shall discharge fuel oil into any other vessel lying at any dock, Pier or Wharf except from sunrise to sunset from October 1st to April 1st; and from April 1st to October 1st, between the hours of 7:00 o'clock A. M. and 7:00 o'clock P. M.

80. No vessel engaged in the business of supplying fuel oil shall be allowed when empty to haul or lie alongside any vessel, dock, pier or wharf, and vessels after having discharged oil, must immediately haul away from vessel or structure.

BY-LAWS

OF THE

CHAMBER OF COMMERCE

OF SAN FRANCISCO.

ADOPTED MAY 12TH, 1868; AS AMENDED TO DATE.

ARTICLE I.

MEETINGS.

The Regular Meetings of the Chamber shall be held every three months, to wit: On the third Tuesdays in January, April, July, and October, at such hour as the Board of Trustees shall order.

ANNUAL MEETING.

The next Annual Meeting shall be the Regular meeting in January, 1874, and thereafter the Regular Meeting in the month of January in each year shall be the Annual Meeting. The Officers and Trustees elected in May, 1873, shall hold office until the Annual Meeting in January, 1874, and until their successors are installed.

Special Meetings may be held at any time on the call of the President, who shall call such meetings whenever requested to do so by any five members. At all meetings of the Chamber fifteen members shall constitute a quorum.

ARTICLE II.

OFFICERS.

The Annual Election for officers shall be held on the second Tuesday of January, in each and every year, under the supervision of a Committee to be appointed by the Board of Trustees. The polls shall be open from 12 M. to 3 o'clock P. M. on the day of election. There shall be elected fifteen Trustees, one of whom shall be designated on the ballot as President, another as Vice-President, and another as Second Vice-President, who shall be, respectively, President and Vice-President of the Corporation and Board of Trustees. Said Trustees so elected shall constitute a Board, to be known and designated as "The Board of Trustees of the Chamber of Commerce of San Francisco." And said Officers and Trustees shall hold their offices for one year from the third Tuesday of January following their election, and until their successors are duly installed.

The Board of Trustees shall have power to manage all the financial affairs of the Corporation. They shall elect or appoint from among the members of the Chamber, or otherwise, a Secretary, a Treasurer, a Librarian, and such other agents and servants as the business of the Corporation shall require, who shall hold their offices at the pleasure of the Board, and shall receive such compensation as said Board shall affix to their respective offices. Said Board shall also have the power to levy and collect assessments, and to fix the amount of dues to be paid by the members, which shall not be less than twelve dollars per annum. They shall also have power to elect and admit members of the Corporation. They shall have the general charge of all the funds and other property of the Corporation. *Provided* that the collection of any assessment levied by the Board of Trustees shall be suspended upon the written dissent thereto of ten members, addressed to the President, until such assessment has been affirmed by a vote of the Chamber, at either a regular or special meeting.

VACANCIES.

Any Trustee ceasing to be a member of the Chamber, or failing to attend three consecutive meetings of the Board, unless debarred by sickness or absence from the city, his office shall thereupon become vacant. All vacancies shall be filled by a new election at the next regular meeting of the Chamber.

BOARD MEETINGS.

The regular meetings of the Board shall be held the second Tuesday in each and every month. Special meetings may be called by the President at any time, who shall call such meeting whenever requested by any three Trustees. At all meetings of the Board of Trustees, five members shall constitute a quorum.

ARTICLE III.

PRESIDENT.

It shall be the duty of the President to preside at all meetings of the Board of Trustees and of the Chamber; to call special meetings, as elsewhere in these By-Laws provided, and to present at the annual meeting a report reviewing the action of the Chamber upon the various matters which shall have been under consideration during the preceding year, and making such suggestions as in his judgment the interests of the Chamber may require. In addition to his vote as a member, he shall have a casting vote at all meetings, both of the Board of Trustees and of the Chamber.

VICE-PRESIDENTS.

The Vice-Presidents, in the order of their rank, shall, in the absence of the President, perform all his duties.

CHAIRMAN PRO TEM.

In the absence of the President and both Vice-Presidents from any meeting, a Chairman *pro tem.* shall be appointed for such meeting.

CITIZENSHIP.

The President and Vice-Presidents shall be citizens of the United States and of the State of California.

ARTICLE IV.

SECRETARY.

The Secretary shall keep a fair record of all the proceedings of the Chamber; shall present at its meeting such of the communications made to him officially as the Board of Trustees shall select for that purpose; and give proper notice of the meetings of the Board and of the Chamber, and report at the annual meeting the existing number of members, together with the deaths resignations and additions of members during the year.

He shall act as Secretary of the Board of Trustees, and shall keep a fair record of their proceedings. He shall attend all meetings of the Committee of Arbitration and Appeals, and shall record the points at issue in the cases submitted to them, and the decisions given. All his records shall at all times be open to the inspection of any member of the Chamber.

He shall perform such other duties as may be assigned him by the Chamber, or by the Board of Trustees.

All communications proceeding from the Chamber shall be signed by the President and Secretary, and attested by the seal of the Chamber.

ARTICLE V.

TREASURER.

The Treasurer shall collect, or cause to be collected all dues, fines and assessments, and take charge of the funds of the Chamber, and pay out the same, under the direction of the Finance Committee of the Board of Trustees; and shall also deposit any surplus funds belonging to the Chamber, in some savings institution, with the approval of said Finance Committee and the President of the Chamber. He shall keep regular accounts of money received and expended, and report at each meeting of the Board of Trustees the condition of the Treasury. He shall render a detailed account at the annual meeting of the Chamber, which shall be certified to by the Finance Committee of the Board of Trustees, showing all the transactions during the previous year.

ARTICLE VI.

LIBRARIAN.

The Librarian shall make and keep a catalogue of all the books, maps and charts which may belong to the Chamber, and attend to their preservation. He shall allow of their proper use by the members of the Chamber. He shall report, at the annual meeting, the additions that shall have been made during the previous year, specifying separately such books as shall have been purchased, and such as shall have been donated, and the names of the parties contributing the same. The same person may be eligible to the three offices of Secretary, Treasurer and Librarian.

LIBRARY.

The Board of Trustees shall have power to employ any funds of the Chamber, not required for necessary expenses, or otherwise appropriated for the purchase of maps, and financial, commercial and statistical books for the Library.

ARTICLE VII.

OF THE BOARD OF TRUSTEES.

At the first regular or special meeting of the Board of Trustees, held after the adoption of these By-Laws, and thereafter at the first regular or special meeting following the annual meeting of the Chamber, the President shall appoint, from among the members of the Board, eight Standing Committees for the year, as follows:

1st. A committee of three, on "Finance," whose duty it shall be to supervise the accounts of the Treasurer; to examine all bills before payment (and none shall be paid without their approval); to recommend assessments when they shall deem them necessary, and to certify to the statement of the Treasurer to the annual meeting of the Chamber.

2d. A committee of three on "Library." This committee shall have general supervision of the Library, and shall also have the general charge of the rooms and furniture.

3d. A committee of three on "Membership," whose duty it shall be to receive all applications for membership, and report thereon to the Board.

4th. A committee of five, on "Arbitration," to whom may be referred all cases of mercantile disputes arising between members of the Chamber, or between parties not members, which may be submitted to the Chamber for settlement This committee shall meet at the call of its chairman. All parties claiming its service shall make statements of their points in writing, and shall have the right of producing witnesses, under the regulations and direction of the Committee,

5th. A committee of five, on "Appeals," to whom appeal may be made from the decisions of the Committee on Arbitration, under such regulations as the Board of Trustees may at any time adopt; but no decision of the Committee on Arbitration, shall be appealed from, unless the appeal be made in writing within five days after the delivery to the parties interested, of the decision of the Committee on Arbitration.

6th. A committee of three on "Foreign Commerce and the Revenue Laws."
7th. A committee of three on "Internal Trade and Improvements."
8th. A committee of three on "Harbor and Shipping."
9th. A committee of three on "Reception and Entertainment."

Their duty shall be to examine into and make report upon such subjects as may be referred to them, or they may originate and report to the Chamber such views as they may deem proper for its consideration. A majority of each committee shall be a quorum thereof. Vacancies in any committee shall be filled at the next regular meeting of the Board.

ARTICLE VIII.
MEMBERSHIP.

Any mercantile firm, merchant, merchandise broker. manufacturer, banker, or officer of a local insurance company, resident in the States of California, Oregon, Nevada, or Washington, may become a member of this Chamber on a proposal signed by a member in writing, addressed to the Committee on Membership, who shall report thereon to the Board at the next regular meeting thereof, when a ballot shall take place, and the candidate shall be declared to be admitted unless three negatives shall appear against him; in which case he cannot again be proposed during the ensuing twelve months. Any other person may be elected a member of the Chamber upon the unanimous recommendation of the Committee on Membership and the unanimous vote of the Board of Trustees. *Honorary Members* may be elected by the unanimous recommendation of the Committee on Membership and the unanimous action of the Board of Trustees, confirmed by a two-thirds vote of the Chamber. Such Honorary Membership shall be conferred only in acknowledgment of eminent services rendered the Republic or for aid given the Chamber on behalf of public interests germane to its organization, and not over two such Honorary Memberships shall be conferred in any one year. The vote for Honorary Membership shall be by ballot.

The Secretary shall forthwith notify all successful candidates of their election; and invite them to sign these By-Laws, in a book to be provided for that purpose. Without such signature in person or by attorney, within one month after his election, the candidate elected shall be deemed to have declined his election.

Every membership shall be entitled to one vote at all meetings and elections of the Chamber.

All elections of persons or firms to membership requiring the unanimous recommendations of the Committee on Membership and the unanimous vote of the Board of Trustees, shall be held by secret paper ballot and in no such case shall a motion be entertained that the ballot be cast by the Secretary.

ARTICLE IX.

DUES AND ASSESSMENTS.

Every member shall pay to the Treasurer, on demand, for the use of the Chamber, such sum (which shall not be less than three, or more than six dollars, payable quarterly in advance) as the Board of Trustees shall assess for the payment of current expenses.

No dues shall be deemed to be remitted or abated by reason of absence from the State.

A member refusing or neglecting to pay fines, dues or assessments, for three months after the same become due or payable, or guilty of any conduct unbecoming his calling, may be expelled from the corporation by a two-thirds vote of the entire Board of Trustees.

ARTICLE X.

RESIGNATIONS.

Any member desirous of resigning his membership, shall address a letter of resignation to the Secretary, which shall be his warrant for erasing the name of such member from the rolls. But no such resignation shall be deemed valid unless all the dues and assessments chargeable against the member resigning shall have been fully paid.

ARTICLE XI.

ARBITRATION FEES.

The Secretary shall be entitled to five dollars for his services in calling a meeting of the Committee on Arbitration or Appeals, and a further sum of five dollars for each copy of an award he may be called on to furnish. In addition to the said compensation of the Secretary, each of the parties shall pay such fee, not less than ten dollars nor more than one hundred dollars, as the Committee shall deem reasonable with reference to the importance of the case. When either of the parties litigant is a member of the Chamber, he shall pay one-half the committee-fee that would otherwise be chargeable under this section.

All fees for arbitration, or an appeal, shall be paid to the Treasurer—one-half for the use of the Chamber, and the balance to be equally divided among such members of the Committee on Arbitration as shall have been in regular attendance during the examination in which the fees in question shall have accrued. All awards by either of these committees shall be reported at the next regular meeting of the Chamber.

ARTICLE XII.

ELECTIONS.

All elections, by either the Chamber or Board of Trustees, shall be by ballot. At elections for Trustees the fifteen receiving the highest number of votes shall be elected; and those receiving the highest number of votes for President and Vice-Presidents shall be elected to those offices respectively; *Provided*, nevertheless, that twenty votes shall be necessary in all cases to elect an officer or Trustee. In case fifteen Trustees are not chosen at the annual election, the others may be elected at the annual, or a subsequent, meeting of the Chamber.

ARTICLE XIII.

SEAL.

The Board of Trustees shall devise and procure, as soon as possible after the adoption of these By-Laws, a suitable seal for the Chamber.

ARTICLE XIV.

AMENDMENTS.

These By-Laws may be amended in the following manner:

1st. The proposed amendment shall be first passed by a two-thirds vote of the members present at a regular meeting of the Board of Trustees.

2d. It shall then be passed by a majority vote of the members present at the next regular meeting of the Chamber.

ARTICLE XV.

All persons who were members of "The Chamber of Commerce of San Francisco" previously to the adoption of these By-Laws, shall be invited by he Secretary to sign the same, either in person or by proxy, failing wherein, after notice and opportunity so to do, they shall be deemed to have declined to continue their membership.

AMENDMENT ADOPTED JULY 18, 1893.

POLITICAL QUESTIONS.

Political questions that are partisan in their nature are prohibited from consideration or action by the Chamber.

RULES OF ORDER.

ARTICLE I.

At all regular meetings of the Chamber, the order of business shall be as follows:
1. Reading of minutes.
2. Presentation of communications.
3. Election to fill vacancies.
4. Reports of Committees on Arbitration and Appeals
5. Reports of other Committees.
6. Unfinished business.
7. New business.

At the Annual Meeting of the Chamber, the order of business shall be
1. Reading of minutes.
2. Report of the Secretary.
3. Report of the Treasurer.
4. Report of the Librarian.
5. Report of the President.
6. Election to fill vacancies.
7. Miscellaneous business.

ARTICLE II.

RULES OF ORDER AT BOARD MEETINGS.

At all regular meetings of the Board of Trustees, the order of business shall be as follows:
1. Roll call.
2. Reading of minutes.
3. Reports of Secretary, Treasurer and Librarian.
4. Report of Committee on Membership, and balloting for new members
5. Filling of vacancies.
6. Presentation of communications.
7. Reports of Committees.
8. Unfinished business.
9. New business.

ARTICLE III.

These rules of order may be suspended for any meeting, of either body by a vote of two-thirds of the members present at such meeting.

ARTICLE IV.

MANUAL.

Cushing's Manual shall be the authority for the decision of all parliamentary questions that may arise at meetings, either of the Chamber or of the Board of Trustees.

ARTICLE V.

NAMES TO BE ENTERED.

At all the meetings, both of the Chamber and of the Board, the Secretary shall enter on the minutes the names of the members present; and no member shall leave the meeting previous to adjournment without permission from the Chair

OFFICERS AND TRUSTEES
OF THE
CHAMBER OF COMMERCE OF SAN FRANCISCO,
FROM DATE OF ORGANIZATION.

	1851-2.	1852-3.	1853-4.	1854-5.	1855-6.
President	Beverly C. Sanders	Beverly C. Sanders	D. I. Ross	J. B. Thomas	J. B. Thomas
1st Vice do	*	*	*	*	J. R. Rollinson
2d Vice do	*	*	*	*	H. F. Dana
Secretary, Treasurer and Librarian	Lewis W. Sloat	Lewis W. Sloat	Lewis W. Sloat	John H. Williams	Wm. R. Wadsworth
Membership	*	*	*	*	*

	1856-7	1857-8.	1858-9.	1859-60.	1860-1.
President	F. W. Macondray	Dan'l Gibb	Dan'l Gibb	Albert Dibblee	Albert Dibblee
1st Vice do	H. F. Dana	*	*	Jas. De Fremery	Geo. H. Kellogg
2d Vice do	H. Carlton, Jr	*	*	Geo. H. Kellogg	C. J. Dempster
Secretary, Treasurer and Librarian	Wm. R. Wadsworth	Wm. R. Wadsworth	Wm. R. Wadsworth	Wm. R. Wadsworth	Wm. R. Wadsworth
Membership	*	*	*	May 1859—65	May 1860—93

†The Records of the Chamber having been lost in 1859, the Secretary has been unable to obtain this information.

List of Officers.

LIST OF OFFICERS OF THE CHAMBER OF COMMERCE FROM 1861 to 1868

	1861-2.	1862-3.	1863-4.	1864-5.
President	G. H. Kellogg	G. H. Kellogg	Jas. De Fremery	Jas. De Fremery
1st Vice do	C. J. Dempster	C. J. Dempster	C. Adolphe Low	C. Adolphe Low
2d do	Jas. De Fremery	Jas. De Fremery	J. Y. Halleck	R. Gibbons
Executive Committee	C. J. Dempster	J. W. Clark	J. B. Thomas	J. B. Thomas
	Wm. C. Ralston	Wm. C. Ralston	Geo. F. Bragg	R. G. Sneath
	J. W. Clark	C. J. Dempster	R. G. Sneath	Geo. F. Bragg
Secretary, Treasurer and Librarian	Wm. R. Wadsworth	Wm. R. Wadsworth	Wm. R. Wadsworth	Wm. R. Wadsworth
Membership	May 1861—111	May 1862—111	May 1863—114	May 1864—105

	1865-6.	1866-7.	1867-8.
President	J. A. Donohoe	R. G. Sneath	R. G. Sneath
1st Vice do	W. Meyer	Robt. B. Swain	R. B. Swain
2d do	C. W. Brooks	J. W. Stow	J. W. Stow
Executive Committee	R. G. Sneath	Albert Miller	John Everding
	L. B. Benchley	W. Bartlett	W. Bartlett
	Albert Miller	A. L. Tubbs	J. W. H. Campbell
Secretary, Treasurer and Librarian	Wm. R. Wadsworth	Wm. R. Wadsworth	Wm. R. Wadsworth
Membership	My 1865—114	May 1866—235	May 1867—237

LIST OF OFFICERS OF THE CHAMBER OF COMMERCE FROM 1868 to 1873.

	1868-9.	1869-70.	1870-1.	1871-2.	1872-3.
President	James Otis	James Otis	Robt. B. Swain	Robt. B. Swain	C. Adolphe Low
1st Vice-President	I. Friedlander	I. Friedlander	C. Adolphe Low	C. Adolphe Low	Wm. T. Coleman
2d Vice-President	G. W. Beaver	Geo. W. Beaver	Alex. Weill	Wm. T.	I. Friedlander
Trustee	Wm. F. Babcock	Wm. F. Babcock	W. F. Babcock	Wm. F. Babcock	Wm. F. Babcock
Trustee	Ira P. Rankin	Ira P. Rankin	H. P. Blanchard	C. A. C. Duisenberg	H. P. Blanchard
Trustee	Thos. H. Selby	Fk. H. Selby	Albert Dibblee	Jas. Otis	C. Christiansen
Trustee	R. Gibbons	R. Gibbons	Jas. Linforth	J. C. Merrill	Albert Dibblee
Trustee	J. W. H. Campbell	C. Adolphe Low	Ira P. Rankin	I. W. Raymond	Horace Davis
Trustee	Robt. B. Swain	Ro. B. Swain	Levi Sachs	J. H. Redington	O. Eldridge
Trustee	L. Sachs	L. Sachs	L. B. Benchley	Albert Dibblee	James Otis
Trustee	Jas. DeFremery	Jas. DeFremery	Jas. DeFremery	Horace Davis	Thos. H. Selby
Trustee	Jas. Linforth	Jas. Linforth	C. T. Hopkins	J. T. Dean	J. W. tSw
Trustee	Fred. L. Castle	Fred. L. Castle	James Otis	W. W. Montague	Robt. B. Swain
Trustee	H. B. Williams	H. P. Blanchard	L. Sachs	James Otis	Levi Sas.
Trustee	O. Eldridge	O. Eldridge	Jml H. Wise	L. Sachs	John Wise
Secretary, Treasurer, and Librarian	C. T. Hopkins	W. Bartlett	W. Bartlett	W. Bartlett	W. Bartlett
Membership	May 1868—237	May 1869—239	May 1870—240	May 1871—246	May 1872—225

List of Officers.

LIST OF OFFICERS OF THE CHAMBER OF COMMERCE FROM 1873 to 1878.

	1873-4.	1874-5.	1875-6.	1876-7.	1877-8.
President	Wm. T. Coleman	W. F. Babcock	W. F. Babcock	I. Friedlander	I. Friedlander
1st Vice-President	Wm. F. Babcock	I. Friedlander		J. C.	J. C. Merrill
2d Vice-Pres't	I. Friedlander	J. D. Walker	J. C.	L. W. Raymond	L. W. Raymond
Trustee	H. P. Blanchard	J. C. Merrill	C. Adolphe Low	Horace Davis	E. D. Heatley
Trustee	C. Christiansen	M. J.	L. W. Raymond	W. N. Olmsted	W. N.
Trustee	Jas. DeFremery	L. W. Raymond	M. P.	Ira P. Rankin	Ira P. Rankin
Trustee	O. Eldridge	H. B.	Jas. C. Patrick	Geo. F. Bragg	Geo. F. Bragg
Trustee	James Otis	G. H. Eggers	A. L. Tubbs	Levi Stevens	Levi S
Trustee	J. W. Stow	N. C.	Fred. L. Castle	W. N. Hawley	W. N. Hawley
Trustee	G. F. Bragg	M. P.	J. C.	D. C. McRuer	D. C.
Trustee	Albert Dibblee	R. C.	W. Norris	C. Adolphe Low	C. Adolphe Low
Trustee	J. C. Merrill	Jas. C. Patrick	W. N.	W. C. Talbot	W. C. Talbot
Trustee	Jas. C.	H. B.	N. C. Fassett	W. W. Dodge	W. W. Dodge
Trustee	Wm. H. Selby	Fred. Roeding	Horace Davis	D. D. Shattuck	D. D.
Trustee	John H.	C. L. Taylor	C. L.	Alfred P. Elfelt	Alfred P. Elfelt
Secretary, Treasurer, and Librarian	W. Bartlett	Henry Mel	Henry Mel	Henry Mel	Henry Mel
Membership	May 1873—238.	Jan'y 1874—234.	Jan'y 1875—241.	Jan'y 1876—232.	Jan'y 1877—227.

LIST OF OFFICERS OF THE CHAMBER OF COMMERCE FROM 1878 to 1883.

	1878-9.	1879-80.	1880-1.	1881-2.	1882-3.
President	Jas. C. Patrick	Geo. C. Perkins	W. F. Babcock	Wm. F. Babcock	Wm. F. Babcock
1st Vice-President	J. C. Merrill	J. C. Merrill	A. P. Williams	A. P. Williams	A. P. Williams
2d Vice-President	I. W. Raymond	I. W. Raymond	A. D. Walker	Fred. L. Castle	E. D. Heatley
Trustee	W. N. Olmsted	Wm. N. Olmsted	A. B. Forbes	Wm. Dibblee	Aw Welch
Trustee	Sam'l Hart	Sam'l Hart	G. W. McNear	Wm L. Merry	A. Cheesebrough
Trustee	Robt. Balfour	R. Balfour	Mrs Heller	Jas. DeFremery	S. L.
Trustee	H. P. Bd	H. P. Bd	Edward Kruse	R. B. Forman	Claus Spreckels
Trustee	W. B. Hooper	W. B. Hooper	Fred. L. Castle	Eugene DeSabla	Robt. Balfour
Trustee	Chas. Goodall	Chas. Goodall	Chas. Gall	W. H. Dimond	Alfred P. Elfelt
Trustee	S. L. Jones	S. L. Jones	Jas. R. Kelly	Fred'k Jacobi	Eugene DeSabla
Trustee	W. W.	W. W. Montague	Jabez Ms.	E. L. G. Steele	W. W. Dodge
Trustee	Chs Sel ds	Claus Is	F. W. Macondray	W. W. Dodge	W. J.
Trustee	Kalman Haas	Wn Is	A. McKinlay	W. W. Montague	Jas. DeFremery
Trustee	J. J. McKinnon	J. J. McKinnon	Gb T. Fay	John Kentfield	A. Scrivener
Trustee	A. B. Forbes	A. B. Forbes	J. J. McKinnon	J. N. Knowles	
Secretary, Treasurer, and Librarian	Henry Mel	Morris Marcus	Mrs M ms	Mrs Marcus	Morris Marcus
Membership	Jan'y 1878—221.	Jan'y 1879—214.	Jan'y 1880—161.	Jan'y 1881—156.	Jan'y 1882—171.

LIST OF OFFICERS OF THE CHAMBER OF COMMERCE FROM 1883 to 1888.

	1883-4.	1884-5.	1885-6.	1886-7.	1887-8.
President	Hoe Davis	Hoe Es	Hnry L. Dodge	Henry L. Dodge	William L. Merry
1st Vice-President	D. J. Stap d	D. J. Staples	Wllm L. Mr	Wllim L. Mry	E. L. G. Steele
2d V-President	Aw W dh	Aw Wch	E. L. G. Steele	E. L. G. Se	Gs Gdall
Te	J. L. McKinnon	J. J. En	J. N. Ms	J. N. Knowles	C. L. Taylor
Te	G. W. eBr	G. W. Mar	Alfred P. Elfelt	Alfred P. Elfelt	Am Gt
Te	H. Beveridge	C. L. Taylor	W. H. Ed	W. H. Ed	John L. Howard
Tstee	A. Chesebrough	J. N. Knowles	A. E. Ht	A. E. Hecht	W. J. Ms
Trustee	Alfred P. Elfelt	Alfred P. Elfelt	C. L. Taylor	C. L. Tr	Ira P. En
Trustee	Be DeSabla	Eugene DeSabla	Bt Miller	Bt Miller	E. W. Ell
Te	Aw Gd	Aw Gd	E. W. El	E. W. Ball	Fred. L. Ge
T te	H. L. E. Meyer	H. L. E. Meyer	Fred. L. Ge	Fred. L. Ge	W. W. Montague
Be	J ms De Fremery	William L. My	J. J. McKinnon	J. J. McKinnon	Gs Br
Be	R. Hr	Chas. W. Whitney	W. W. Me	W. W. Mgue	J. M. Roma
1 Te	E. L. G. Se	E. L. G. Steele	L. L. Baker	L. L. Baker	C. B. t Se
Te	b S. Tr	Jacob S. Tr	Hugh Craig	Hugh Craig	H. L. E. Meyer
Ry, Treasurer, ad Librarian	Morris Marcus	Morris Marcus	Morris M	Ms Ms	E. J. Haynes
Membership	Jan'y 1883—168.	Jan'y 1884—156.	Jan'y 1885—169.	Jan'y 1886—175.	Jan'y 1887—220.

LIST OF OFFICERS OF THE CHAMBER OF COMMERCE FROM 1888 to 1893.

	1888-89.	1889-90.	1890-91.	1891-92.	1892-93.
President	Willam L. ...	Ira P. ...	G. C. Perkins ...	C. L. Taylor ...	E. B. Pond ...
1st Vice-President	E. L. G. t Sle ...	... Gall	C. L. Taylor ...	W. H. Dimond ...	W. H. Dimond ...
2d ...	C. ...	C. L. Taylor ...	G. W. ... Dr	J. F. Ch rn ...	J. F. ... an
...	C. L. ...	R. B. F ... rn	W. T. Y. ... eSk	Wm. L. Merry ...	W. L. ... Mry
...	E. Balfour ...	W. H. ... Bt	Geo. H. Sanderson ...	W. T. Y. Schenck ...	W. T. Y. Schenck ...
...	...s Carol an...	... Gn	W. H. Harries ...	W. W. Spaulding ...	A. J. Ralston ...
Trustee	Fred L. ... Ge	Ed. L. ... Ge	J bn D. S els ...	Gs. R. All n ...	W. W. Montague ...
...	Robt. Watt ...	Bt. ... Mt	A. J. Ralston ...	A. J. Ral sm ...	Barry ... En
...	Ira P. Rankin ...	W. T. Y. Schenck ...	John Rosenfeld ...	J hn Rosenfeld ...	C. L. Taylor ...
...	W. W. Montague ...	W. W. Montague ...	Arthur R. Briggs ...	Arthur R. ... gs	Mr R. ... gs
Trustee	G. W. McNear ...	G. W. McNear ...	as F. ... n	J. J. ... Mn	dn Rosenfeld ...
...	as F. ... Gn	as F. ... Gn	Robert ... t	Robert Watt ...	M. P. Jones ...
...	H. L. E. Meyer ...	C. L. Dingley ...	E. W. eWhall ...	C. B. Stone ...	J. J. ... Mn
...	R. W. Simpson ...	A. R. ... gs	as G ... n	imes ... Glan	dn F. Merrill ...
...	E. W. ... ll	E. W. ... hall	W. E. ... Idl wy	Gs B. Parrott ...	Gs B. ... B.
Sey, Treasurer, and Lib ian	Thos. J. Haynes	Thos. J. Haynes	Thos. J. Haynes	Ths. J. Haynes	Ths. J. Haynes
Membership	Jan'y 1888—231.	Jan'y 1889—247.	Jan'y 1890—239.	Jan'y 1891—259.	Jan'y 1892—310.

LIST OF OFFICERS OF THE CHAMBER OF COMMERCE FROM 1893 to 1898.

	1893-94.	1894-95.	1895-96.	1896-97.	1897-98.
President	E. B. Pond	W. H. Dimond	W. H. Dimond	Hugh Craig	Hugh Craig
1st Vice-President	W. H. Dimond	Jas. F. Chapman	Hugh Craig	Jm L. Howard	John L. Howard
2d Vice-President	Jas. F. Chan	Hugh Craig	W. T. Y. Schenck	his B. arott	his B. arott
Trustee	Wm. L. Merry	E. B. Pond	E. B. Pond	W. H. Dimond	Louis Sloss, Jr.
Trustee	A. J. Ralston	R. D. Laidlaw	W. L. Merry	W. L. Merry	Charles M. Yates
Trustee	W. T. Y. Schenck	Louis B. Parrott	A. J. n	Jas. F. afman	George A. Newhall
ee	hur R. Briggs	Chas. Nelson	his B. Parrott	Chas. Nelson	Charles Nelson
e	C. L. Taylor	C. L. Taylor	Geo. A. Newhall	A. J. Ralston	W. E. Mighell
Trustee	Charles n	iWam Merry	Walter M. Castle	Go. A. Ne all	A. G. Towne
Trustee	J. J. McKinnon	J. N. Knowles	Jas. F. Chapman	ohis Ss, Jr.	A Gerberding
e	his B. Parrott	W. T. Y. Schenck	C. L. Taylor	A. G. Towne	Len Blum
Trustee	J. N. Knowles	C. Carpy	J. J. McKinnon	H. T. Scott	Edward Coleman
stee	John Dolbeer	A. J. Ralston	is. Nelson	A. B. Field	Oscar T. Sewall
ee	C. Carpy	J. J. McKinnon	Louis Ss, Jr	F. W. Van Sicklen	A. B. Field
ee	H. B. Hunt	Go. A. all	Arthur G. Towne	Chas. M. s	W. L. Merry
Secretary, Treasurer and Librarian	Tos. J. Haynes	Ts. J. Haynes	L. H. Clement	W. L. Merry	Wm. L. Merry
Membership	Jan'y, 1893—310.	Jan'y, 1894—315.	Jan'y, 1895—308.	Jan'y, 1896—342.	Jan'y, 1897—406.

List of Officers of the Chamber of Commerce from 1898 to 1901.

	1898-99.	1899-1900.	1900-1901.	1901-1902.	1902-1903.
President	Hugh Craig	Geo. A. Newhall	Charles Nelson	Geo. A. Newhall	G. A. Newhall
1st Vice-President	Charles Nelson	H. F. Allen	Geo. A. Newhall	Henry F. Allen	E. R. Dimond
2d Vice-President	Geo. A. Newhall	Leon Blum	H. F. Allen	Wm. E. Mighell	Wm. E. Mighell
Trustee	H. F. Allen	Frank L. Brown	Wakefield Baker	Wakefield Baker	C. H. Bentley
"	Frank L. Brown	E. R. Dimond	E. R. Dimond	E. R. Dimond	W. J. Dutton
Trustee	Leon Blum	A. B. Field	A. B. Field	W. J. Dutton	A. B. Field
"	Edward Bannan	R. D. Fry	Henry F. Fortmann	A. B. Field	Wm. L. Gerstle
"	E. R. Dimond	Geo. W. McNear, Jr.	William Haas	Wm. L. Gerstle	Rufus P. Jennings
"	A. B. Field	Wm. E. Mighell	W. H. Marston	William Haas	Wm. H. Marston
Trustee	H. Rosenfeld	M. A. Newell	W. H. Marston, Jr.	C. Ed Hooker	G. W. McNear, Jr.
Trustee	Edwin Gill	H. Rosenfeld	Geo. W. McNear, Jr.	W. H. Marston	Gus Rosenfeld
Trustee	Wm. E. Mighell	Fred Tillman, Jr.	Wm. E. Mighell	Geo. W. McNear, Jr.	Henry Rosenfeld
"	Fred. Tillman, Jr.	A. G. Towne	H. Rosenfeld	H. Rosenfeld	James B. Smith
"	A. G. Towne	Chas. M. Yates	A. G. Towne	A. G. Towne	A. G. Towne
"	Charles M. Yates		Chas. M. Yates	Chas. M. Yates	Chas. M. Yates
Secretary, Treasurer and Librarian	E. Scott	E. Scott	E. Scott	E. Scott	E. Scott
	Honorary Members 12	Honorary Members 12	Honorary Members 12	Honorary Members 12	Honorary Members 12
	Active 396	Active 412	Active 432	Active 443	Active 616
	Total Membership 408	Total Membership 424	Total Membership 444	Total Membership 455	Total Membership 628

LIST OF OFFICERS OF THE CHAMBER OF COMMERCE FOR 1903 to 1905.

	1903-4.	1904-5
President	Geo. A. Newhall	Geo. A. Newhall
1st Vice-President	E. R. Dimond	E. R. Dimond
2nd Vice-President	Wm. E. Mghell	C. H. Bentley
Trustee	C. H. Bentley	Frank L. Brown
"	W. J. Dutton	W. J. Dutton
Trustee	A. B. Field	J. A. Folger
"	Wm. S. Gerstle	Wm. L. Gerstle
"	Rufus P. Jennings	Rufus P. Jennings
"	Wm. H. Marston	H. D. Loveland
"	Geo. W. Mr, Jr.	W. H. Marston
Trustee	James Otis	Thos. Rickard
"	Henry Rosenfeld	James Rolph, Jr.
"	James B. Smith	Henry Rosenfeld
"	E. L. Eyre	Jas. B. Smith
Trustee	Chas M. Yates	Wm. R. Wheeler
Secretary, Treasurer and Librarian	E. Scott	E. Scott
Honorary Members	11	11
Active Members	592	6.2
Total Membership	603	643

LIST OF MEMBERS

OF THE

CHAMBER OF COMMERCE

SAN FRANCISCO

HONORARY MEMBERS.

Hon. W. W. Morrow, U. S. Circuit Judge, Appraisers' Building.
Prof. Geo. Davidson, 530 California St.
A. G. Menocal, Civil Engineer, U. S. Navy, Washington, D. C.
Hon. Warner Miller, ex-United States Senator, New York City.
A. E. K. Benham, Rear Admiral, U. S. N., 1508 Ninth St., Washington, D. C.
Hon. John T. Morgan, United States Senator, Washington, D. C.
President American Chamber of Commerce, Paris, France.
George Dewey, Admiral, U. S. N., Washington, D. C.
Hugh Craig, 210 Sansome St., San Francisco.
Hon. Wm. L. Merry, United States Minister to San Jose, Costa Rica.
Charles Nelson, 6 California St., San Francisco, Cal.
*Lewis A. Kimberly, Rear Admiral, U. S. N.
*Daniel Ammen, Rear Admiral, U. S. N.
*Col. Geo. H. Mendell, U. S. Engineer.
*Hon. Lorenzo Sawyer.
*Hon. Wm. H. Webb.

*Deceased.

MEMBERS.

Name.	Firm.	Place of Business.
Adams, W. J.	Lumber and Shipping	6 California.
Alaska Commercial Co.		310-312 Sansome.
Alaska Packers' Ass'n		308 Market.
Allen, Chas. R.	Wholesale Coal Dealer	144 Steuart.
Allen, E. T.	Sporting Goods, etc.	414 Market.
Alexander, Edgar	Ins. Mgr. Parrott & Co.	318 California.
Alexander & Baldwin	Commission Merchants	308 California.
Alexander, S. T.		308 Market.
Allen, Henry F.	Shipping and Com. Mer.	202 California.
Albion Lumber Co.		Fifth and Channel.
Adams, Edson F.	Far. and Mer. Sav. Bank	Oakland, Cal.
American Steel & Wire Co.		Sixteenth and Folsom.
American Biscuit Co.		Broadway and Battery.
Anglo-California Bank		NE. cor. Sansome-Pine.
Anglo-American Crockery Co.		108 Pine.
Armsby, J. K. Co.	Commission Merchants	138 Market.
Andros, Milton	Attorney-at-Law	320 Sansome.
Atlantic Gulf & Pacific Co.	Contractors	220 Market.
Avery, Wm. H.	Toyo Kisen Kaisha	421 Market.
Ames & Harris	Manufacturers Bags, etc.	101 Drumm.
American Beet Sugar Co.		123 California.
Ames Mercantile Co.	Manufacturers' Agents	Luning Bldg.
American National Bank		Mills Bldg.
American Can Co.	H. W. Phelps, Mgr.	214 Mission.
Aronson, A.	Capitalist	340 Post.
American Milling Co.	Flour and Mill Products	Union and Battery.
American-Hawaiian Engineering and Construction Co.		Rialto Bldg.
Alaska Codfish Co.		17 Davis.
Alameda Sugar Co.		132 Market.
Associated Oil Co.		Hayward Bldg.
Arnstein, Simon & Co.	Importers Cloths, etc.	585 Market.

Name.	Firm.	Place of Business.
Bank of California		NW. cor. Cal.-Sansome.
Bank of British North America		120 Sansome.
Bates, Morris U.	Commercial Pub. Co.	463 Mission.
Baker, Wakefield	Baker & Hamilton	Pine and Davis.
Barton, Wm. F.	Union Pacific Salt Co.	218 Sacramento.
Birmingham, John	Pres't Cal. Powder Wks.	330 Market.
Beebe, Chas. W.	Trumball & Beebe	419 Sansome.
Bertheau, Cesar	Fire Insurance Agent	423 California.
Bee, Everett N.	Otis, McAllister & Co.	109 California.
Bennett & Goodall	Shipping, etc.	204 California.
Bishop, Chas. R.	Vice-Pres't Bank of Cal.	Occidental Hotel.
Bissinger & Co.	Hides, Wool, etc.	401 Front.
Bissell, Wm. A.	Santa Fe R. R. System	641 Market.
Blake, Moffitt & Towne	Wholesale Paper Dealers	55 First.
Blanchard & Page	Imp. Teas and Matting	623 Sansome.
Bley, Mel. A.	"Pacific Coast Merchant"	212 Sansome.
Boole, W. A. & Son	Shipbuilders	20 California.
Brandenstein, M. J.	M. J. Brandenstein & Co.	Spear and Mission.
Brown, A. A.	Merchandise Broker	202 Market.
Brown, J. Dalzell	Vice-Pres't Cal. Safe Dep.	Cor. Cal. and Mtgy.
Britton & Rey	Lithographers	525 Commercial.
Brigham, Hoppe & Co.	Dairy Dealers	205 California.
Briggs, A. R.	Bank of California	400 California.
Buckingham & Hecht	Shoe Manufacturers	225 Bush.
Bunker, C. D. & Co.	Ship, Frt. and Cust. Brok.	435 Battery.
Bunker, Wm. M.	1417 G St., N. W.	Washington, D. C.
Butler, Geo. E.	Insurance Agent	200 Pine.
Butler, A. H.	20 Broad St.	New York City, N. Y.
Byxbee & Clark	Commission Merchants	48 Market.
Beadle, Donald, Beadle & Co.	Shipping Merchants	22 Market.
Bailey, Jas. D.	Ins. Co. of North Am.	202 Pine.
Boesch Lamp Co.		585 Mission.
Borel, Ant. & Co.	Bankers	Nevada Block.
Boston Woven Hose and Rubber Co.		14 Fremont.
Bosworth, Chas. J.	Gen. Agt. The F. & C. Co.	318 California.
Brann & Prior	Sailmakers	56 Clay.
Brooks-Follis Electric Co.		527 Mission.
Blake, Anson S.	Secretary Blake Co.	6 California.
Burns, Isidor	Shipsmith	20 Steuart.
Balfour, Guthrie & Co.	Shipping and Commission	316 California.
Bartnett, W. J.	Pres't S. F. T. Ry. & F. Co.	Safe Deposit Bldg.
Boyd, John F.	Real Estate	Nevada Block.
Baumann, John D. & Co.	Fibres, Gums, etc.	409 California.
Bass-Heuter Paint Co.		816 Mission.
Bekeart, Phil B. Co.	Arms and Ammunition	114 Second.
Bickford, C. E.	Coffee Broker	38 California.
Bliss & Faville	Architects	Crocker Bldg.
Bovee, Toy & Co.	Real Estate	117 Montgomery.
Boyd, George D.	Real Estate	22 California.
Bradford, Brodie M.	Sec'y A. & S. J. R. R.	515 Safe Deposit Bldg.
Bonestell, Richardson & Co.	Wholesale Paper	401 Sansome.
California Cotton Mills Co.		310 California.
California Fruit Canners' Ass'n		Pine and Battery.
California Powder Works		330 Market.
California Shipping Co.		42 Market.
California Wine Ass'n		661 Third.
Canadian Bank of Commerce		Cal. and Sansome.
Castle Bros.	Wholesale Grocers	First and Mission.
Catton, Bell & Co.	Com. and Insurance	406 California.
Challenge Glue Co.		218 California.
Chapman, Jas. F. & Co.	Shipping Merchants	303 California.
Chapman, Wilfred B.	Commission Merchant	123 California.
Chesebrough, A.	Williams, Dimond & Co.	202 Market.
Christensen, Chas.	Am. Central Ins. Co.	220 Sansome.
Chesebrough, H. C.	Tacoma Mill Co.	300 California.
Church, Seymour R. Co.	Pig Iron, Coke, etc.	307 Sansome.
Clabrough, Golcher & Co.	Sporting Materials	538 Market.
Clark, W. D.	Williams, Dimond & Co.	202 Market.
Clark, N. & Sons	Sewer Pipe, Brick, etc.	17 Spear.
Cole, Daniel T.		NE. cor. Sac.-Davis.

List of Members.

Name.	Firm.	Place of Business.
Coleman, Edward	Capitalist	NW. cor. Franklin-Cal.
Compressed Air Machinery Co.		24 First.
Connor, F. F.	Agt. P. R. R. & S. S. Co.	421 Market.
Conradi & Goldberg	Leaf Tobacco, etc.	730 Montgomery.
Cornwall, P. B.	Black Diamond C. M. Co.	204 Front.
Crane Co.	Hdw. and Plumbers' Sup.	23 First.
Crocker Estate Co.		Crocker Bldg.
Crocker-Woolworth National Bank		Post and Market.
Crothers, R. A.	Proprietor. "Bulletin"	233 Kearny.
Cunningham, Curtis & Welch.	Paper Dealers	Cor. Sansome-Halleck.
Curtis, A. A.		205 Crocker Bldg.
Cox, Thos. A.	Cox Seed and Plant Co.	413 Sansome.
Capelle, Robert	North Ger.-Lloyd S. S. Co.	140 Montgomery.
California Barrel Co.		327 Market.
California Ink Co.		413 Commercial.
Connecticut Fire Ins. Co.		411 California.
Cahill & Hall Elevator Co.		133 Beale.
Cahn, Nickelsburg & Co.	Mnfgs. Boots and Shoes.	129 Sansome.
California Fireworks Co.		219 Front.
California Fruit Evaporating Co.		313 Davis.
California Hydraulic Engineering and Supply Co.		17 Fremont.
Campe, Henry & Co.	Wholesale Liquor Dealers.	54 Drumm.
Chrestofferson & Tway	Shipsmiths	420 Beale.
City Street Improvement Co.		5th Floor, Mills Bldg.
Clinch, C. G. & Co.	Paints, Oils, etc.	9 Front.
Code Portwood Canning Co.		101 Front.
Continental Building and Loan Association		301 California.
Cook Belting, H. N. Co.		126 Fremont.
Crocker, H. S. Co.	Stationers, Printers, etc.	215 Bush.
Cudahy Packing Co., The		424 Townsend.
California and Hawaiian Sugar Refining Co.		204 California.
Crocker, Henry J.	Capitalist	Crocker Bldg.
Chamberlain, W. G.	Remington Typewriter Co.	228 Bush.
Chevalier Co., The F.	Liquor Merchants	9 Beale.
Comfort, J. V. C.	Agt. China Com. S. S. Co.	204 Front.
California Door Co.		20 Drumm.
Columbia Marble Co., The		516 Rialto Bldg.
Corbus, A. T.	Purchasing and Com. Agt.	Mills Bldg.
Central Trust Co. of Cal.		42 Montgomery.
California Sugar and White Pine Agency		515 Rialto Bldg.
Clark & Bros., W. F.	Shipping and Commission.	311 California.
Clausen, John H. N.	Agt. Con. Life Ins. Co.	230 Montgomery.
Caswell, Geo. W. Co.	Importers Tea, Coffee, etc.	412 Sacramento.
California Canneries Co.		125 California.
Danforth Warehouse Co.		Cor. Battery-Broadway.
Davis, Horace	Pres't Sperry Flour Co.	133 Spear.
Davis, J. B. F. & Son	Insurance Brokers	215 Sansome.
Deere Implement Co.		209 Market.
De Bernadi & Co.	Wholesale Dairy Produce	409 Front.
De Fremery, James & Co.	Commission Merchants	410 Battery.
Devlin, Frank J.	Atlas Insurance Co.	309 Sansome.
De Young, M. H.	"Chronicle"	Chronicle Bldg.
Dieckmann & Co.	Imp. Coffee and Hardwood.	421 Market.
Dickie, John W.	Shipbuilder	125 Steuart.
Dimond, E. R.	W., D. & Co., Shipping Mer.	202 Market.
Dinkelspiel, Samuel L.	D. & Co., Dry Goods.	37 Battery.
Dollar, Robert	Dollar Steamship Co.	134 California.
Dornin, George D.	National Fire Ins. Co.	Hayward Bldg.
Doyle, John T.	Attorney-at-Law	916 Market.
Doyle, Henry & Co.	Fishermen's Supplies.	513 Clay.
Dow, Geo. E.	Dow Steam Pump Works.	First and Natoma.
Dunham, Carrigan & Hayden Co. Hardware.		17-19 Beale.
Dutton, W. J.	Fireman's Fund Ins. Co.	401 California.
Dean, Walter E.	Capitalist	Nevada Block.
De Lamare, A. J.	Commission Merchant	132 California.
Dickson, Frank W.	Mgr. Royal Ex. Assur. Co.	501 Montgomery.
Drum, Frank G.	Agent Tevis Estate.	Mills Bldg.
Drake, E. E.	Union Metalic Cartridge Co.	86 First.
Doak, D. P.	Ry. Const. and Supplies.	708 Market.
Dodge, Sweeney & Co.	Dairy Produce	114 Market.
Donohoe, Jos. A.	Banker	Sutter and Montgy.

Name.	Firm.	Place of Business.
Dunsmuir's Sons Co., R.	Coal	340 Steuart.
De la Montanya Co., J.	Hardware, Metals, etc.	214 Jackson.
Day, Thomas Co.	Gas Fixtures	719 Mission.
Doble, Abner Co.	Iron, Steel, etc.	200 Fremont.
Easton, Wendell	Real Estate	638 Market.
Eastman, Frank & Co.	Printers	509 Clay.
Ehrman, M. & Co.	Wholesale Grocers	104-110 Front.
Emporium and Golden Rule Bazaar.	Department Store	825 Market.
Eschen, J. C.	Eschen & Minor, Stevedores.	204 California.
Evans, Evan C.	Commission Merchant	308 California.
Everding, John J.	Manufacturers Starch etc.	48 Clay.
Earl, D. W. & Co.	Forwarding Agents	Crocker Bldg.
Eichbaum, W. P.	Mgr. Pac. Branch H. R. W.	148 First.
Electrical Railway and Manufacturers' Supply Co.		68 First.
Evans, C. H. & Co.	Machine Works	183 Fremont.
Eddy, Falk and American Trading Co.		123 California.
Eberhard, The Geo. F. Co.	Manfacturers' Agents	12 Drumm.
Erlanger, Simon	Commission Merchant	300 Davis.
Fairbanks, Morse & Co.	Scales, Windmills,etc.	310 Market.
Ferris, John W.	Engineer and Contractor	320 Sansome.
First National Bank		Sansome and Bush.
Flood, Jas. L.	Capitalist	Nevada Block.
Foard, Lorentz	Ship Chandlery	26 East.
Folger, J. A. & Co.	Spices, Flav. Extracts, etc.	104 California.
Foster, A. W.	Pres't Cal. N. W. Ry.	Mutual Life Bldg.
Frank, S. H. & Co.	Hides, etc.	406 Battery.
Fredericks, Jos. & Co.	Carpets	649 Market.
Freese, Andrew C.	Stevedore	55 Mission.
Fry, R. D.	Cal. Safe Dep. & Trust Co.	Cal. and Montgomery.
Fuller, Wm. P.	W. P. F. & Co.,Paints, etc.	Pine and Front.
Fairbanks, N. K. & Co.	W. W. Saint, Manager	304 Sacramento.
Fair Heirs		230 Montgomery.
Fargo, E. A. Co.	Whse Wines and Liquors	316 Front.
Farnsworth & Ruggles	Teaming and Forwarding	25 Davis.
Fife, Geo. Storrs		1201 California.
Finn Metal Works, John		313 Howard.
Fleishhacker, A. & Co.	Paper Box Mnfgs., etc.	520 Market.
Froelich, Christian	Agt. R. D. Wood & Co.	202 Market.
Fisher, L. P. Advertising Agency		425 Montgomery.
Ferguson, J. C. H.	The Midvale Steel Co.	220 Market.
Garcia & Maggini	Commission Merchants	100 Washington.
Gas Consumers' Association		455 Sutter.
Getz Bros.	Wholesale Produce	111 California.
Ghirardelli Co., D.	Mfrs. Chocolate, Etc.	104 Pine.
Girvin & Eyre	Grain and Ins.Brokers	426 California.
Gladding, McBean & Co.	Terra Cotta and Brick	Rialto Bldg.
Goodall, Edwin, Goodall, Perkins & Co.		22 California.
Goodyear Rubber Co.		577-579 Market.
Goodman, Geo.	Mfr. Art. Stone, Cement	307 Montgomery.
Golden State and Miners' Iron Works		237 First.
Gould, C. W. & Co.	Produce and Com. Mer.	314 Washington.
Grace, W. R. & Co.	Shipping and Commission	Cal. and Battery.
Gray, Geo. D.	Wholesale Lumber	421 Market.
Grant, Jos. D., Murphy, Grant & Co.		Bush and Sansome.
Gray, Geo. F., Pres. Gray Bros., Contractors		Hayward Bldg.
Greenebaum, M., Greenebaum, Well & Michels, Men's Furnishings.		17 Sansome.
Griffin, Skelley Co.	Fruits and Raisins	132 Market.
Grinbaum, M. S. & Co.	Commission Merchants	215 Front.
Gundlach, Bundschu Wine Co.		434 Bryant.
Gutte, I.	Gutte & Frank. Ins. Agents.	303 California.
Grant, Geo. F.	London Assurance Cor.	216 Sansome.
German Savings and Loan Society, The		526 California.
Germania Life Insurance Co.		4th floor, Mills Bldg.
Guggenhime & Co.	Dried Fruits, etc.	118 Davis.
Geberding, A. & Co.	Grain and Commission	222 Sansome.
Goldberg, Bowen & Co.	Grocers	426 Pine.
Golden Gate Brick Co., The		501 Rialto Bldg.
Garratt & Co., W. T.	Brass Founders	Fremont and Natoma.
Gettleson & Rhine	Whse Candy Mnfgrs	210 Sacramento.

List of Members.

Name.	Firm.	Place of Business
Golden State Asparagus Co.		22 California.
Guittard Manufacturing Co.	Coffees, Teas, Spices, etc.	119 Front.
Gutta Percha and Rubber Manufacturing Co.		26 Fremont.
Haas Bros.	Grocers.	100-102 California.
Hall, A. I. & Son.	Manufacturers' Agents.	645 Market.
Hamilton, Alexander.	B. & H., Hardware.	Pine and Davis.
Hanify, J. R. & Co.	Whse Lumber and Shipping.	16 California.
Harries, W. H.	H. & S. Banking Cor.	401 Montgomery.
Harris Bros. & Co.	Wholesale Grocers.	40 Spear.
Haven, C. D.	L., L. & Globe Ins. Co.	422 California.
Hawaiian Commercial and Sugar Co.		308 Market.
Hay & Wright.	Shipbuilders.	35 Steuart.
Heise, Chas. E. & Co.	Custom House Brokers.	528 Battery.
Hecht Bros. & Co.	Bond and Investment Secur.	310 Pine.
Helvetia Milk Condensing Co.		3 California.
Hendry, C. J. Co.	Ship Chandlers.	8 California.
Herold, Rudolph Jr.	Hamburg.Bremen Ins. Co.	415 California.
Herring Hall Marvin Co.	Safes.	605 Market.
Hicks, Judd Co.	Printers, etc.	23 First.
Hume, R. D.	Pres't K. P. & T. Co.	421 Market.
Hirschman, A.	Jewelry.	712 Market.
Hoffman, Rothschild & Co.	Wholesale Clothing.	9 Battery.
Holbrook, Merrill & Stetson.	Hardware.	237 Market.
Holmes, C. S.	Renton, Holmes & Co., Lum.	10th floor, Mills Bldg.
Holt Bros. & Co.	Wagons, etc.	30 Main.
Hooker, C. G.		967 Bush.
Hooker & Co.	Wagons, etc.	16 Drumm.
Ho Yow.		
Howard, H. Z.	Sup't Oceanic S. S. Co.	Company Dock.
Hubbard, Samuel.	Capitalist, 98 Montecito Ave.	Oakland.
Hooper, C. A. & Co.	Wholesale Lumber.	Cor. Cal. and Front.
Hartter, Hayes & Co.	Wholesale Grocers.	216 Front.
Haviside, J. J. & Son.	Ship Riggers, etc.	46 Clay.
Hechtman, A. J.		504 Hayward Bldg.
Hromada, Adolph.	Candy Manufacturer.	222 Battery.
Harrison, M. C. & Co.	Adjusters and Underwriters.	319 California.
Harvey, J. Downey.	Capitalist.	916 Market.
Heller, Bachman & Co.	Importers Dry Goods.	112 Sansome.
Henshaw, Bulkley & Co.	Engineers.	Cor. Fremont and Mis.
Herzog & Co.	Agts. H.-A. L. & E. R. R. Co.	401 California.
Heywood Bros. & Wakefield Co.		659 Mission.
Hulme & Hart.	Commission Merchants.	690 Fifth.
Healy, Tibbitts & Co.	Engineers and Contractors.	22 Market.
Huddleston, H. & Co.	Great Am. Imp. Tea Co.	52 Market.
Hunt Bros. Co.	Commission Merchants.	3 California.
Harron, Rickard & McCone.	Machinery.	21 Fremont.
Heyneman, Herman.	Wholesale Tobacco.	204 Sacramento.
Hooper, Geo. K.		536 Taylor.
Hilmer & Bredhoff.	Commission Merchants.	34 California.
Hooke-Field Co.	Commission Merchants.	12 Front.
Hellman Bros. & Co.	Commission Merchants.	12 Front.
Haslett Warehouse Co.		206 California.
Havens, F. C.	Mgr. The Realty Syndicate.	14 Sansome.
Hills Bros.	Dairy Produce, Commission.	23 California.
Hendy Machine Works, Joshua.		42 Fremont.
Hilbert Mercantile Co.	Commission Merchants.	213 Market.
Hind, Rolph & Co.	Shipping and Commission.	302 California.
Halloran, J. F.	"Mining & Scientific Press".	330 Market.
Hammer & Co.	Commission Merchants.	212 Sacramento.
Ivancovich & Co.	Fruit, Commission.	211 Washington.
Isaacs, William B.	Iron, Steel and Ry. Supplies.	226 Market.
Illinois-Pacific Glass Co.		10 Main.
International Banking Corporation.		Cor. Bush and Sansome.
Jacobi, J. J.	L. & J., Wines, etc.	Cor. Bryant and Second.
Jensen, Jacob.	Shipping and Commission.	6 California.
Jerome, James.	Mgr. Saginaw Steel S. S. Co.	Claus Spreckels Bldg.
Johnson-Locke Mercantile Co.		123 California.
Johnson, J. C. & Co.	Harness, Leather, etc.	120 First.
Jones, Everett D.	S. L. Jones & Co., Com. Agts.	207 California.

List of Members.

Name.	Firm.	Place of Business.
Josselyn, G. M. & Co.	Ship Chandlers	36-40 Market.
Judson Manufacturing Co.	Iron Works	Cor. Howard-Beale.
Jackson, Byron	Byron Jackson Mach. Wks.	411 Market.
Jennings, Rufus P.	Importer and Exporter	6 California.
Jesse Moore Hunt Co.	Whse Wines and Liquors	Sac. and Davis.
Jones-Paddock Co.	Coffee, Teas, etc.	26 Fremont.
Kauffman, Leon	Grain Broker	206 Sansome.
Kentfield, Edwin E.	J. Kentfield & Co., Lumber	318 Steuart.
Kelley, Jas. R.	Pres't Hibernia S. & L. S.	Jones and McAllister.
Kohlberg & Co.	Leaf Tobacco	526 Washington.
Koshland, S. & Co.	Wools, Bags, etc.	426 California.
Kruse, Emil T.	Shipping, etc.	207 Front.
Kullman, Salz & Co.	Leather, etc.	580 Mission.
Kutner, Goldstein Co.	General Merchandise	Room 2, 4 Sutter.
Keystone Boiler Works		Cor. Main and Folsom.
Kelley-Clarke Co.	General Agents	130 California.
Keithley, E. A.	Manufacturers' Agent	409 Rialto Bldg.
Kunz, Henry	Charles Meinecke & Co.	314 Sacramento.
Lastreto, L. F., Consul Ecuador and	Commission Merchant	280 California.
Laton, Chas. A.	Fresno Canal Irrigation Co.	Safe Deposit Bldg.
Le Count Bros.	Stationers	533 Market.
Levison, J. B.	Fireman's Fund Ins. Co.	401 California.
Lewis, Wm. & Co.	Cigars and Tobacco	24 California.
Liebes, H. & Co.	Furriers	133 Post.
Lilienthal, E. R.	L. & Co., Hop Dealers-Com.	73 Beale.
Livingston, Smith & Co.	Ins. and Com. Agents	317 California.
Lloyd, Reuben H.	Attorney-at-Law	Nevada Block.
Loaiza, W. & Co.	Commission and Insurance	202 Sansome.
London and San Francisco Bank		424 California.
London, Paris and American Bank		1 Sansome.
Lougee, F. W.	Fireman's Fund Ins. Co.	401 California.
Lukens, Ed. G.	Judson Dynamite and Powder Wks.	200 Market.
Lund, Henry	H. L. & Co., Ship. and Com.	214 California.
Landers, Wm. J.	Agt. Imp. and Lion Ins. Co.	205 Sansome.
Leist, Chas. J. & Co.	Flour, Grain and Produce	201 Davis.
Lewis, Soloman	Capitalist	320 Sansome.
Linen Thread Co., The		224 Bush.
Locomobile Co. of the Pacific		1622 Market.
Lewis, Anderson, Foard & Co	Ship Chandlers	24 East.
Lowden, W. H., Mgr. Pac. Dept. Norwich	Union Life Ins. Co.	314 California.
Landers, John	Mgr. Manhattan L. Ins. Co.	240 Montgomery.
Livingston & Co.	Wholesale Liquors	206 Davis.
Lyons, E. G. & Raas Co., The	Wines, Liquors, etc.	549 Mission.
Lovell, Mansfield Co.	Shipping and Commission	22 California.
London & Lancashire Fire Insurance Co.		324 Montgomery.
Loveland, H. D.	Mgr. Pac. T. & C. Ass'n	Hayward Bldg.
Macondry & Co.	C. & Ins., N. C. Ins. Co.	116 California.
Madison, M. J.	Sec. Pac. Dredging Co.	35 Steuart.
Main, Chas.	M. & W., Leather, etc.	214-216 Battery.
Malm, C. A. & Co.	Trunks, Bags, etc.	220 Bush.
Marston, Wm. H.	Welch & Co.	220 California.
Marcus, Geo. & Co.	Commission and Insurance	418 California.
Martin, John	Martin Pipe and Foundry Co	31 New Montgomery.
Matson, Wm.	Matson Navigation Co.	327 Market.
McNear, Geo. W.	Flour, Shipping and Com.	326 California.
McNear, Geo. W. Jr.	Flour, Grain, etc.	326 California.
McLaughlin & Co.		185 Crocker Bldg.
McNab & Smith	Draying	205 Davis.
Meese & Gottfried Co.	Machinery, etc.	167 Fremont.
Mendocino Lumber Co.		40 California.
Metcalf, John	Surveyor Lloyd's Register	303 California
Meyer, Daniel	Banker	214 Pine.
Meyer, Wilson & Co.	Shipping and Commission	210 Battery.
Meyerstein Co.	Mnfrs. Furnishing Goods	2 Battery.
Mighell, Wm. E.	Pres't Cal. Shipping Co.	42 Market.
Mills, W. H.	Southern Pacific Co.	Wells-Fargo Bldg.
Mitsui & Co.	Commission Merchants	222 Sansome.
Montague, W. W.	W. W. M. & Co., Hard., etc.	309-317 Market.
Montealegre & Co.	Imps. and Com. Merchants	410 Hayward Bldg.

List of Members.

Name.	Firm.	Place of Business.
Moore, Chas. C. & Co.	Engineers	67 First.
Moore, Ferguson & Co.	Commission Merchants	310 California.
Moore, J. J. & Co.	Commission Merchants	416 California.
Morgan, Parmelee & Co.	Commission Merchants	405 Front.
Morse, I. H.	City Warehouse Co.	Lombard and Battery.
Morse, Lester L.	Seeds, etc.	Santa Clara, Cal.

Mullins, C. F.	Insurance and Commission	416 California
Mutual Label and Lithograph Co.		Second, near Bryant.
Mann, C. M.	Successor to I. de Turk	220 Sacramento.
Morton Draying and Warehouse Co.		112 Battery.
Mack & Co.	Wholesale Druggists	13 Fremont.
Martin, Dangers & Camm.	Dairy Produce, etc.	101 California
Mayhew, F. E. & Co.	I. R. and C. H. B.	424 Battery.
McCreery, Andrew B.	Capitalist	211 Sansome.
Meyer, C. H. & Bros.	Mnfs. Hats and Caps	28 Sansome.
Miller & Lux	Wholesale Cattle	508 California.
Mitchell, Geo. M. & Co.	Agts. H. & W. Ins. Co.	210 Sansome.
Moore, Arthur W.	Stock and Bond Broker	407 Montgomery.
Murray Bros. Machine Work		Cor Folsom and Beale.
Magnesia Asbestos Sup. Co.	Steam Covering	157 Spear.
McAllister, M. H.	Otis, McAllister & Co.	109 California.
Maybeck, B. R.	Architect	307 Sansome.
Moore, Geo. A. & Co.	Commission Merchants	208 California.
Mailliard & Schmeidel	Commission Merchants	307 Sansome.
Mugan, Wm. G.	Dolbeer & Carson	6 California.
Maldonado & Co.	Importers	419 California.
Magee, Thomas & Sons	Real Estate	5 Montgomery.
Meyer & O'Brien	Architects	Crossley Bldg.
Mattoon & Co.	Custom House Brokers	532 Battery.

Nathan-Dohrman Co.	Wholesale Crockery	122 Sutter.
Neustadter Bros.	Whse. Furnishing Goods	Pine and Sansome.
Nevada National Bank of San Francisco		Pine and Mtgy.
Newell, M. A.	Agt. Tokio Marine Ins Co.	318 California.
Newhall, H. M. & Co.	Ship., Com. and Ins	309 Sansome.
Nunan, Matthew	Hibernia Brewery	1225 Howard.
Naber, Alfs & Brune	Wholesale Wines, etc.	323 Market.
Nason, R. N. & Co.	Paints, Oils, etc.	115 Front.
Nelson, Chas. Co., The	Shipping and Lumber	6 California.
Newell & Bros.	Manufacturers Soap, etc.	217 Davis.
New York Life Insurance Co.		Mills Bldg.
New Zealand Insurance Co.		312 California.
Northern Commercial Co.		645 Market.
Newman Bros.	Shipping and Com. Mer.	126 Davis.
Neal, Geo. F.	Mgr. Commercial Pub. Co.	463 Mission.

Otis, James	O. M. & Co., Com. Mer.	109 California.
Overland Freight Transfer Co.		203 Front.
Otis Elevator Co.		509 Howard.
Osborn, Russell W., Mgr. Pac. Coast Dept. Pa. Fire Ins. Co.		508 California.
Osborn, D. M. & Co.	Mnfrs. Farming Machinery	13 Main.
Onffroy, R.	Pres't P.-A. T. & Coal Co.	214 Rialto Bldg.

Pacific Acetylene Gas Co.		182 First.
Pacific Coast Co.	Coal Importers	401 California.
Pacific Mail Steamship Co.		421 Market.
Pacific Mutual Life Insurance Co.		Mtgy. and Sacramento.
Pacific States Telephone and Telegraph Co.		216 Bush.
Pacific Steam Whaling Co.		30 California.
Pacific Surety Co.		326 Montgomery.
Page Bros.	Ship Brokers	302 California.
Paraffine Paint Co.		Second and Stevenson.
Parrott & Co.	Shipping and Commission	306 California.
Parsons, Thos. J.	Del Monte Milling Co.	Front and Clay.
Partridge, John	Stationer	306 California.
Payot, Upham & Co.	Stationers	Battery and Pine.
Payson, A. H.	Asst. to Pres't Santa Fe Ry.	641 Market.
Perkins, Geo. C.	Goodall, Perkins & Co.	22 California.

Name.	Firm.	Place of Business.
Perrin, Howard	Agt. Wash. Life Ins. Co.	Chronicle Bldg.
Phelan, James D.	Capitalist	Phelan Bldg., Market.
Piper, Aden, Goodall Co.	Shipping Merchants	24 Clay.
Plummer, Geo. C.	Shipping and Commission	51 Steuart.
Pond, E. B.	Capitalist	530 California.
Pollard, Thos.	Lumber and Shipping	22 California.
Pacific Coast Syrup Co.		717 Sansome.
Pacific Improvement Co.		Crocker Bldg.
Pacific Metal Works		155 First.
Pennell-Suydam Co.	Wholesale Grocers	16 Spear.
Pioneer Soap Co.		220 California.
Pollitz, Edward & Co.	Stocks and Bonds	403 California.
Port Costa Milling Co.		326 California.
Price, Thomas & Son	Analytical Chemists, etc.	526 Sacramento.
Pacific Hardware and Steel Co.		Mission and Fremont.
Pike, Chas. W. & Co.	Commission Merchants	124 California.
Pacific Steel and Wire Co.		100 Front.
Pacific Coast Casualty Co.		408 Safe Deposit Bldg.
Pacific Coast Rubber Co.	H. C. Norton, V.-P. and Mgr.	453 Mission.
Pacific Lumber Co.		308 Rialto Bldg.
Pacific Portland Cement Co.		508 Rialto Bldg.
Pascal, Dubedat & Co.	French Wines, etc.	222 California.
Payne, Theodore F.	Capitalist	330 Pine.
Phoenix Raisin Seeding and Packing Co.		3 California.
Raymond, Armstrong & Co.	Real Estate	Mills Bldg.
Redington & Co.	Wholesale Druggists	Second and Stevenson.
Roeblings, John A. Sons Co.	Wire Rope	25 Fremont.
Rosenberg Bros. & Co.	Dried Fruits	211 California.
Rosenfeld, John Sons	Shipping and Commission	605 Montgomery.
Reid Bros. & Co.	Architects	Claus Spreckels Bldg.
Roth, Blum & Co.	Provision Packers	201 California.
Roth & Co.	Wholesale Liquors, etc.	316 Market St.
Richards, John W.		328 Montgomery.
Rix Compressed Air and Drill Co.		396 Mission.
Rosenblatt Co., The	Cal. Wines and Brandies	113 Pine.
Rehfisch & Hochstadter	Stock and Bond Brokers	413 California.
Risdon Iron Works		Steuart and Folsom.
Rollins, E. H. & Sons	Bankers, etc.	335 Pine.
Realty Syndicate, The		14 Sansome.
Renters' Loan and Trust Co.		Room 214, 328 Mtgy.
Rinaldo Bros.	Wholesale Cigars	300 Battery.
Rowley, Forrest S.	Rowley Investment Co.	10th floor, Mills Bldg.
Rosenthal, Louis	Insurance	315 California.
Sachs Bros. & Co.	Notions, etc.	Bush and Sansome.
San Francisco Breweries, Ltd.		240 Second.
San Francisco Gas and Electric Co.		415 Post.
San Francisco National Bank		Pine and Sansome.
San Francisco Savings Union		532 California.
Sanborn, Vail & Co.	Stationers	745 Market.
Sanders & Kirchman	Shipping and Commission	22 California.
Saroni, Louis	Whse. Candy Manufacturer	Second and Folsom.
Sbarboro, Andrea		518 Montgomery.
Schoenfeld, Jonas & Co.	Leaf Tobacco	516 Washington.
Schwartz Bros.	Commission Merchants	421 Market.
Schilling, A. & Co.	Wholesale Coffee, etc.	Folsom and Second.
Scott & Van Arsdale	Lumber	Fifth and Brannan.
Selby Smelting and Lead Co.		416 Montgomery.
Sewall, Oscar T.	Williams, Dimond & Co.	202 Market.
Shainwald, Hermann	S. B. & Co., Real Estate	Mills Bldg.
Shreve & Co.	Jewelry	Market and Post.
Siegfried, J. C.	Tea Importer	202 Market.
Simpson, A. M.	Simpson Lumber Co.	14 Spear.
Simpson, John		36 Steuart.
Slade, S. E.	Slade Lumber Co.	6 California.
Sloane, W. & J. & Co.	Whse. Furn. and Carpets	116 Post.
Smith, A. A.	F., S. & C., Commission	104 Sutter.
Snow, Louis T.	Wholesale Grocer	210 California.
Sonntag, Julian	Sonntag Bros., Real Estate	232 Montgomery.
Spaulding, Geo. & Co.	Printers	414 Clay.

List of Members.

Name.	Firm.	Place of Business.
Spear, Ed. S. & Co.	Auctioneers	31 Sutter.
Sperry, Geo. B.	Insurance	322 Pine.
Spreckels, Claus		327 Market.
Spreckels, John D.		327 Market.
Spreckels, Rudolph		421 Market.
Spring Valley Water Co.		Geary and Stockton.
Sroufe & Co.	Wholesale Liquors	208-210 Market.
Stafford, W. G.	Coal, Coke, etc.	216 East.
Stallman, Chas.	Pacific Tool and Supply Co.	First and Mission.
Standard Oil Co.		Rialto Bldg.
Sierra Railway of California		Crocker Bldg.
Storror, L. W.	Supt. Postal Telegraph Co.	534 Market.
Strauss, Levi & Co.	Dry Goods	14-16 Battery.
Stubbs, D. D.	O. & O. S. S. Co.	421 Market.
Studebaker Bros. of Cal.	Carriages, etc.	Market and Tenth.
Sumner, F. W.	H. B. S. & Co., Hides, Leather, etc.	Front and Jackson.
Sussman, Wormser & Co.	Wholesale Grocers	123 Market.
Sierra Lumber Co.		320 Sansome.
Swayne & Hoyt	Custom House Brokers	426 Battery.
Sherwood & Sherwood	Wholesale Grocers	212-214 Market.
Shea & Shea	Architects	26 Montgomery.
South San Francisco Packing and Provision Co.		117 Davis.
Southern Pacific Milling Co.		224 California.
Security Savings Bank		Mills Bldg.
Silverberg, S.	Wholesale Butcher	320 Sansome.
Simonds Saw Co.		31 Main.
Standard Biscuit Co.		Cor. Front and Pacific.
San Francisco News Co., The		342 Geary.
Siebe Bros. & Plageman	Whse Wines and Liquors	322 Sansome.
Smith, Francis & Co.	Sheet Iron and Steel Pipe	83 Fremont.
Stevens, Jno. H., Gen. Agt. Accident Dept. Aetna Life Ins. Co.		328 Montgomery.
Stockton Milling Co.		112 California.
Swift & Co., of Chicago	C. W. Sherwood, Agt.	640 Fifth.
San Francisco Dry Dock Co.		302 California.
Shipowners' and Merchants' Tugboat Co.		302 California.
Smellie, William		303 California.
Scott & Gilbert Co.	Manufacturing Chemists	300 Davis.
Smith, James B.	Western Fuel Co.	318 California.
Smith, Frank E.	Western Electrical Instruments Co.	183 Jessie.
San Francisco Stevedoring Co.	John Whitney, Mgr.	326 Clay.
Schulz, Niggle & Co.	Dairy Produce, etc.	221 Front.
Sloane, The Chas. F. Co.	Electrical Supplies	Mills Bldg.
Smith, F. M.	Capitalist	101 Sansome.
Spruance-Stanley Co.	Wholesale Liquors	410 Front.
Sonntag, Henry P.	Sonntag Bros., Real Estate	232 Montgomery.
Shields, A. M.	Equitable Life Ass. Society	Crocker Bldg.

Talbot, Wm. H.	Pope & Talbot, Lumber	314 California.
Tatum & Bowen	Machinery	34 Fremont.
Taylor, C. L.	Pres't Sun Insurance Co.	218 Sansome.
Thayer, I. E.	Shipping	28 California.
Thornley, Wm. H.	Custom House Broker	322 Washington.
Tillmann, Frederick Jr.	T. & B., Wholesale Grocers	Clay and Battery.
Tosawa, K.	Mgr. Yokohama Specie Bank	514 Montgomery.
Toplitz, Robt. L. & Co.	Wholesale Millinery	549 Market.
Transatlantic Fire Insurance Co.		213 Sansome.
Tubbs Cordage Co.		611 Front.
Tuft, Jas.		22 California.
Turner, Matthew	Shipbuilder	40 California.
Tyson, Geo. H.	Ger. Ins. Co. of New York	214 Sansome.
Tyler, S. H. & Son	Coffee, Spices, Mills, etc.	310 Front.
Taylor, James I.	Agt. Everett Pulp and Paper Co.	404 Sansome.
Taussig, Louis & Co.	Wholesale Liquors	26 Main.
Thompson, R. R.	Capitalist	Clunie Bldg.
Triest & Co.	Importers Hats and Caps	116 Sansome.
Tetzen, Chas. & Co.	Shipping and Commission	318 Battery.
Thomson Bridge Co.		129 Mission.
Troy Laundry Machinery Co., Ltd.	W. E. Cumback, Mgr.	581 Mission.
Tay, Geo. H. Co.	Plumbers' Supplies	50 First.

List of Members.

Name.	Firm.	Place of Business.
Union Gas Engine Co.		244 First.
Union Iron Works		222 Market.
Union Lumber Co.		23 Crocker Bldg.
Union Pulp and Paper Co.		414 Sansome.
Unna Co., The Harry	Brushes, Brooms, Woodware	113 Battery.
United Carriage Co.		12 New Montgomery.
United Engineering Co.		254 Spear.
Umbsen, G. H. & Co.	Real Estate	20 Montgomery.
Union Oil Co. of California		Mills Bldg.
Van Bergen, N. & Co.	Wholesale Liquors	418 Clay.
Voss, Conrad & Co.	Insurance Agents	204 Sansome.
Von Rhein Real Estate Co.		513 California.
Vulcan Iron Works		505 Mission.
Walter, Isaac N.	D. N. & E. Walter & Co.	529 Market.
Warfield, R. H.	California Hotel	Bush.
Watt, Robert, Langley & Michaels Co., Druggists.		38 First.
Watt, Rolla V.	Royal and Norwich Union	Pine and Sansome.
Weil, Raphael & Co.	Dry Goods	Kearney and Post.
Weil, Wm. M.	Distribution Agent.	106 Pine.
Welch & Co.	Shipping	220 California.
Welch, A. P.	Welch & Co.	220 California.
Wellman, Peck & Co.	Wholesale Grocers	Market and Main.
Wells, Fargo & Co.'s Bank		Market and Sansome.
Western Commercial Co.		204 California
Western Expanded Metal and Fire Proofing Co.		Rialto Bldg.
West Side Flume and Lumber Co.		175 Crocker Bldg.
Whittell, George	Capitalist	40 Montgomery.
Whittier, W. F.	Capitalist	20 Fremont.
Williams, A. P.		Palace Hotel.
Wilmerding, Loewe & Co.	Wholesale Liquors	40 First.
Wilson, T. D. E.	O. & O. S. S. Co.	2226 Grove.
Wolf, Wm. & Co.	Commission	216 Mission.
Worden, Clinton E. & Co.	Manufacturers Drugs	Mills Bldg.
White Bros.	Hardwood Lumber	Spear and Howard.
Warren, Charles A.	General Contractor	230 Montgomery.
Williams, J. B.	Rep. Am. Tin Plate Co.	Mills Bldg.
Western Union Telegraph Co.		Mtgy. and Pine.
White, L. E. Lumber Co.		303 California.
Wickson, G. G. & Co.	Dairy and Farm Machinery.	34 Main.
Woods, H. F.	Woods Estate	508 California
Western Repair and Supply Co.	Ship Chandlers	63 Steuart.
Western Fuel Co.		318 California
Western Engineering and Construction Co.		408 Rialto Bldg.
Wells, Fargo & Co.'s Express		Cor. 2d and Mission.
Western National Bank		805 Market.
Western Meat Co.		Sixth and Townsend.
Williams, H. A. Co., The	Commission Merchants	308 Market.
Yates & Co.	Paints, Oils, etc.	117 Market.
Young, Alexander	Capitalist	Rose Crest, Oakland.
Young, Harry R.	Stevedore	204 California.
Zeile, F. W.	Pres't Mercantile Trust Co.	464 California.

INDEX

A

	PAGE
Addition to Library	16
Almonds	209
Annual Statistics	113
Appendix	242
Apples	207
Apricots	207
Annual Banquet	60
Area of Counties	206
Asphalt, Production	214
American Commerce	225, 226 and 227
Arbitration, international	68
Arbitration Clause, Bills of Lading	,94, 95-101
American National Exposition, Shanghai	68-107
American Shipping, Revival of	96-101
Alaska Wagon Road	106
American Vessels for Public	111

B

Banks of San Francisco and the State	116-123
Barley, Exports of	154 and 161
Beet Sugar Production	210
Bonds and Stocks, Sales of	200 and 201
Brokerage and Commission Rates	242 to 244
Butter Receipts of	193
By-Laws	253 to 259
Banquet, Annual	60
Bank Clearings	114 and 115
Banks of California	122
Brandy and Wines	172, 173 and 174
Brandy, Production of	175
Borax, Production of	214
Bituminous Rock, Production of	214
Barley Quotations	160
Bills of Lading, Arbitration Clause	94, 95, 101
Bills of Lading, Signing	69
Bunker, Wm. M., Reports. etc	28, 49, 83, 85, 88, 90, 92, 93

C

	PAGE
California Property	205 and 206
Call for Meeting	64
Canned Fruits, Yearly Pack	164
Cereal Exports	161
Cheese, Receipts of	193
Clearances of Tonnage	152
Clearing House Business	114 and 115
Climatological Data	237, 238, 239, 240 and 241
Coal, Coke and Iron	186
Coffee	182
Coinage	168 and 169
Commerce, San Francisco	125
Commerce, American	225, 226, and 227
Commercial Banks, San Francisco	116
Commercial Banks, Interior	119
Commissions and Brokerage	242 to 244
Copper	214
Correspondents	65
Crude Oil, Production of	187 and 188
Customs Receipts	165
Commercial Prospects of California	38
Coal	215
Clay (Pottery)	215
Corn, Exports of	161
Canned Goods, Shipments of	170
Consuls, U. S.	107
Consular Reform	68
Cable, Submarine in Alaska	69
Cuban Reciprocity	70, 73 and 96
Customs Duties	76-102
Chinese Treaty	76
Canal Commission	80
Cable Companies' International Vocabulary	84
California Delegation, Thanking	85
Cable, Pacific	70, 91-103
Canal, Isthmian	80, 106
City Sanitation	78

D

Dairy Produce	193 and 194
Dockage, Rates of	246 and 247
Dried Fruits, Shipments of	170

Index.

	PAGE
Dried Fruits, Production of	207, 208, 209 and 210
Drawback Customs Duties	102

E

Eggs, Receipts of	194
Exports of Merchandise	126 to 131
Exports of Flour, Wheat and Barley	154
Exports of Treasure	136 and 137
Export and Import, Summary	135
Exports of United States	225, 226 and 227
Electric Power	189 and 190
Exports of Cereals	161
Exposition, Shanghai	68 and 107

F

Figs, Dried	208
Flour and Grain Exports	154 and 161
Flour, Receipts of	217 and 218
Freights, Grain	162
Fruit and Canned Goods Shipments	170
Form of Call for Meeting	64
Fruit Shipments, Fresh	171
Flour and Wheat	155, 157 and 158
Fruits, Canned	164
Fuel Oil, Rules for Handling	252

G

Gold, Yearly Production	212
Grapes, Dried	209
Grain and Flour Shipments	161
Grain Freights	162
Grain Freights, Average	162
Grain Quotations, Wheat	159
Grain Options	163 and 164
Grain Quotations, Barley	160
Grain Crop, Wheat	157
Gypsum, Production	215
Granite, Production	216
Governmental Transportation	71, 77, 87
Governmental Transports, Stoppage at Honolulu	90

H

	PAGE
Honey	210
Hops, Exports	195
Hops, Production	209
Harbor Commissioners	73, 75
Harbor Improvements	73, 75, 78, 79, 100, 103, 105
Harbor Police Boat	83

I

Imports of Foreign Merchandise	132 to 134
Imports of United States	225, 226 and 227
Imports of Treasure	138
Interest on Deposits	201
Internal Revenue Collections	166
Import and Export Summary	135
Insurance	202
International Arbitration	68
Instruction Camp, Military	68
Islais Creek	79
Indian Supplies	80, 95, 98
Isthmian Canal	80, 106
International Cable Co., Vocabulary	84

L

Lead Production	216
Lemons, Productino	210
Library, Additions to	16
Lumber	196, 197 and 198
Lime Production	216
Lightship	97
Life Saving Station	105

M

Members, List of	271 to 282
Merchandise, Delivery of	244
Merchandise, Exports of	126 to 131
Merchandise, Imports of Foreign	132 to 134
Merchandise, Payment of Freight	242
Merchandise, Rates of Stevedores	245
Metals, Precious	213
Mint, Coinage	168 and 169
Mineral Products by Counties	213
Mineral Products, Yearly Production	213, 214, 215 and 216
Manchuria, Trade With	103-106

Index. 285

N

	PAGE
National Banks of San Francisco	118
Nectarines	208
Normal Climatological Data	237 to 241
Naval Construction	219
National Banks of California	123
Navy, Increase of Officers	71-74
Navigation Laws, Philippine Islands	109-110

O

Oats, Exports of	161
Officers and Trustees	3
Oil and Whalebone	184 and 185
Oil, Crude	187 and 188
Oranges	210
Oriental Trade	139 to 150
Oil, Rules for Handling	252
Officers, Yearly Lists	261 to 270
Oakland Harbor	105

P

Pacific Coast Trade	224
Peaches	207
Pears	208
Plums	208
Precious Metals	213
Precipitation, Monthly and Seasonal	233, 234, 235 and 236
President's Report	5
Private Banks	121
Produce Receipts	218
Produce, Dairy	193 and 194
Prunes	207
Products, Annual Yield	207
Pacific Ocean Trade	124
Petroleum, Crude	187 and 188
Population of Counties	206
Property in California	205 and 206
Pilotage, Rates of	246
Pacific Ocean Cable	70-91-103
Parcels Post, Foreign	88-97-105
Philippine Islands Navigation Laws	109-110

Q

	PAGE
Quicksilver	191 and 192

R

Rainfall in San Francisco	228
Raisins	211
Rates of Dockage	246 and 247
Rates of Pilotage	246
Rates of Stevedores	245
Rates of Tolls	248 to 251
Real Estate	203 and 204
Receipts of Wheat and Four	217 and 218
Receipts of Leading Products	217
Receipts of Dairy Products	193 and 194
Report of President	5
Report of Secretary	13
Report of Treasurer	15
Reports, etc., of Washington Bureau	28-49, 83, 85, 88, 90, 92, 93
Rice	183
Rules of Order	260
Receipts of Lumber	196 and 198
Rye Exports	161
Rules for Handling Fuel Oil	252

S

Sales of Oil Stocks	201
Salmon	176 and 177
Savings Banks, Interior	120
Savings Banks, San Francisco	117
Secretary's Report	13
Ship Building, Yearly	220, 221, 222 and 223
Silver	167
Statistics, Annual	113
Stevedore Rates	245
Stocks and Bonds	200 and 201
Sugar	181
Synopsis of Transactions	68-111
Standing Committees	3
Summary of Exports and Imports	135
Silver, Yearly Production	212
Ship Building Summary	219
Sanitation, City	78
Siuslaw Harbor	104-110
Shipping, American	96-101

Index.

T

	PAGE
Tea	179 and 180
Temperature	229, 230, 231 and 232
Tolls, Rates of	248 to 251
Tonnage according to Nationality	153
Tonnage Movement	151
Transactions, Synopsis of	68-111
Treasure, Exports of	136 and 137
Treasure, Imports of	138
Treasurer's Annual Report	15
Trustees, List of	3
Trade with Orient	139 to 150
Taxation, State Rates	205
Taxation, County Rates	206
Transportation, Governmental	71-77-87
Transports, Governmental, Stoppage at Honolulu	90
Tonnage Dues	76

V

Vocabulary, International Cable	84

W

Walnuts	209
Whalebone and Oil	184 and 185
Wharfage, Rates of	251 and 252
Wheat Exports	154 and 161
Wheat and Flour	155, 157 and 158
Wines and Brandies	172, 173 and 174
Wool	199
Wheat, Receipts of	156
Wheat Crops and Distribution	157
Wheat Quotations	159
Wines, Production	175
Wines, California, in Cuban Treaty	70
Water Front	See Harbor
Washington Bureau Reports	28-49, 83, 85, 88, 90, 92, 93